born with a question mark
in **your heart**

OSHO

Extemporaneous talks given by Osho in
Rajneeshpuram, Oregon, USA

AUTHENTIC LIVING

born with a question mark
in **your heart**

DVD: *Is Spiritual Guidance an Absolute Necessity?*
(*From Darkness to Light,* #10)
Copyright © 1985, 2010 OSHO International Foundation

This book is a transcript of a series of original talks by Osho given to a live audience. The talks in this edition were previously published as *From Personality to Individuality* (Chapters 1-10). All of Osho's talks have been published in full as books, and are also available as original audio recordings. Audio recordings and the complete text archive can be found via the online OSHO Library at www.osho.com/library

OSHO is a registered trademark of OSHO International Foundation
www.osho.com/trademarks

OSHO MEDIA INTERNATIONAL
New York • Zurich • Mumbai
an imprint of
OSHO INTERNATIONAL
www.osho.com/oshointernational

Distributed by Publishers Group Worldwide
www.pgw.com

Library of Congress Catalog-In-Publication Data is available

Print edition: ISBN-13: 978-0-9836400-5-9
eBook edition: ISBN-13: 978-0-88050-428-7

Printed in China

10 9 8 7 6 5 4 3 2 1

Contents

About the Authentic Living Series

T he "Authentic Living" Series is a collection of books based on Osho's responses to questions from his international audience at meditation events.

About this process of asking questions, Osho says:

How do you ask a question which can be meaningful – not simply intellectually but existentially? Not just for verbal knowledge, but for authentic living? There are a few things which have to be remembered:

Whatever you ask, never ask a ready-made question, never ask a stereotyped question. Ask something that is immediately concerned with you, something that is meaningful to you, that carries some transforming message for you. Ask that question upon which your life depends.

Don't ask bookish questions, don't ask borrowed questions. And don't carry any question over from the past because that will be your memory, not you. If you ask a borrowed question, you can never come to an authentic answer. Even if an answer is given, it will not be caught by you and you will not be caught by it. A borrowed question is meaningless. Ask something that you want to ask. When I say "you," I mean the you that you are this very moment, that is here and now, that is immediate. When you ask something that is immediate, that is here and now, it becomes existential. It is not concerned with memory but with your being.

Don't ask anything that once answered will not change you in any way. For example, someone can ask whether there is a God: "Does God exist?" Ask such a question only if the answer will change you – so that if there is a God then you will be one type of person, and if there is no God you will be a different person. But if it will not cause any change in you to know whether God is or is not, then the question is meaningless. It is just curiosity, not inquiry.

So remember, ask whatever you are really concerned about. Only then will the answer be meaningful for you.

Preface

The personality is just hodgepodge: something is put by your mother, something by your father, something by your neighbors, friends, wife, teachers, priests, leaders. It is a patchwork, it is not indivisible. It is almost falling apart – any moment, a small accident and it will fall apart. It has no soul connecting all its parts; it has no wholeness, it is only parts.

Against personality I use the word individuality, meaning indivisibility. Individual means indivisible: you cannot divide it, there are no parts – it cannot fall apart. It is solid rock; seen in comparison with personality, it is one piece.

But that is only one aspect. Seen from the universal, you are no longer individual either. Even that much demarcation disappears. You are the whole. The winds, the trees, the moon are not separated anywhere; neither are you. You are breathing every moment. Existence is not separate from you, even when you think you are separate.

When you know that you are not separate, it is a tremendous realization. Then all fear of losing your face, all fear of losing your personality – which is always slipping – disappears. You have come to the origins. You have come to the eternal, to the universal. This is what I call enlightenment.

Osho
Beyond Psychology

CHAPTER 1

Man Is Born with a Question Mark
in His Heart

Osho,
What place has mysticism in your religion?

M y religion is pure mysticism, there is nothing else in it.
Other religions have no place for mysticism in them; they
cannot have, for the simple reason that they have answers for every
question – bogus answers with no evidence, with no argument. But
they are consoling for the gullible humanity; they demystify existence. All knowledge demystifies existence.

I don't teach you knowledgeability. On the other hand, all the
religions do just that; they make you knowledgeable. They have a
God as the creator. They have messengers of God bringing all the
answers from the original source, indubitable, infallible. These religions could exploit humanity for the simple reason that man feels a
kind of inner unease when there are questions and there is no way to
find an answer. Questions *are* there – man is born with questions,
with a big question mark in his heart – and it is good.

It is fortunate that man is born with a question mark, otherwise
he would be just another species of animal. Buffaloes have no

questions; they accept whatever is, unquestioningly – they are really faithful, religious. Trees have no questions, birds have no questions; it is only man and man's prerogative, his privilege. In the whole of existence he alone is capable of asking a question. The old religions have been trying to destroy your privilege. They have been forcing you down to the level of the animals. That's what they call faith, "undoubting faith." They want you to be buffaloes, donkeys, but not men – because the only special quality that defines man as separate from animalhood is the question mark. Yes, it is a turmoil.

Certainly to live without any questions is peaceful, but that peace is a dead peace, it has no life in it. That silence is the silence of a cemetery, of the graveyard. I would prefer man to be in a turmoil, but *alive*. I would not like him to become a graveyard. That peace, that silence is at a great cost: you are losing your life, you are losing your intelligence, you are losing all possibility of discovering an ecstatic way of life. That question mark is not there without significance. It is not the work of the Devil that each child is born with doubt and not with faith. Doubt is natural.

Each child asks a thousand and one questions. The more a child asks questions, the more potential he shows that he will be able to discover something. There are dumb children too – not literally dumb, but psychologically dumb. Parents like them very much because they don't create any trouble, they don't ask any questions – even a small child can destroy all your knowledgeability.

I am reminded of my own childhood and so many things that will help you to understand the beauty of the question mark. And unless you understand the question mark as something intrinsic to your humanity, to your dignity, you will not understand what mysticism is.

Mystifying is not mysticism. Mystifying is what the priests have been doing. They have taken away your question mark; they have destroyed your possibility of exploring the mystery of existence. But they have to give you some substitute, some lollipop that is mystifying. And that is what all the scriptures have been doing; their basic methodology has been the same. For example, in Hinduism the scriptures are written in a very difficult language, Sanskrit. Not a single Indian speaks it; it is a dead language. And as far as I am concerned, I have tried hard to find out whether it has ever been alive and I have not found a single piece of evidence. It has always been dead from the very beginning; it was born dead. It was invented by the priests. People have never used it, people cannot use it. It is so sophisticated, so grammatical, so mathematical, so phonetical that people cannot use it.

When people use a language, the language starts becoming less grammatical but more alive; less mathematical but more meaningful. It becomes raw, it is no longer polished and sophisticated – and it starts to grow. Sanskrit has never grown. A dead thing cannot grow. It is exactly where it was five thousand years ago – no growth. Obviously a dead thing cannot grow.

A living language used by people goes on growing. Its words become more and more rounded, just like stones slipping into the river become round. The continuous flow of the river, the continuous hitting against other rocks, against other stones, gives them a roundness. When a language is growing, that can be seen; you can immediately describe, define which languages are dead and which languages are living.

Dead languages will always be perfect; living languages will never be perfect – because living languages are used by imperfect, fallible, human beings, and they go on changing from mouth to mouth. They become more and more usable.

For example, English was introduced into India from the outside. A few words were bound to go into people's use – for example, the word *station*. Now there had never been anything like a station in India before; it came after the English language had already come. Then the railways were introduced and of course the word *station* was there. But if you move all over India, in the villages you will never find a single Indian – I mean of the ninety-eight percent of Indians who don't know English – using the word *station*. It is too difficult, too sophisticated. Through use, they have made – without anybody actually making it, just by use – they have come to the word *tesan*. That is simple. *Station* seems to be a little difficult, it is a strain, so *tesan*.

The word *report* came with the English language, the police stations and your having to "report." But go to the villages and you will be surprised: nobody uses the word *report*, they use the word *rapat*. It has become rounded, *rapat* – the sophistication of *report*, the difficulty of *report* is gone. *Rapat* seems to be human. So many words, and they tell a tremendously meaningful story: when words are used by people then they start taking a shape of their own. They go on changing by mere usage.

Sanskrit remains static. Hebrew, Arabic, Greek, Latin, all remain static, far above people's heads, far above their hands. Sanskrit was never the language of the people and it was mystifying; the whole country depended on the priesthood and they would be saying pure rubbish – in Sanskrit. Once you know it, you will be surprised – what is sacred about it? But chanted in Sanskrit, you don't know what it means, you are mystified.

To keep the scriptures sacred it was necessary to keep them secret. They should not reach the people, people should not be able to read them. Whenever they have a need, the priest is available, he will read the scripture. When printing was introduced Hindus were very reluctant for their scriptures to be printed: what would happen to the mystifying that they had maintained for thousands of years?

Hindus have mystified the whole country with the idea that they have all the secrets in their sacred books – but of those sacred books, ninety-nine percent is simply cow dung! For Hindus it may be holy, but for nobody else is it holy. When those sacred books were translated into other languages the mystifying process stopped; Hinduism lost its height, its glory, because then you could read it in any language – all the scriptures were available.

Mahavira never spoke in Sanskrit, Gautam Buddha never spoke in Sanskrit – for the simple reason that they were trying to defy the priesthood. They spoke in the language of the people. They were condemned by the priesthood: "This is not the right way. You should speak in Sanskrit. And both of you are perfectly well educated" – both were sons of great kings – "you know Sanskrit, so why do you speak ordinary people's languages?"

They said, "For a certain reason: we want people to know that this mystifying has to be exposed. There is nothing in your scriptures, but because they are in a language which nobody understands, it is left to the people's imagination."

Even the priest may not understand what he is reciting because Sanskrit has to be learned by memorizing, not by understanding. There is a great difference between the two. Sanskrit has to be learned by rote, by memory; you have to memorize it. Its whole emphasis is on memory, not on understanding. There is no need to be bothered with what it means; all that you should be concerned about is how it is chanted.

And of course Sanskrit is a very beautiful language, with the quality of singing. You can memorize a song more easily than the same length of prose. Poetry is easily memorized; hence, all the languages which have depended on memory are all poetic, they look like songs, they sound beautiful. Meaning? – you should not ask, because the meaning may be just as stupid as any of today's newspapers, perhaps even worse because it is a five-thousand-year-old newspaper.

When a brahmin is chanting you will be mystified by his chanting; it creates a certain atmosphere of song. And what is the meaning of what he is chanting? Perhaps the passage he is chanting is a prayer to God that means: "Please destroy the crops of my enemy, and let my crops double over last year's. Let the milk disappear from my neighbor's cows and let all that milk come to my cows." When you understand the meaning, you will say, "What nonsense! Where is the sacredness? Where is the religion? This is religion?" – but the meaning is not to be bothered about.

If you listen to a Mohammedan calling from the tower of his mosque, you will be thrilled with its singsong quality. Arabic is tremendously touching, goes directly to the heart. It is meant to go there, it is not meant to go to your intellect, your reason. It is meant to touch your feelings, and it certainly touches them. So when you hear Arabic you will be thrilled, "There must be something immensely beautiful in it." If just the sound makes you so thrilled and excited, what about the meaning? But please don't ask the meaning...

Hence it is not to be allowed that the people learn the sacred language, the holy language. It is only for the priesthood – that is their monopoly.

This is the mystifying. This is a substitute to satisfy you, because they have taken away something of immense potential – the question mark – which would have made the whole existence a mystery. They had to give something as a substitute, a toy to play with. And they are ready with every kind of answer. Even before the child has asked, they start stuffing him with answers. Just look at the process. If the question has not been asked, the answer is irrelevant.

This is what I was going to tell you...

In my childhood they started giving me answers – because there was a special class for Jainism in the Jaina temple and every child had to attend it for an hour every evening. I refused.

I told my father, "In the first place I don't have those questions for which they are supplying answers. This is stupid. When I have questions, I will go and learn their answers and try to find out whether they are correct or not. Right now I am not even interested in the question. Who created the world? My foot! – I am not interested. I know one thing for certain: I have not created it."

My father said, "You are a strange child. All the children from the family are going; everybody from the neighborhood is going."

Jainas tend to live in a neighborhood, a close neighborhood. Minorities are afraid of the majority so they remain close to each other; it is more protective. So their temple is in the middle of the neighborhood and all the children of the neighborhood go. That too is for protection, otherwise if it is in a Hindu neighborhood or in a Mohammedan neighborhood it can be burned any day. And it will become difficult otherwise: if there is a riot you cannot go to your own temple.

There are people who will not eat without going to the temple. First they have to go to the temple and worship, only then can they eat. So Jainas live in small sections of the town, city, village, with their temple in the middle and their whole community surrounding it.

"Everybody is going," my father said.

I said, "They may have questions, or they are idiots. I am not an idiot, and I don't have those questions, so I simply refuse to go. And I know what the teacher goes on teaching the children is absolute rubbish."

My father said, "How can you prove that? You always ask me to prove things; now I ask you, how can you prove what he says is rubbish?"

I said, "Come with me." He had to go many times to many places; it was just that the arguments had to be concluded.

When we reached the school, the teacher was teaching that Mahavira had three qualities: omnipotence, all-powerful; omniscient, all-knowing; omnipresent, everywhere-present.

I said, "You have listened, now come with me to the temple." The class was just by the side of the temple, a room attached to the temple. I said, "Now come into the temple."

He said, "But what for?"

I said, "Come, I will give you the proof."

What I had done was I had just put a *laddu* on Mahavira's statue – that is an Indian sweet, a round sweet, just like a ball. I had put a *laddu* on Mahavira's head, so naturally two rats were sitting on Mahavira's head eating the *laddu*. I said, "This is your omnipotent Mahavira. And I have seen these rats pissing on his head."

My father said, "You are just impossible. Just to prove this, you did all that?"

I said, "What else to do? How else to prove it? Because I cannot find Mahavira. This is a statue; this is the only Mahavira I know and you know and the teacher knows. And he is omnipresent so he must be present here, seeing the rats and what they are doing to him. He could have driven those rats away and thrown away my *laddu*. I was not here, I had gone to pick you up – I had all the arrangements to make. Now prove to me that this man is omnipresent. And I'm not bothered at all – he may be. Why do I care?"

But before a child even asks a question, you stuff his head with an answer. That is a basic and major crime of all the religions. This is what programming is, conditioning is. These religions condemn me, that I am conditioning people; I am simply deconditioning people. They have done the conditioning: they have already filled your mind with all kinds of answers. I am simply destroying those answers so you can find your question. They have covered the question completely, so completely that you have forgotten that you had any question.

In fact you have never asked any questions. No chance has been given to you to be acquainted with your question, with your questioning intelligence. The religions are so afraid that once you start questioning – just once – then it is going to be difficult to force answers against your will, because that questioning intelligence will be raising doubts; it will raise more questions against their answers than you could have imagined. So the best way is to commit this basic crime: the child should be caught – the earlier the better – and he should be spoon-fed theology, dogmatics, doctrines, catechisms. Before he becomes even aware of the question he knows all the answers.

If you are a Christian how do you know that there is a trinity? That God the father, the Holy Ghost, and the son make the highest power monopoly – that they dominate the world, that they are the real dictators. How do you know it? It has been told to you. Perhaps you have forgotten who told you. It was told to you so early that unless you go deeper than that, further back than that, you will not be able to find who this fellow was who corrupted your mind.

The virgin birth... If you are not a Christian, you will immediately object: how can a virgin give birth to a child? But if you are a Christian, you simply don't question it because before your questioning arose, the answer was put into you. They behaved with you as if you are a computer – they just go on feeding in the answers. If somebody says anything against Christianity, you are ready to kill or be killed for this rubbish that you are not even responsible for discovering on your own. And the person who forced it on you did not himself know either: the same was done to him.

For centuries it goes on and on. Each generation goes on giving all its stupidities and superstitions to the new generation, thinking that they are helping you to become knowledgeable. And once you become knowledgeable, the doors of mysticism are closed for you.

Mysticism means looking at existence without any prejudice.

Hence I say no so-called religion can be really mystic – mystifying of course, but never mystic because they cannot fulfill the basic condition to be a mystic. You have to drop all your knowledge, all that you have taken on faith has to be thrown down the drain. Nothing is valuable in it, so don't be worried; it is not a treasure, it is a tragedy. If you can get rid of it you will feel light, you will feel suddenly unburdened, your eyes fresh like a child's eyes.

All these layers of knowledge: Hindu, Christian, Mohammedan, Jewish... All these layers of knowledge – it does not matter who has committed the crime against you; all the religions are in the same boat, committing the same crime. And because they are all committing the same crime, nobody objects. The whole of humanity is in their grip.

Whenever a person like me objects, obviously he is to be condemned by all, criticized by all – but not answered. Nobody has ever answered me. From my childhood I have been continually asking. Nobody has even answered a single question – there are no answers. When you understand that all answers are arbitrary, created by man just to make you feel at ease...

It is just like the mother telling the child who is not ready to sleep alone in the room, "Don't be worried, Jesus is with you. You can sleep. You are not alone." How can the child think that the mother is deceiving him? His own mother? Nor does the mother think that she is deceiving; *she* believes it. Her mother poisoned her; she is doing the same to her own child. Naturally, what else can you do?

The child is afraid to be alone, but he has to learn to be alone, to sleep alone. Soon he will be going to a boarding school; he has to learn to stand on his own. For how long can he go on clinging to his mother's frock? She finds a good reason for saying it: "If he starts feeling the presence of Jesus or God and goes to sleep..."

The child will also feel at ease, less afraid. Nothing has changed – it is the same room, he is alone, the darkness is there – but now there is a little comfort, that Jesus is looking after him, that God is looking after him, that God is everywhere. His own mother says so, his father says so, his teacher says so, his priest says so; everybody cannot be wrong. And God is invisible so you cannot see him, but a certain at ease-ness comes to him.

That's what all this knowledge has been doing to you. It relieves you from inquiring, and inquiry is troublesome. In this world you cannot get anything unless you are ready to risk something to get it. You have got God so cheaply, without even asking. Now what value can this God have? You have got religion so cheaply. This religion, this God, are ways of mystifying existence so that your question remains repressed. My effort here consists in demystifying.

Perhaps that is why the question of what place mysticism has in my religion has arisen – because I am continuously demystifying. The questioner does not understand the difference between mysticism and mystifying. He thinks they are synonymous. They are not: they are against each other. It is mystifying that prevents mysticism from growing. And there is no other way except to destroy mystifying completely, uproot it completely.

Then there is no need for me to give you any answer. Your question is there, and existence is there. Who am I to come between you and existence? Face existence. Look at the sunrise, the sunset. Then you don't have any answers – you just see what is there: a tremendously beautiful sunset.

You will be overwhelmed. You would love to sing or dance or paint or just lie down there on the grass and not do anything, just to go on looking. And a certain communion between you and the beauty of the sunset starts happening. Something transpires – this is mysticism. You know nothing, and yet you know.

There is knowledge which does not know at all. And there is an ignorance which knows everything, because ignorance is innocence.

I can say to you, blessed are the ignorant; but the second part of my sentence cannot be that they shall inherit the kingdom of God. No, because that will be mystifying. I will say: blessed are the ignorant, for theirs is the kingdom of God already, now, here. It is not a question that they shall inherit sometime, somewhere in some life after death – that is mystifying.

Mysticism is cash. Mystifying is a promissory note. Nobody knows whether you will be able to cash this promissory note. The government may fail, the bank may go bankrupt. Only banks can go bankrupt, who else? And this promissory note can be cashed only after death; that is the condition on it. "In God we believe. In God we trust." And the pope promises you that this much will be given to you after death but it is always after death. They have been exploiting people with such a simple means of exploitation that anybody who has a little bit of intelligence can see it.

Life is mystery; scriptures are mystifying. Scriptures are dead and the priesthood lives on these dead scriptures. A real authentic man lives life, not scriptures. And by sheer living, intensively, totally, he is surrounded by mystery all over. Each moment is a mystery. You can taste it, but you cannot reduce it to objective knowledge. That's the meaning of mystery: you have a certain way of knowing it, but there is no way to reduce it to knowledge. It never becomes knowledge, it always remains knowing. You have a sense of knowing, but if somebody insists, "If you know, then give me the answer," and you are a true, honest man, you will say, "I have a sense of knowing but I also have another sense that it cannot be reduced to knowledge."

That's why Lao Tzu refused to write anything his whole life – for the simple reason that the moment you write it, it is something else. But this can be detected only by one who has some acquaintance with mystery.

It is not a question of scholarship: a scholar cannot detect anything wrong in Lao Tzu. Confucius was a great scholar in Lao Tzu's time, his contemporary. The world knows Confucius more than Lao Tzu, naturally: he was a great scholar, a well-known wise man. Great emperors used to visit him for advice. The emperor of China, who must have been the greatest emperor of those days – because China has always been a continent unto itself – appointed Confucius to be his prime minister, so that he was always available to him for advice. But when Confucius went to see Lao Tzu, do you know what happened? He came back almost in a nervous breakdown...

Lao Tzu was known at least to those people who were in search. And when the disciples of Confucius came to know that he was going to Lao Tzu they waited outside – Lao Tzu was living in a mountain cave.

Confucius did not want anybody else to accompany him because he knew that the man was strange, unpredictable. How he may behave, what he will do, what he will say, nobody knows. And he may cut you to pieces before your own disciples. It is better to go alone first.

So he said to his disciples, "Wait outside. Let me go in." When he came out, he was trembling.

The disciples asked, "What happened?"

He said, "Just take me home. I am not myself. That man is a dragon, never go to that man."

What had happened inside the cave? Lao Tzu's disciples were there, that's why we know what happened, otherwise a great meeting would have been missed. Lao Tzu's disciples were also very shocked – even *his* disciples, because Confucius was older than Lao Tzu, far more well-known, respected. Who knew Lao Tzu? – very few people.

The way Lao Tzu behaved with Confucius was simply outrageous. But not for Lao Tzu. He was a simple man, neither arrogant nor humble, just a pure human being. And if his purity, his innocence, and his ordinariness hit hard on Confucius, what could he do?

If you go to a mirror and the mirror shows your face to be ugly, is it the fault of the mirror? You can do one thing, you can avoid mirrors – never look in a mirror. Or you can manufacture a mirror that makes you look beautiful. That is possible. There are hundreds of types of mirrors, concave and convex, and who knows what: you can manage to look tall, and you can manage to look fat, you can manage to look small, and you can manage to look beautiful. Perhaps the mirrors you have are deceiving you. Perhaps the manufacturers are creating mirrors to give you a consolation – that you are so beautiful. Women particularly, standing before the mirror, forget everything else. It is very difficult to take a woman away from a mirror. She goes on looking in the mirror. It must be something in the mirror, otherwise people are just homely.

Lao Tzu's disciples asked, "What did you do?"

He said, "I have not done anything, I simply reflected; it was my response. That idiot thinks he knows, and he is only a scholar. Now what can I do if I made it clear to him that all scholarship is rubbish, and told him, 'You don't know anything at all?'"

When you face a man like Lao Tzu you cannot be dishonest either, at least in front of him. Confucius remained just like a statue, frozen, because what Lao Tzu was saying was right: "Scholarship is not knowing. You are quoting others, have you anything to say on your own?" And Confucius had nothing to say on his own. He was a great scholar he could have quoted all the old ancient scriptures – but on his own? He had never thought about it, that anybody was going to ask, "Have you something to say of your own?"

When Lao Tzu looked at him, Confucius knew that that man could not be deceived. Confucius asked him about something; Lao Tzu said, "No, I don't know anything."

Then Confucius asked, "What happens after death?"

Lao Tzu was just like a flare, became aflame, and he said, "Again! Are you going to drop your stupidity or not? You are alive – can you say what life is? You are alive – can you reduce your experience of life into objective knowledge and make a statement of what life is? And remember that you are alive, so you must know. You don't know life while you are alive and you are bothering about death! You will have enough time in your grave. At that time you can meditate on what death is. Right now, live! And don't live lukewarm."

Many people go on living on dimmer switches. They go on dimming, dimming. They don't die, they simply go on dimming; they simply fade out. Death happens to only a very few people, those who have really lived and lived hot. They know the difference between life and death because they have tasted life, and that experience of life makes them capable of tasting death too. Because they know life, they can know death. If living, you miss life; dying, you are going to miss death.

"You are wasting your time; just go out and live!" said Lao Tzu to Confucius. "One day you will be dead; don't be worried, I have never heard of anybody living for ever, so one day you will be dead. Death makes no exceptions – that you are a great scholar or a prime minister. You will die, that much I can predict. Nothing else is predictable but that much can be predicted easily – that you will die. In your grave, silently, meditate on what death is." Confucius was trembling.

The king also asked him, "You have been to Lao Tzu – what happened?"

Confucius said, "All that I was afraid of happened. He made me look so idiotic that even after forty-eight hours I am still trembling. I am still afraid of that man's face – I had nightmares for two nights! That man is following me, and, it seems, will go on following me. And he had some eyes! They go into you just like swords." He said, "One thing I can say to you as your adviser: don't ever think of meeting this man. He is a dragon, he is not a man."

Mysticism is to know life, without knowledge standing in between you and living.

But you go on living a borrowed kind of life, as if somebody else is living. You are like a zombie, sleepwalking, a somnambulist. And this whole situation has been created by the religions. The trouble is that people think that the religions have been a great blessing to the world; just the contrary – they have been the greatest curse to humanity. They destroyed all that was living in you and replaced it with something dead. Your question was a living phenomenon. Your doubt was breathing, beating in your heart. But they told you, "Don't doubt – otherwise you will suffer."

My father used to tell me, "I am concerned about you. You use such words against religion, God, heaven, and other doctrines, that I am concerned you may suffer for it."

I told him, "I am ready, but before that suffering happens, let me live my life, and I will not have any grudge, I will not complain. In fact, I should be concerned about you, because all this knowledge is hocus-pocus and you think this boat made of paper is going to take you to the further shore. I tell you, you will drown.

"I am from the very beginning trying to swim – I am not depending on any paper boat. If I drown, okay, it is my own choice. Nobody else is responsible for it, and I have no complaint. I enjoyed life. I enjoyed denying all that was bogus and borrowed. I enjoyed being myself. And if this is the reward that existence gives to an authentic man, I take it with grace.

"But what about you, when your boat – made of paper, holy paper, made out of scriptures – is sinking? You missed your life. You cannot feel grateful, because for what will you feel grateful? Life, that may have made you feel gratitude, has slipped out of your hands, and now you are drowning and you don't know how to swim because you never doubted the boat. I have every chance of reaching the other shore if I can swim."

He was a good swimmer himself. And I loved swimming so much that whenever my family wanted to find me they had to go to the side of the river to find where I was – because I had to be somewhere in the river. For four to six hours every day I was in the river. Once in a while we both used to go for a swim. I used to invite him, particularly in the rainy season.

And he would say, "Don't do that," because in the rainy season the river was a mountainous river. It would suddenly become so wide, and so big; otherwise it was a small river. In the summer you could not conceive how much bigger it would become: a hundred-fold at least, miles broad. And the current was so heavy that if I wanted to cross the river – and I have crossed that river hundreds of times in the rainy season – it would take me at least two to three miles downstream. Only then would I be able to reach the other shore. To move directly from this point straight to the other side was impossible. The current was so strong that crossing it I would be carried at least three miles down river.

But I said, "I manage it, and you are certainly a better swimmer, with more strength than me. I am just a child. You are a strong man, you can make it. He came with me only once, and that too because I created a situation where he had to come.

My sister had married and her husband had come to visit us. He was a wrestler; he was the university champion. It was a joke in the university, because when I entered the university – it was his last year, final MA – I stayed in his room. So it became a joke because two champions... I was the university champion in debate, and he was a wrestler.

But everybody was worried about how we would manage because I was continually arguing and he knew only one argument: fighting. He was accepted by the university and passed all the examinations, but it was not that he *was* passing those examinations: the university wanted him to remain in the university because he was the all-India champion. Champions are valuable; they raise the credit of your university.

He knew nothing of what the examinations were about. From the morning, he was doing hours of exercises; in the evening, more exercises – and he was continuously wrestling with people, and his teacher. He was certainly a very good wrestler. I have seen him fighting. He finally became our sannyasin, but unfortunately he died very early. He was not more than fifty-five when he died.

He had come with me from the university and I said to my father, "Today, we are both going swimming. He is a swimmer as well as a wrestler. You have to come." He could not say no in front of his son-in-law – that would have looked a little as if he was afraid. And the son-in-law could not say anything because the father-in-law was coming – an old man. And I was very young and he was an all-India champion wrestler; so how could he expose that he was afraid?

When he saw the river he said, "Really, are we going to cross it?"

I said, "Of course."

My mother was trying to prevent us; my sister was trying to prevent her husband, but I was all for it. I said, "This chance will never come again; let us see what happens. At the most we'll be taken three, four miles down stream; we will just have to walk four miles up again." So when I jumped in, they had to jump.

It was terrible – the current was so strong that my brother-in-law said, "It would have been better if I had said that I was afraid before; to go back now is impossible. We are right in the middle, and I don't see any hope of reaching the other side."

My father said, "I always knew that one day this boy was going to create some trouble for everybody."

But I said, "When we have crossed half, it is proof enough: we can cross the other half because we have already crossed half." Many times they both agreed to turn back, but I said, "You are being absolutely foolish, because to return is still the same distance. And for your whole life you will be known as a coward. What is the point of returning now? In the same time, with the same energy, we will reach the other shore. Even if you return, I am going to the other shore."

That pulled them out of it; they felt, "He is going to make it because he has been going across continually. If he goes on and reaches the other shore and we turn back now, he will spread the rumor in the whole city: 'Look, this is the all-India wrestling champion, and this is my father, who has been swimming his whole life. They both turned back from the middle of the river leaving a small child to go alone to the other side.'"

"Now," they said, "whatsoever happens, even if death happens, there is nothing to do but follow him. He will not turn back." My father said to my brother-in-law, "You don't know him, he is not the type to go back on anything. He would rather die – and we are both going to die with him! We have unnecessarily got ourselves into trouble. I have been avoiding this for years, but just because of you, I agreed."

And my brother-in-law said, "Just because of you, I agreed. He played a trick on both of us."

But finally we reached the bank and I said, "Now, what do you say? Just a little courage and a little readiness to take the risk, and to go into the unknown... And you were trying to go back, which was the same distance – but it was known. That shore was known, so you felt that perhaps it was easier because it was known, and this side was unknown. The unknowability made you afraid, otherwise what arithmetic is this?"

We reached the other shore. We walked three, four miles up again, but they were not prepared to swim back because if we wanted to reach the other shore at the same point we started, then we would have had to go on four miles further. They said, "Four more miles walking? – and this experience of almost dying? We are going to catch the boat from here!" – because that was the point from where the boat used to leave to the other shore, to take passengers from this side to that side.

They said, "Now whatever you want to do, you can. If you want to go four miles on, go; we are not coming. We have decided – we both have decided – that whatsoever happens, if people call us cowards, okay."

I said, "No, I am not going to spread the rumor about you, and I am not going four miles just to prove you cowards. This is my usual practice: I walk up again, and then from four miles further up, I swim across and reach the spot where I have left my clothes. But I will not do that; that will be too much.

"I have already done more than is supposed of a son; I will not do that. But remember one thing: it is better to be ready to swim rather than to wait for boats which are unreliable; better to rely on your own hands than to rely on some knowledge which may be just arbitrarily created by clever people."

Mysticism needs no other qualification except a simple open mind.

You are not a Hindu, you are not a Mohammedan, you are not a Jaina, you are not a Buddhist – you are simply you. And then see: life has no answers; all answers are mystifying.

Life can be lived, can be loved, can be danced, can be drunk, can be tasted. You can do so many things with life. Just remove the dimmer switch.

Livva – not a little hot, livva real hot! And life immediately becomes a mystery. My religion is pure mysticism.

Osho,
Many things which once gave a person a sense of belonging are disappearing: the tribe, the family marriage, even friendship. What is happening? What will happen next?

It is something beautiful that is happening, something really great. Yes, the tribe is disappearing. The family is disappearing, marriage is disappearing, friendship is disappearing. So far so good – because it leaves you alone to be yourself.

The tribal man is just a number in the tribe. The tribal man is the most primitive man, the most unevolved, closer to animals than to man. He lives only as a number in the tribe. It is good that tribes have disappeared. The disappearance of the tribe created families. At that stage, the family was a great advantage because the tribe was a big phenomenon; the family was a small unit. You had more freedom in the family than in the tribe. The tribe was very dictatorial and very powerful. The head, the chief of the tribe was all-powerful, even enough to kill you.

There are still a few tribes in very undeveloped countries. In India there are a few tribes of aboriginals and I have been to those tribes. I got myself appointed in Raipur as a professor just because not far from Raipur is the nearest and the most primitive tribe in India, in Bastar. It is a small state, a tribal state. People still live naked and eat raw meat. Perhaps these are the people from the time when fire had not been discovered, and they have carried on the idea of eating raw meat.

They are very simple, innocent; but as far as the tribe, its conventions and its traditions are concerned, absolutely orthodox. There is no question of anybody rebelling against the tribe. He will be immediately killed, sacrificed to a god, because anybody going against the tribe means he is angering the god – and the tribe cannot afford to make the god angry.

The tribe is carrying on the tradition created by the god himself. They don't have scriptures, they don't have any written language; so the priest, who is also the chief, has all the powers. And it is impossible in that tribe to rebel and still remain alive.

You cannot escape, because outside you will not be accepted at all. They don't know any language that is spoken outside their tribe, they are naked... They put on small wraparound clothes only on the twenty-sixth of January every year, when a small group of them goes to Delhi, to participate in the celebrations for Republic Day, when India became a republic.

Just a small group is trained to speak a little Hindi and to wear some clothes: "Don't be naked in Delhi, particularly when you are passing before the president and the prime minister and all the ambassadors and the invited guests from the world. At least at that time you should be properly dressed." So a small group is trained. The same group goes every year because nobody else wants to bother with all this.

Raipur was so close that I used to visit those people just to see how the tribe has a hold over its people. It has an absolute hold because it does not leave you in a position to revolt. You can leave the tribe, but you cannot live outside the tribe. All that you know is the tribal way of living. If you are caught outside the tribe eating raw meat – they simply kill the animal and start eating it – you will be immediately taken by the police. Naked, you cannot go outside – you will immediately be caught.

They don't know any language, they don't know any skills. All the skills that they do know are useful only in their tribe. For example, a certain dance, a certain kind of drumming; but that is not used anywhere else except in their tribe. So nobody can move out of the tribe; mobility is impossible.

Living inside the tribe, and going against the tribe and its conventions is impossible. The moment the chief finds out, he has found a sacrifice for the god. Then the whole tribe gathers together, dances and creates so much noise – and a bonfire. And the man is pushed into the bonfire as a sacrifice to the god. The tribe was a collective mind. It is still existent in your collective unconscious.

The family was a development at that time because it made you part of a smaller unit, gave you a little freedom. And your family became protective toward you. Now the family is also disappearing because something which is protective at one point is bound to become prohibitive at another point.

It is just like when you grow a small plant and you put a protective fence round it. But don't forget to remove it when the tree is grown up, otherwise the same fence will not allow the tree to grow. When you put it there, the tree was thin like a finger; that's why you put a small fence around it, it protected it from animals, from children. But when the tree trunk grows wider then the fence then that which was protective becomes prohibitive, and you have to remove it.

That time has come. The family is no longer protective. It is prohibitive. It was a great step out of the tribe. Now another step has to be taken: from the family to the commune. The commune can give you all the freedom that you need, and all the protection that is needed without prohibiting you at any point.

So I say it is good that the tribe has disappeared, that the family is disappearing. Yes, you will miss it because you have become addicted; these are addictions. You will miss the father, the mother, but that is only a transitory period. When there are communes established around the world, you will be immensely surprised that you have found so many uncles and so many aunts, and you have lost only one mother and one father. What a gain!

Having one father and one mother is psychologically dangerous because if the child is a boy, he starts imitating the father; if a child is a girl, she starts imitating the mother, and great psychological problems arise.

The girl imitates the mother but she hates the mother, because the girl is a woman; she loves the father. This is an absolutely, biologically solid, scientifically proven fact: the girl loves the father and hates the mother. But the girl cannot imitate the father, she is a girl; she has to imitate the mother.

The boy loves the mother because he is a man, and she is a woman – and the first woman in his life. He loves the mother, he hates the father. He is jealous of the father too because the father and mother are in love; he cannot tolerate it. Small children show it in many ways: if the father and mother are sleeping in bed, the boy will come and sleep just in the middle of both. It is not just that he wants both. No, he is separating them: "Get away!"

The girl is also jealous of the mother. She would like to take the place of the mother and be the father's beloved. And this is not only about the child. If the father shows too much love to the daughter, the mother immediately starts giving him a headache. If the mother is too loving toward the boy, the father starts feeling left out.

But the father and the mother are fading out: soon they will be gone. But they will leave this whole psychological mess in the children. Now the girl will hate her mother her whole life, and anything that appears to be similar to the mother, she will hate. Strangely enough, she will behave exactly like the mother, so she will hate herself too. She will see her face in the mirror and she will remember her mother. She will look at her behavior and she will remember her mother. And the same is going to happen to the boy. This mess is creating almost fifty percent of the psychological diseases in men and women around the world.

A commune will have a totally fresh psychological health. This is possible only in a commune, because the child... Of course the child will be born of a mother and will have a father, but that will not be the only boundary around him. He will be moving in the whole commune and all men of the age of his father will be his uncles – and an uncle is a nice person. The father is always a little nasty, just because of his function. He is a powerful man and has to show that power; he has to discipline the boy.

The same is true about the mother: she has to discipline the girl. She is afraid of what the girl is going to be like if she is not forced into a certain ideal which fits with the society, so she disciplines out of love, with good intentions. But the uncle is not trying to impose anything. When there are so many uncles and so many aunts, a very great phenomenon comes into existence: you are not carrying a single person's image in your mind.

The boy carries the mother's image in his mind: he would like a woman exactly like his mother to be his wife. Now, where can you find your mother again? So he will fall in love with a woman who has some similarity, but just similarity is not going to function. People become attracted to strange things: the color of the hair, the way the woman walks, the color of her eyes, the length of her nose, the cut of her face; something is similar. But only some things can be similar; what about everything else?

So, you fall in love with the similar. But you are also falling in love with the whole person, not just the way she walks. She will also cook, and it's not going to be your mother's cooking. Then you will know that just walking is not going to help. She screams also, she shouts also. She is not behaving like your mother. She is your wife, why should she behave like your mother? She has not come to baby-sit.

She has been in search of a husband, and because there was something in you similar to her father – the length of your nose, the length of your ears – she fell in love with you. Now what to do with your ears? How long can she go on playing with your ears? And you won't like it either: "What nonsense is this? I am not just ears, I am a whole person!" But she has no desire for the whole person.

This is the trouble that exists, and it is because of a certain reason: every boy has an idea of a woman, and that woman is his mother; every girl has an idea of a man, and that man is her father. That's why all love affairs are bound to fail. No love affair can succeed, because the basic psychology is against its success.

So the only successful love affair is one which remains only in your mind, but never materializes. The great lovers of the world – Laila and Majnu, Romeo and Juliet, Shiri and Farhad, Soni and Mahival – are great lovers whose story the world has remembered. But if they had married, finished; nobody would ever have heard of their love story. Because they could not materialize their relationship into actuality, it remained only in their minds. The society and the parents or something came in between, and they had to remain apart, separated. The love remained aflame because it was only in imagination.

In imagination there is no problem. You create your lover the way you want. Now, in your imagination your lover cannot say, "No! I am *going* to smoke" – because it is your imagination. If you want him to smoke, he will smoke; if you don't want him to smoke, he will not. But a real husband will smoke even if you say he should not smoke, that it stinks, that if he smokes you cannot sleep with him in the bed. The more you insist, the more he will resist: "Go to hell, sleep anywhere." His cigarette is far more important than you. It is far more significant for him because it gives him support, help, friendship, company – thousands of things in such a small cigarette. And what can a woman do? So if there is a choice he will choose the cigarette and leave the woman. But in your imagination you can manage whatsoever you want.

The man goes on imagining the woman: in his imagination she does not perspire, needs no deodorant. In his imagination she never becomes a pain in the neck because imagination cannot go to the neck, imagination remains in the head. And it is just your painting, so whatsoever color you want to put there, you go on putting. There is no problem. There is no resistance from the painting like: "I am not going to take this color" or, "I am not going to wear this sari."

So the only love affairs which are famous in the world are the love affairs which never materialized. What happened to all the other love affairs? – nobody bothers about them. In every story, when the lovers get married the last sentence is: "Then they lived happily ever after." It's strange: every lover in every story then lives happily ever after? In fact, after that the real story begins, before that the story was all imagination.

It is good that the family is disappearing. And with it nations will disappear because the family is the unit of the nation. So I am tremendously happy whenever I see the family disappearing, because I know behind it will go the nation. With it will go the so-called religions, because it is the family which imposes religion, nationality, and all kinds of things on you. Once the family is gone, who is going to force Christianity on you, Hinduism on you? Who is going to insist that you are an American, that you are an Oregonian?

Once the family is gone, much of the psychological disease will be gone, much of the political insanity will be gone. You should be happy that they are disappearing. Marriage was an invention against nature. It has tortured man long enough, but there was a time when it was needed.

It was needed because there were powerful people and there were weaker people. The powerful people used to collect all the beautiful women for themselves, and the weaker people remained without wives. Their biology remained unsatisfied. So marriage had to be invented – it was invented by the weaker men. The weaker men got together, must have got together some time in the past and must have decided on it, because when weaker men are together then the stronger man is no longer the stronger. He is stronger than a single man, but he is not stronger then the whole mass of weak people.

The weak people got together and they said, "One man, one wife" – because that is the ratio in which children are born. It was forced by the weaker man on the stronger people; otherwise it was bound to be that they would collect all the beautiful women to their harems and the weaker people would remain sex-starved. That situation was not good. The family helped, and the monogamous family came into being. It was of great importance that the weaker people were no longer sex-starved.

But now the family is no longer needed, now it is phony. It is possible now that the woman can earn, the man can earn; they need not depend on each other. It is possible for a woman not to have children. It is possible for a woman to hire another woman to have her children grow in the other woman's womb, or she can arrange for a test-tube baby. Sex and children are no longer connected. You can have sex and it does not mean that you have to suffer children too. Now the family is absolutely out of date. The commune has the future.

A commune means many independent individuals, not belonging to each other in the old ways of family, tribe, religion, nation, race – no. Only in one way are they related to each other: that they are all independent. They respect your independence, and the same they expect from you: to respect their independence.

That is the only relationship, the only friendship, the only thing that is the cementing force in a commune: that we respect each other's individuality, independence. The other's way of life, his style of life is absolutely accepted, respected. The only condition is that nobody is allowed to interfere with anybody else in any sense.

So it is good that all this dead past is disappearing, and freeing us to create a new man, a new humanity, a new world.

CHAPTER 2

To Define Is to Confine – Existence Has No Boundaries

Osho,
Why do I feel that life is meaningless and empty? It seems that I am deathly afraid of being alone. How can I go totally into my aloneness with joy instead of fear?

The word *meaning* is irrelevant to life. Life is neither meaningful nor meaningless. But for centuries, man's mind has been conditioned to believe that life has great meaning. All that meaning was arbitrary. Hence only in this century, for the first time in the whole history of man, has the question, "What is the meaning of life?" become one of the most important, because all old lies are exposed.

Life was meaningful with a God. Life was meaningful with a life beyond death. Life was meaningful because the churches, synagogues, temples, mosques, were continuously hammering the idea into man's mind.

A certain maturity has come to man; not to all, but to a very small minority.

I would like you to remember five significant names. The first is Søren Kierkegaard. He was the first man who raised this question and was condemned universally, because even to raise the question created suspicion in people. Nobody had ever dared to ask, "What is the meaning of life?" Even the atheists who had denied God, who had denied the afterlife, who had denied the existence of the soul had never asked what the meaning of life is. They said, "Eat, drink and be merry, that is the meaning of life." It was clear to them that these joys – eat, drink, be merry – were what life is all about.

But Søren Kierkegaard went very deeply into the question. He unknowingly created a movement: existentialism. Then followed the four other names: Martin Heidegger, Karl Jaspers, Gabriel Marcel, and the last but not the least important – in fact the most important – Jean-Paul Sartre. These five people went on hammering on the whole intelligentsia of the world that life is meaningless.

Now, anybody who has some kind of intelligence is bound to come across this question, and he has to find some way to encounter it. I do not agree with these five great philosophers, but I give them the respect that they deserve. They were courageous, because once you take meaning out of life, religion disappears – because religion up to now has been nothing but an effort to give meaning to your life: to fill it so that you don't feel empty; to surround you with God and angels so that you don't feel lonely. You have not been going to the church, the synagogue and the temple without a reason.

For thousands of years man has not been bowing down to the priests without a reason. He was gaining something. Of course they were exploiting him, but even in their exploitation man was finding a certain consolation. He was not alone, he was being looked after. Life was not futile, it had tremendous meaning, spiritual, esoteric, profound – so high and so deep that your intellect could not comprehend it.

Still, the majority of people, ninety-nine percent, are not bothered by the question. How can they be bothered? They easily find consolation from the dead past. To them it is not a dead past.

I have told you about Bishop Jenkins of England who declared that there was no resurrection, that it is a myth; that there was no virgin birth, it is an absolute lie, and that there is no need for anybody to believe in all these mythologies to become a Christian. Of course, there he is not right because he says, "I don't need all these things – I can still believe in God." I can't see what reason he can give for his faith in God.

Christians were not fools to go on believing in absurdities for two thousand years. The reason was, without those absurdities you cannot support God, the ultimate absurdity. Now, it is like taking your legs and your hands and your head and everything away and saying I still believe in you. Nothing is left behind. All the theologians, from Thomas Aquinas to any modern preacher, understand perfectly well that God needs support. Every lie needs support.

Only truth can stand on its own feet.

A lie cannot stand on its own feet. It needs borrowed legs, a borrowed head, a borrowed heart – everything borrowed. If you go on taking things away piece by piece, and then you say in the end that all these things are not needed, that you still have faith in God... So for a Christian, according to Jenkins, these things should not be required as a fundamental part of Christianity. I don't know whom he is befooling. Certainly he is befooling himself, because these are the supports, and if you take away all the supports, the house will fall down. And he has not given a single reason now for faith in God.

But I have remembered him again today because a few days ago lightning struck one of the most beautiful cathedrals in England, York, and the majority of the masses believe that it is not a coincidence: it is God punishing the church for installing a man like Jenkins as a bishop. He was the fourth in the hierarchy; he had just to pass two people to become the archbishop of England, and it would not have been difficult to pass these two people. Life is so full of accidents – they may die or something – one can always hope. And he was not so far away, just close.

But now, all over England, it is believed that God has punished the church. But this is a strange God, and a strange punishment, because Jenkins was not the bishop of this cathedral. This is strange. Jenkins was two hundred miles away. Your God is such a great shot – he missed him by two hundred miles. A master archer!

And what has the cathedral of York to do with Jenkins' statement? The lightning should be on Jenkins or on the cathedral or church where he was the bishop, or on the Archbishop of Canterbury because he had appointed him. This cathedral in York is in no way connected. But people have found a relationship – it is not a coincidence. Then life becomes related to profound realities, even your small stupidities. Now, even if God is there, do you think he will bother about Bishop Jenkins? And if he does bother then what kind of anger is this? He should at least learn a little marksmanship; he must have been doing this for millions of years, so much training.

I am reminded...

A king who was a very great lover of archery – and he himself was a master archer – always wanted to meet anybody who was better than him. But his whole life he could never find anybody who was better than him. One day when he was passing through a small village, he saw on every tree a strange thing – perfect marksmanship, a master far better than him. On every tree, on the wooden fences, everywhere, he found a round circle with an arrow just exactly in the middle.

He stopped his chariot and asked, "Where is this great archer? I would like to honor him. I will take him to the palace – he should be my master. I have been in search but I have never found anybody better than me. But this man seems to be a hundred percent accurate. Not even by a minute part of an inch does he miss; he exactly hits the center."

He went to a few trees and measured and it was the exact center. He asked one of the villagers who had gathered, to see why the king was there with his golden chariot. He asked, "Where is this great archer?"

They all laughed, they said, "He is no archer, he is the idiot of this village." They said, "You don't understand."

"You are all idiots!" the king said. "Such a great archer and you call him an idiot?"

They said, "First, try to understand. He is no archer, he is just a fool. First he shoots the arrow and then he draws the circle. Of course he is perfect, he draws the circle afterwards. So wherever the arrow goes, there he makes the circle. Don't get worried about him, just go on your way. He is a complete idiot.

"We have been telling him that this is not the way of archery. First you make the circle and *then* you shoot, but he goes on doing it his own way: he shoots first. He says, 'What does it matter which you do first and which you do second? This way it is always perfect. Your way does not work at all, I have tried it.'"

Now, for millions of years, God has been threatening people with lightning, killing people with lightning. Hinduism believes that lightning is nothing but the arrow of the Lord Shiva. So whenever there is lightning they have to make a sacrifice to Shiva, to pray or do some rituals, because lightning is the perfect symbol that Shiva is angry, and they have to find the person who has made him angry.

But in the twentieth century, in this last part of the twentieth century, in one of the most educated and sophisticated countries like England, most of the people believe that it is a punishment sent by the lord to Bishop Jenkins! If this is God's archery then I don't think any man is a lesser archer than him. You won't miss by two hundred miles! Even that idiot who discovered the right way was far more intelligent than this God.

But why do people go on believing in such things? It is not without reason. The reason is that all these things are giving meaning to their lives. A God above makes you feel safe, secure. If there is no God then the whole sky is empty, and you are left alone. You are so tiny, and the emptiness is so vast. Fear is bound to strike you – just think of the emptiness of the sky, which is infinite, because there cannot be any boundary anywhere. The old religions all believed there is a boundary, but that is absolutely illogical. A boundary means there must be something beyond it, otherwise how can you make a boundary? Yes, you can make a boundary around your house because of the neighbor's house. You can create a fence around your house because the earth continues beyond your fencing.

But if you are creating a fence where the earth ends, and there is nothing else beyond your fencing, your fencing will fall into the emptiness. How will it be supported from the other side? To create a boundary, two things are needed; one on this side and one on the other side. Obviously existence cannot have any boundary. It is fearful to conceive of infinity, the emptiness continuing forever and ever. You will never come to a point where you can say, "Now we have reached the end." There is no end and there is no beginning.

Now, think of a story which has no beginning and no end. It was one of my pastimes... I have never been interested much in novels, but once in a while when I had nothing else to read I had my own way of reading a novel – just from the middle, because that gave it some authenticity. With no beginning, you have to work out what must have preceded because you start suddenly in the middle. And I would never go to the end. Again I would stop halfway – halfway through the second half. First I would try to figure out what the beginning could be and what the end could be; then I would start reading from the beginning.

And I was puzzled that I always managed to figure out the beginning and the end. I never missed, not only in details but on all the basic points, because it is a man-created thing, and the mind works in a certain fashion. It has a routine way of working. If this is the middle, created by a human mind, and if I understand the human mind, I can figure out what the beginning will be and what the end will be.

Yes, if the book is written by a madman, then certainly I will not be able to figure it out. But madmen don't write books. That is very compassionate of them. But in fact if they start writing books, their books will be far more interesting than the books written by scholars, intellectuals, because the intellect has a certain way of working.

I am not in favor of all these five "existentialists"– in quotes – because I am not even ready to call them existentialists. Kierkegaard never really lived, or if you call his life, life, then it was worse than death. He came out of his house only once a month, and the house was not much, just a small room. His father, seeing that his son seemed to be a little crazy – continuously reading and writing – tried to read his books, and threw them away because he could not manage to figure out what he wanted to say. Kierkegaard goes on and on about nothing, much ado about nothing.

Kierkegaard never married. One foolish woman was in love with him – must have been foolish, because he was an ugly man in the first place, and a strange type, eccentric, who lived in the darkness of his room. Once a month he had to go out because, before he died, his father had put money in the post office, and made an arrangement that every month Kierkegaard could draw a certain amount. He knew that Kierkegaard was not going to earn any money; he would simply die in his room, so his father sold everything and deposited the money in the post office. That's why Kierkegaard had to go out once every month; he would go out the first day of the month.

He lived in Copenhagen, and the whole town waited because Kierkegaard coming out of his room was a rare opportunity. The children used to follow him to the post office; it was almost a procession. He had written a book, *Either Or*, which had just been published and that had become his nickname in Copenhagen. So the children would be shouting "Either-or" – that was his real name to them – "Either-or is going to the post office!"

It was a great insight on the part of the children to name this man Either-or, because he was exactly that. That's why he could not marry the woman, because he continued to think: "Either-or." All the favorable points for marriage and all the unfavorable points for marriage all balanced out. He could not decide. The woman waited for three years, but he said, "Forgive me, I cannot decide. It is still either-or."

Now, this man, who had never loved, who had not a single friend, who had not in any way contacted nature, who never communed in any way with existence, if *he* feels life is meaningless, no wonder – it has to be meaningless. But he is projecting his feeling of meaninglessness on everybody.

And then came these four other so-called existentialists. I am calling them "so-called" because they had no communion with existence at all. The only way to have communion with existence is silence; and they didn't know the language of silence – how could they commune with existence? So what were they doing? They were exposing the lie that the religious people have imposed on humanity. And it *was* a lie.

The meaning that religious people have given to human life is arbitrary. These people are exposing the arbitrariness of the religious people's meaning – but that does not mean that life is meaningless. It simply means that the meaning that was given to life up to now was found invalid: God is not the meaning of life. Life beyond death is not the meaning of life. Jesus Christ is not the meaning of life. That does not mean that life has no meaning. But because you have been thinking that this *is* the meaning of life, when suddenly it falls apart, you pick up the polar opposite idea of meaninglessness.

I want you to remember *my* standpoint. I am an existentialist. And I say to you that life is neither meaningful nor meaningless. The question is irrelevant. Life is just an opportunity, an opening. It depends what you make of it. It depends on *you* what meaning, what color, what song, what poetry, what dance you give to it.

Life is a creative challenge and it is good that it hasn't any fixed meaning, otherwise there would be no challenge. Then it would be just a ready-made thing: you are born and the meaning of life is given to you and you carry it your whole life; this is the meaning of your life. No, existence is far more profound than any meaning.

Existence is just a challenge to creativity. It allows you all the space that you need – and you think it is empty? Just try to use the right words, because words have a certain context. *Empty* is a sad word; it seems something is missing, something that should have been is not there. But why call it empty? Why in the first place expect that something should be there waiting for you? Who are you? Give it the right name.

It is one of the basic arts of living to call things by their right name, the right word, to make the right gesture, because even a slightly wrong word brings wrong associations. Now, *empty* – the very sound of the word reminds you of something futile. No, I give it a different word: it is *spaciousness*, uncluttered with anything. Existence is so spacious that it allows you absolute freedom to be whatsoever you want to be, whatsoever you have the capacity to be. It allows you an unhindered space to grow and to blossom. It does not impose anything on you.

God imposes things on you. He wants you to be a certain kind of man, having a certain kind of personality, morality, ethics, etiquette. He wants to put you into a cage. And you think to be caged is to have found meaning? To be caged is to be dead.

Nietzsche is far truer when he says, "God is dead and I proclaim to humanity that now man is free." He is saying two things: "God is dead" – that is the least important part of his statement, which has angered all the religions of the world. The most important part is the second part: "Hence man is free." Just think a little bit about it. God is equivalent to slavery. No God is equivalent to freedom. And freedom is bound to be spacious – don't call it empty. Yes, it is empty of any hindrance. It is empty of any structure. It is empty of any guidance. It does not force you to move in a certain direction, to be someone.

No, life gives you all the space you need, perhaps more space than you need. Space out, rather than bothering about why life is empty. This spaciousness without boundaries, with no guidelines, with no map is good. You can move like a cloud in the sky: untethered, unforced. Wherever the wind takes you, wherever you reach, that is the goal.

Ordinarily we have been taught that there should be a goal and then you start moving toward it; if you reach then you have succeeded. But really you have missed immense opportunities. In going for this particular goal you have lost immensely the whole richness of life.

Why does one feel life is meaningless? – because in the first place you expect some meaning to be there. Who told you that you have to expect some meaning? This is what I call the wrong that religions have done to man. They have told you there is meaning; you accepted it – and when you don't find it, you are frustrated, you feel lost.

So many intelligent people go on committing suicide. The greatest number of suicides in any single profession is in the profession of philosophy. More philosophers commit suicide than any other profession. Strange! Professors should be wise people, philosophers particularly so. But what goes wrong? – their expectation of finding meaning. They try hard to find it, and it is not there. It was never there in the first place.

Other people don't try to find meaning, that's why they need not commit suicide: they never feel frustrated. They know that they have not tried to find it, so they feel they are sinners, that something is wrong with them, but they never feel that they have to commit suicide because life is meaningless. They have not searched; meaning was always there. They have not cared. They have not listened to the priest, to the wise guys who are all around, who are giving advice freely – although nobody takes it. Advice is the only thing in the world that everybody gives and nobody takes. And everybody knows it.

These people – Jaspers, Marcel, Heidegger, Sartre – have moved to the opposite polarity. Religions say that life is meaningful because God cannot create a meaningless life; it has an intrinsic meaning, a significance. You have to fulfill it, and you will be rewarded for it. Religions gave this hope but these people found that there is no God, that nobody has created a meaningful life, that there is no destiny – man is just driftwood going nowhere. So they moved to the opposite polarity: life is meaningless.

Just see the point: religions say life is meaningful, and these so-called existentialists have impressed on the intelligentsia of the world that life is meaningless. But to me they are both making the same mistake. I say that meaning is irrelevant to life. Let me explain to you. Now, what is the smell of the color red? You will say, "It is irrelevant, smell has nothing to do with color." And if you start searching for a certain smell in the color red – because scriptures say, priests say, religions say, and thousands of years of traditions say that the color red has a certain fragrance – you will find that there is no fragrance. Color and smell are totally different dimensions; they never meet. Neither smell has any color, nor color have any smell. That does not mean that color is futile, throw it away.

Life and meaning are totally different. Meaning is a logical concept, and life has nothing to do with logic. People who want to live have to put logic aside; otherwise you cannot live. Logic will come in everywhere preventing you from living: "either-or." You will think much, but you will not live much. And the more you think, the less is the possibility of living.

Living needs a little transcendence from thinking.

Zorba the Greek says to his boss, "Boss, only one thing is wrong with you – you think too much." And he is right; even his boss realizes finally that he is right. The whole day Zorba works hard, labors – and then he dances and plays some instrument. What is it in Italian...? *Santuri*? Or in Greek...? *Santuri*? I think whatever it is, *santuri* is a good name! Anyway all names are made up. I will just use *santuri*.

He plays the *santuri*, he dances, he goes mad, dancing – and the boss simply sits. One day Zorba says, "What are you doing sitting there? There is a full moon, there is the river, the sands are calling, and the winds are so cool – come along with me." With very hesitant feet the boss goes with him because Zorba is dragging him, and Zorba is a very strong man.

The boss is just a boss as bosses are supposed to be: a rich man, intellectual, but not strong. Zorba just pulls him and starts dancing and playing on his *santuri*. The boss also tries a little bit, finds it exhilarating – the wind, the moon, the river, the sand, and the mad way Zorba plays his *santuri*, and the mad way he dances. Slowly, slowly he forgets that he is the boss and starts dancing. It takes a little time to slip out of the mind, but he slips out. It is only for a few moments, but now he too knows that life has a different taste.

Life is not available to thinking. Perhaps it is available to dancing, to singing. One thing is certain, that thinking is the driest dimension of your life. It is a desert with no oasis.

If you feel that life is meaningless, it simply means you don't know how to live. You don't know that meaning has nothing to do with life. This has to be a fundamental principle: life has nothing to do with meaning. It is not arithmetic. It is not logic. It is not philosophy.

Living in itself is such an ecstasy – who cares for meaning?

Can't you visualize experiences which are intrinsically so joyous that even to ask the question about meaning will look idiotic? Nobody asks, "What is the meaning of love?" But these people who are asking, "What is the meaning of life?" are bound to ask, "What is the meaning of love?"

There is a Russian story, a small story...

In a village a young man, is called an idiot by everybody. From his very childhood he has heard that he is an idiot. And when so many people are saying it – his father, his mother, his uncles, the neighbors, and everybody – of course he starts believing that he must be an idiot. How can so many people be wrong? And they are all important people. But when he becomes older and this continues, he becomes an absolutely sealed idiot; there is no way to get out of it. He tries hard but whatsoever he does is thought to be idiotic.

That is very human. Once a man goes mad he may become normal again but nobody is going to take him as normal. He may do something normal but you will suspect that there must be something insane about it. And your suspicion will make him hesitant and his hesitancy will make your suspicion stronger; then there is a vicious circle. So that man tried in every possible way to look wise, to do wise things, but whatsoever he did people would always say it was idiotic.

A saint was passing by. The man went to the saint in the night when there was nobody about and asked him, "Just help me to get out of this locked state. I am sealed in. They don't let me out; they have not left any window or door open so that I can jump out. Whatsoever I do, even if it is exactly the same as they do, still I am an idiot. What should I do?"

The saint said, "Do just one thing. Whenever somebody says, 'Look how beautiful the sunset is,' say, 'You idiot, prove it! What is beautiful there? I don't see any beauty. Prove it.' If somebody says, 'Look at that beautiful roseflower,' catch hold of him and tell him, 'Prove it! What grounds have you to call this ordinary flower beautiful? There have been millions of roseflowers. There are millions, there will be millions in the future; what special thing has this roseflower got? What are your fundamental reasons which prove logically that this roseflower is beautiful?'

"If somebody says, 'This book of Leo Tolstoy is very beautiful,' just catch hold of him and ask him, 'Prove where it is beautiful; what is beautiful in it? It is just an ordinary story – just the same story which has been told millions of times, just the same triangle in every story: either two men and one woman or two women and one man, but the same triangle. All love stories are triangles. So what is new in it?'"

The man said, "That's right."

The saint said, "Don't miss any chance, because nobody can prove these things; they are unprovable. And when they cannot prove it, they will look idiotic and they will stop calling you an idiot. When I return the next time, just tell me how things are going.

And the next time when the saint came back, even before he could meet the old idiot, people of the village informed him, "A miracle has happened. We had an idiot in our town; he has become the wisest man. We would like you to meet him."

And the saint knew who that "wisest man" was. He said, "I would certainly love to see him. In fact I was hoping to meet him."

The saint was taken to the idiot and the idiot said, "You are a miracle-worker, a miracle man. The trick worked! I simply started calling everyone an idiot, stupid. Somebody would be talking of love, somebody would be talking of beauty, somebody would be talking of art, painting, sculpture, and my standpoint was the same: 'Prove it!' And because they could not prove it, they looked idiotic.

"It is a strange thing. I was never hoping to gain this much out of it. All that I wanted was to get out of that confirmed idiocy. It is strange that now I am no longer an idiot, I have become the most wise man. I know I am the same, and you know it too."

But the saint said, "Never tell this secret to anybody else. Keep the secret to yourself. Do you think I am a saint? Yes, the secret is between us. This is how I became a saint. This is how you have become a wise man."

This is how things go on in the world.

Once you ask, "What is the meaning of life?" you have asked the wrong question. Obviously somebody will say, "This is the meaning of life" – and it cannot be proved. Then one thing is proved automatically: that life is meaningless. But that is a fallacy. That's why I say that all these five existentialists – great names because theirs is the only great philosophical school that has arisen in these last few decades – have defeated all other philosophical schools with the same trick, the same one that the idiot used. About any painting they will say, "Meaningless!" Of any poetry they will say, "Meaningless!" And there is no way to prove beauty; either you see it or you don't see it. There is no way to prove love; if you have to prove it, you are finished. Can you prove your love?

It is good that people take it for granted, at least in the beginning, that they love each other without asking, "Do you really love me? Where is love? Prove it first." Then love would disappear from the world because nobody can prove it. How can you prove it? At the most you can say, "You can listen to my heartbeat." The other person can listen to your heartbeat and say, "I can hear your heartbeat, but I don't hear any love. I don't hear any song or dance or any bells ringing. It is just a heartbeat." You can find a stethoscope and listen to it more accurately, more loudly, so then it becomes really loud, but you will not find any love there. Love is not a heartbeat. Then what is love? Has anybody ever been able to define it? No, there is no way to define it.

There are things which are indefinable; hence I call my religion pure mysticism, because I accept things which cannot be explained, which cannot be defined, which can only be lived, which can only be known by experience. If you try to think about them you are going to miss them.

All these five great philosophers have missed life absolutely because they asked the wrong question, they accepted the wrong answer, they fought the wrong answer and they moved to the polar opposite. And remember, if you move from one wrong thing and to oppose it, you go to the polar opposite, you reach another wrong thing – because only wrong can be the polar opposite of another wrong, not right.

Life is simply an experience.

Your birth is only the beginning. You are not born ready-made; you are born with all dimensions open. That's the beauty and dignity of man.

A dog is born as a dog; he will remain a dog. He comes with a certain structure, lifestyle, morality, religion, philosophy. He brings with him everything ready-made; in fact nature provides him with everything. He never feels meaningless. He never bothers about meaning – it is only man who bothers. Hence he thinks he needs a very great philosophical understanding. The dog comes into the world complete. Man is born incomplete, open; it is left to him what he is going to become, what he is going to make out of his life. This creates

problems, but all those problems are challenges to be accepted, faced.
You have to be in constant effort for your own growth. Yes, many times you will move in a wrong direction, but don't be worried, that's how we learn – by making mistakes.

My father used to stop me, saying, "Don't do that, you are doing it wrong."

I said, "One thing should be settled between us: let *me* find out that it is wrong, and never stop me when I am going to commit a mistake."

He said, "What! You are going to commit a mistake and I am not to stop you?"

I said, "Yes, because without mistakes I will never learn. How long are you going to be with me? Are you going to live for me, on my behalf? I have to live myself. So please be kind enough: let me fall, let me make mistakes, let me go wrong, allow me to see what is right and what is wrong. Yes, I am groping, but only through this groping will I find out. And only that which is found by you is yours."

Jesus may have found truth, Buddha may have found truth, but it is all hogwash, just meaningless to you. You will have to travel the path, many paths, out of which some will take you in the wrong direction and you will have to return to find the right one. But if you go on searching you are bound to find, because when you start finding that the path is wrong, you are already starting to feel what is right. It may not be very clear to you, but the moment you see that something is wrong, side by side somewhere inside you, you have already achieved a glimpse of the right.

To know something as a lie means that you have a vague idea of what is truth. So just moving in wrong directions is not wrong, because it is through that movement that you will slowly, slowly, crystallize the idea of the right. And once you find what is right then you will jump out of your bathtub and run naked in the streets shouting, "Eureka! Eureka! Eureka!"

That's what happened to Archimedes. He ran into the palace of the king, naked, into the court! – shouting just one word, "Eureka! I have found it!"

But the king said, "Don't be so excited – at least you should have put some clothes on. Along the whole street people have gathered and you are standing in the court."

Then he looked and saw that he was naked. He said, "In fact, I was in my bathtub, and that's where I found it." A great present had been given to the king which was made of gold. The king had given him the job of finding some way of telling whether it was pure gold or was there some mixture.

The king said, "I don't want you to destroy it and I don't want you to cut it into pieces. I don't want you to poke into it to find out whether it is also pure gold inside. Work out a method where you don't touch it, and find out whether it is pure gold." And that's what he had found while he was in the tub.

The tub was full of water, absolutely full. When he entered the tub he saw water spilling out. As he lay down in the tub, he saw more water spilling out. And a sudden flash in the mind – he jumped out of the tub and saw how much water had spilled out, and how much the water level had gone down. And he saw it was exactly his volume. He had found the way!

Now, find some pure gold and put it in water. The bath should be full, then water will spill out because you have put the gold into the water. Now weigh the water that has overflowed, and then you know how much water spills out when you add a certain weight of pure gold. Then bring the king's present, and put it into the water. You are not destroying it, not touching it. If exactly the same amount of water spills out as did from the same weight of pure gold, then the present is pure gold. Otherwise it is impure; some other metal is there.

After the discovery he was so ecstatic that he forgot all about the bathroom, and the clothes, and he just ran. And the king could understand. He said, "I can understand when someone finds something on his own, it is so ecstatic." Just a small thing – he had not found God or nirvana or enlightenment. No, he had just found a way to decide whether the gold was pure or not. But even that, the flash of finding something, makes you aware of your own intelligence. The greater the finding, the greater you feel your intelligence.

When you find what life is by living, then you will not find yourself surrounded by emptiness; you will be surrounded by space, pure space, which allows you to grow in every direction. Existence is freedom.

And yes, I agree with Nietzsche: man is free. Up to now the religions have tried to make man a slave – spiritually, psychologically, but a slave all the same.

Nietzsche is not right that God is dead, because God has never been there. It was just his emphasis – I know that he was a man of tremendous insight and could not commit such a mistake. When he says, "God is dead," he does not mean that God was there and is now dead. He wants to emphasize the fact that there is no God: forget about God and forget about all the mythologies that you have lived by up to now. From now onward you are free. Live in freedom, and create yourself.

Why be created by God? Anyway God is not capable of creating you. Just look: he created Eve out of a rib from Adam – a great creator! In the first place is he a certified surgeon? I don't think that he is an FRCS, and he is doing surgery without anesthesia. Adam was just asleep and he took out his rib. But when you are stupid, then you are going to believe in any stupid thing. And from the rib how can you create the woman?

I don't see any way to create a woman from a rib. This is pure crap! – and so insulting to women. Women at least should stop going to all the churches and all the synagogues because God has done such an insult. He cannot be forgiven! Let *him* apologize. What do these liberation women go on doing? They should protest before every church, before every synagogue, that no woman will enter unless that statement from the Bible is removed.

Woman is created from the rib of Adam? Why could he not also create woman the way he has created Adam? The word *Adam* means earth, mud. First he made Adam with earth, and then breathed life into him. Now, when he was making woman, was earth missing? Was all the mud finished with one Adam? It would have been easier to make the woman also from earth. Why take a rib from this poor man?

And after that, you know what used to happen? I have just heard about it, I don't know whether it is true or not. Every night when Adam came home and went to sleep, the first thing Eve would do was count his ribs, because she was afraid God might create another woman. Every night... It was a natural fear because if another rib was missing then Adam would have been in real trouble. But God never did the same operation again.

The past of humanity is full of myth, and a myth simply means an invented story to give you a bogus feeling of meaning. And man, even very educated people, cultured people...

I had a professor, my colleague in the university, who was a great follower of these people: Søren Kierkegaard to Jean-Paul Sartre. He thought himself an existentialist. I asked him, "Do you really think there is no God?"

He said, "Yes, there is no God, no Holy Ghost, no Jesus Christ." He had been a Christian.

I said, "If I can manage some meeting with one of these three fellows…"

He said, "What! A meeting! How can you manage a meeting? Nobody has ever seen them. It is all just superstition."

I said, "Okay, come to my house tonight."

He started becoming a little afraid: "But what will you do?"

I said, "That you don't ask. First let the meeting happen."

He said, "With whom?"

I said, "Don't be bothered – with whomsoever I can get the appointment. I don't know yet with whom I can get the appointment. Come with me tonight. Eat with me, sleep in my house and I will try my best."

He said, "But I am very busy today."

I said, "There is no problem, then tomorrow. It is going to happen one day so this busyness without business won't help – you are not busy."

He said, "That's right, I am not busy. I was just trying to get out of this."

I said, "Why? I am going to make an appointment, and you are trying to get out of it. You deny them, and having denied them then you say life is meaningless. I will make your life meaningful tonight."

He said, "My God! Okay."

But sitting with me in my car, he would look at me again and again, and he would say, "With whom are you going to make…?"

I said, "Don't worry, that is my business. And I have done it many times so don't worry!"

But how could the poor man stop worrying? A minute or two minutes would pass, then again he would say, "You can just tell me. Are you joking, kidding?"

I said, "I am a serious man and this is no joke – making an appointment with one of the fellows in the trinity."

Eating, he was not there, he was just afraid. I told him, "Now I am going to make the appointment. This is the room for you to sleep in. Rest, or you can read. I will be here nearabout ten tonight."

He said, "Where are you going?"

I said, "I have a place where I can arrange to have a contact."

He said, "A place! Are you mad or something?"

I said, "Just wait. It is only a question of one night and it will be decided."

I had a friend in the medical college. I went to him; he was a professor, and I told him that I wanted a skeleton just for the night. He asked, "What are you up to?"

I said, "Don't be worried, nobody will be killed and no problem will arise out of it."

He said, "It is not permissible for me. I have the key; if a skeleton is missing tomorrow I will be caught."

I said, "It will be back here before morning. It is just that I have to make an appointment with a man."

He said, "What appointment?"

I said, "Don't be worried. Just let me finish, don't waste my time. Just give me a skeleton."

He said, "If you insist, take one, but it should be back before morning."

I said, "Don't be worried; perhaps there will be two skeletons. I don't know what will happen, because this is just an appointment. A meeting will happen and then after the meeting nobody knows. It is with the Holy Ghost."

The medical professor said, "I am coming with you. It seems there is some risk."

I said, "You can come. There is just enjoyment, entertainment – no risk. Come with me" – and he did.

I was living in a big bungalow so I had given the professor of philosophy a side room which had a bathroom attached and a small walk-in closet. We reached home. I left the skeleton in the garage. I knocked on the door; he came, looking afraid. He opened the door and said, "What about the appointment?"

I said, "Everything is fixed, the appointment is going to happen. Just rest in your bed and whenever you hear three knocks you should go into your bathroom."

He said, "In the bathroom?"

I said, "What can I do? I tried my best to tell him that there is a good sitting room, but the Holy Ghost is the Holy Ghost."

He said, "I will meet him in the bathroom if you insist."

I said, "I have no objection, and I don't think you have any objection."

He said, "Holy Ghost! – in the bathroom?"

It was possible only in the bathroom, because at the back there was a door so I could bring the Holy Ghost in. Otherwise, from where to bring it into his room? In India, you have to have a door from the outside because the people who clean the bathrooms cannot go through the inside of your house. That is impossible in India. So I had kept that door open from the very beginning.

He went to bed and covered himself with the blanket. I put the light off. He said, "No. Keep the light on."

I said, "Don't be worried, because when the Holy Ghost comes, the light comes on, he is so illuminated. Don't be worried."

He said, "But still, keep the light on. And where will you be?"

I said, "I will be in the next room. If there is any trouble, or if the Holy Ghost does any unholy thing to you, either you can hide in this closet and lock it from the inside so he cannot do anything to you, or if you still have any voice left, you can call me – I will come immediately. But my experience, because this appointment has happened many times before, is that people lose their voices. They want to say something, they want to scream, but they cannot; they are just choked – just the presence of the Holy Ghost!"

He said, "I was an idiot to talk to you about this meaninglessness of life. Perhaps there is meaning."

I said, "No need to change your philosophy so soon. First let the meeting happen."

And the meeting happened. I persuaded him to put the light off because otherwise the Holy Ghost wouldn't come. So I put the light off. I brought the skeleton in through the back door and put it in the right place in the bathroom. Just nearabout twelve – the other professor was also staying with me in my room – we knocked on his door. I had told him, "The moment the Holy Ghost knocks on your door, open the bathroom door and have the meeting. Whatsoever question you have to ask, you can ask. Everything else is then up to you. With the appointment my work is finished."

We knocked on his door. He jumped out of his bed and fell on the floor! In the darkness he could not figure out where he was. He really wanted to get out of the room, but instead he went into the bathroom where I had kept the light on. The skeleton was there. He saw it and just fell down and went unconscious. I called the medical professor and said, "Now you can help – this is the second skeleton! I'll remove the first one to my car, and you take care of this man. That's why I have brought you with me. You thought it was for some other reason, but a medical doctor is always needed when such encounters happen. Now look after him!"

He said, "You are a real trouble. Now I have to look after him, and perhaps he may die or anything may happen and I will be responsible because I am medically attending him."

But he did not die. He opened his eyes, looked at the professor, looked at me, closed his eyes again and said, "Has... Has he gone?" The first thing he asked was, "Has he gone?"

I said, "Who?"

He said, "The Holy Ghost. And I do believe in God the father, the Holy Ghost and Jesus Christ and I will never say anything about it again."

I said, "This is good! I have converted you into a Christian."

He said, "My God! What an experience. My wife will not believe it, nobody will believe it. Even I would not have believed it if I had not seen it. Has he gone?"

I said, "You can look in the bathroom."

He opened the bathroom, looked and said, "Yes, he is gone." That man started going to church and became a very, very religious person. The whole university was amazed at what had happened. I told them, "It is the result of a great encounter."

"What encounter?" they asked, and I spread the whole story.

I told him, "Don't be a fool! Come with me to the medical doctor; he can tell you that I brought a skeleton. There was no Holy Ghost, no appointment. You are simply a coward."

He said, "You cannot befool me now – I have seen with my own eyes. Am I to believe my eyes or your words – or any medical professor? I don't care what anybody says, from now onward I am going to remain a Christian. You cannot destroy my Christianity."

He is still a Christian, very pious, helping others to be Christians – and all that he had seen was only a skeleton! I told him – I brought the medical professor and he told him – "You can come and we will show you the same skeleton so you can recognize it."

He said, "I am not going. You showing something to me..." He said, "I don't trust this man: if he can manage an encounter, a meeting with the Holy Ghost, he can manage anything. Perhaps the Holy Ghost is going to be there again, wherever you are both trying to take me. I am not going again, not before death." And he crossed himself; each time he would say "Holy Ghost" he would make the sign of the cross. Such a conversion!

People have been living under all kinds of superstitions which may have been founded on some reason in the past; but they have not been able to understand that reason clearly. It is true that Jesus did not die on the cross, but it is untrue that there was a resurrection. He was taken down from the cross and he escaped from Judea. While escaping from Judea, of course he met a few people, and certainly a few of his disciples. And they all thought that he was back, he was resurrected!

But he escaped from Judea because he knew perfectly well... That was the suggestion given to him by Pontius Pilate – because he allowed him to escape. The whole credit goes to that Roman governor-general of Judea. It is a strange coincidence that Rome became the citadel of Christianity: it was Rome who crucified Jesus, it was a Roman governor-general who had helped him to escape. But it was made clear to Jesus that he should not be found inside Judea or nearby, because then Pontius Pilate would be held responsible. So he had to escape as far away as possible. And he escaped really far away: he died in Kashmir in India. I have been to his grave. He lived a long life of one hundred and twelve years. But those six hours on the cross were enough: he never tried again to prove that he was the messiah. In India nobody would have bothered about him; a messiah means nothing there. There are hundreds of living incarnations of God any time, any day, any night.

Once I happened to stay in Allahabad. I was attending a Hindu world conference. Somebody by mistake had invited me thinking that I was a Hindu. They found out, but it was too late. By that time I had disturbed everything that they were planning: how to convert the whole world into Hinduism.

I was staying with hundreds of other guests in tents by the side of the Ganges, the beautiful place they had chosen for the conference. In those tents at least five incarnations of God were present. In India it is so easy. Nobody can object – you can declare yourself an incarnation of God. About that India is very nice. Who cares? Who bothers? It is your business. If you think you are an incarnation of God, good: be an incarnation of God. You are not doing any harm to anybody.

But that one experience of Jesus' was so bad, so horrible, that he dropped the idea of being a messiah, and he dropped the idea of solving the problems of the whole of humanity. He had found what happens if you try to redeem humanity – you are crucified!

But his escaping helped a religion to be born. Now, Christians have no report of what happened after his resurrection. If he was resurrected, okay. Then what happened? When did he die? Where did he die? Where is his grave? Why have you not preserved his grave? – because that must be the holiest thing for you. Sheela has just informed me that all they have preserved was the foreskin of Jesus Christ! Because he must have been circumcised...

And even that has been stolen from the Vatican yesterday. The poor Christians... Now they have nothing! It was not much anyway. What can you do with the foreskin? And I don't think it was *his* foreskin; anybody's would do because foreskins are just foreskins. "Jesus Christ" is not written on it – but somebody has done a really great job, stealing it. Now the whole of Christianity is shaken because their greatest treasure is lost.

CHAPTER 3

Beware! I Am Here to Destroy Your Dreams

Osho,
I have heard you say that only Christians dream of Jesus, and
followers of Krishna dream only of Krishna. Sannyasins are
dreaming of you, Osho. Will you comment?

Dreaming is a substitute for the real. It is a mind device to console you.

If you have been fasting, in the night you will dream of a feast because the hunger needs food, and without food sleep will be difficult. The mind has to provide you a substitute, that's what dreaming is. It gives you the feeling that you are no longer hungry; you are eating and you are eating good food, delicious food, food that you like. Now you can sleep without any trouble. The mind has drugged the body through the dream. But a dream is not reality. You can dream of eating but that is not going to nourish you. The mind can befool the body for the time being but the body is going to suffer. Reality is reality, and you need real food.

A Christian dreaming of Christ, a Hindu dreaming of Krishna, or a sannyasin dreaming of me are all doing the same thing. It makes no difference of whom you are dreaming; that is irrelevant. You can dream of anybody: Krishna, Christ, Mahavira or Buddha, Zarathustra. The object of the dream is irrelevant, what is significant is that you are dreaming.

So the first thing to be remembered is that there must be a certain hunger behind it, which the mind is trying to fulfill. Read the message clearly: you are not what nature intends you to be; you are missing something immensely important in you. You are not yet your authentic self. The dream of Christ, Krishna or me is symbolic. It shows that you are groping in the dark: who are you? Krishna? Christ? Me? You are none of these people.

So remember that the dream indicates a certain hunger in you. That is the first thing to remember. It is very significant, because not all people are dreaming of Krishna, Christ and me. Millions of people are dreaming of money, millions of people are dreaming of power, prestige. Men are dreaming of women, women are dreaming of men. And the market is vast, you can choose any commodity to dream about. Somebody is dreaming of becoming the president of a country; somebody is dreaming that he has become the president of the country.

Chuang Tzu has a beautiful story about this. And he was a man not to tell a story but to act it:

Chuang Tzu is one of the rare beings who have happened on this earth – unique in every way. One morning he awoke and sat up in bed very sad. Nobody had ever seen him sad. He was a man of laughter, a very non-serious man. Not only non-serious, he was known as the most absurd man – playing jokes upon himself, upon his people, upon his master, upon his disciples. This too was a joke, but everybody was puzzled because he had never been sad, and they asked, "Why are you sad?"

He said, "I am in such trouble but I don't think any one of you can help me, so what is the point of telling you?"

They became even more curious. They said, "Please tell us! Who knows; we may be able to do something. All together we may be able to find a way. If there is a problem, there must be a solution. If there is a question, somewhere there must be an answer to it."

Chuang Tzu said, "If you insist I will tell you what the problem is. The problem is not a question that you can find an answer for. It is a riddle which has no answer, and I am caught in the riddle; that's why I am sad. Last night I dreamed that I had become a butterfly, flying from this plant to that, from this flower to that flower. And I completely forgot that I was Chuang Tzu, the famous, great master: I was really the butterfly, Chuang Tzu was nowhere at all."

The disciples said, "This is not a problem – everybody dreams. We don't see the riddle."

Chuang Tzu said, "Wait a little, I have not told you the whole thing. Now waking up, the problem has arisen: perhaps now the butterfly has gone to sleep and is dreaming that she is Chuang Tzu, and I am caught in it. What's what? Has Chuang Tzu dreamed of a butterfly or is a butterfly dreaming of Chuang Tzu?"

They were all silent, then they said, "Perhaps you are right that we cannot help you. Nobody can help you."

But he had raised a tremendously important question. His question remained unanswered because I was not there! Naturally, the question has waited for me for twenty-five centuries. It is so simple. If I had been there I would have hit him really hard and awakened him.

The butterfly had no problem; it was not worried about what happened to Chuang Tzu. It was not concerned at all with Chuang Tzu – Chuang Tzu is concerned. The butterfly was alone, but you are not alone. Now you are sitting up in your bed concerned about what is right, what is real; whether you are Chuang Tzu or the butterfly. All these things prove that you are not a dream, you are a reality.

The butterfly was just a dream. In a dream you are asleep; there are no questions, no problems. You don't even think that it is a dream: you *are* it, you are totally identified with it. Now you are not identified with it. You cannot be a butterfly; that is certain, because butterflies are not concerned about such great philosophical problems. It is only the prerogative of man to be puzzled, to be worried, to be riddled.

You dream of Jesus, Krishna, Zarathustra, Mohammed – why? There must be some hunger in you which you feel is fulfilled by Jesus. That's what the Christian has been told: Christ has arrived, and you have not yet arrived. Somehow you have to arrive. But you can never be another Christ; existence never repeats. History repeats because history belongs to idiotic humanity, hence it goes on moving in a circle, doing the same stupidities again and again and again. It never learns. But existence never repeats. It always produces only unique pieces, one of a kind, and that is enough. What is the point of repeating it? It is not an assembly line in a car factory where every minute a car comes out similar to another car and they go on coming off the assembly line exactly the same.

Nature does not manufacture people, things, birds, flowers. There is no assembly line, there is no model; it goes on exploring new dimensions. So it is certain that you are feeling starved: Christ is your food, somebody else's food is Krishna. These are simply different kinds of disease.

A Hindu has become accustomed to a certain dish. Of course, when he is hungry he cannot dream of a dish which he knows nothing about. You can dream only about something you know. Can you dream of something that you don't know? It is impossible, because a dream is only a repetition.

A dream is not creative; yes a dream can be compositive but never creative. See the difference between these two words: *compositive* and *creative*. It can compose something. For example, it can take the head of Jesus and the body of Krishna and compose something which is both Krishna and Christ. That's what people like Mahatma Gandhi have been doing their whole lives: composing – something from the Koran, something from the Bible, something from the Gita, something from Mahavira, something from Buddha and trying to make something that in India is called *khichri*. In English, the closest term is *hodgepodge*, but it is nothing to be compared with *khichri*.

With the legs of one man, the hands of another man, the hair of somebody else, the eyes from somewhere else, you can make *khichri*. You can make a composite man who has everything – eyes, nose, ears, head, legs, everything – but it will still be dead. By composing, you cannot create life, you cannot create consciousness. A dream can be a composite. You can see a horse flying – no horse flies, but there are things that fly: flying saucers, flying planes and flying birds, and it is not very difficult to compose a horse which flies.

What dream is to man, mythology is to society.

The Mohammedans say that Mohammed never died; but then the problem arises, where has he gone? It is time, now that he has millions of followers – six hundred million followers – it is time he came out. Where is he hiding and what is he doing? No, Mohammedans have a myth. A myth is a dream dreamed by the whole race, a collective dream – but it is composite.

Mohammed used to move from one place to another on a beautiful horse; and Arabian horses are the most famous horses in the world. Jesus would have looked very poor because he was just using a donkey. And it is good that Christians have not created the myth that Mohammedans have created: Mohammed never died, one day he simply flew up with his horse toward God. The horse has also gone with him into heaven! It is more fortunate to be a horse with Mohammed than to be a Mohammedan and a man.

And I say it is good that Christians have not dreamed of the same dream, otherwise Jesus would have gone with his donkey. And in heaven what will these horses and donkeys do? – because there are many donkeys from ancient times already there. All your saints and all your sages, what are they?

Now, this is mythology. Prophets die, but Mohammedans have to make something special for Mohammed: that he never dies, he's alive. Every other prophet has entered heaven after death, Mohammed is the only one who goes there alive. He not only goes alive, his horse also goes with him. Naturally, the horse had to fly.

So you will see in the Mohammedan sacred days of Muharram, horses made with wings. Horses don't grow wings but one horse has done it. They cannot make the image of Mohammed because Mohammed is against images; so they simply make the horse with wings, and you have to imagine Mohammed on it. You will only see a horse made of paper; you have to imagine Mohammed on it – and there are Mohammedans who do see him.

My village had a big population of Mohammedans, and in my childhood it was not yet the way it turned out later on, that Hindus and Mohammedans started killing each other. It was because of the same man I told you about – Mirza Allama Iqbal. He is a great poet, there is no doubt about it. I mentioned his name to you because he had written that poem, "My country is the best in the whole world – *Hindostan hamara sare jehan se achchha.*"

He uses the word *Hindostan* for India, but later on the same man created the idea of Pakistan. He was the originator of the idea that Hindus and Mohammedans should separate, that they could not live together because their religions were different, their cultures were different, their languages were different, that there was no need for them to live together, they should separate. Everybody laughed: the whole idea was Don Quixotic, absolutely absurd, because Hindus and Mohammedans had lived together for centuries, and there was no problem.

But soon, a great politician, Mohammed Ali Jinnah, got hold of Allama Iqbal's idea. For thirty years he went on emphasizing, "We need Pakistan, we cannot live with Hindus" – and he created Pakistan. India was divided into two – the same India, Hindostan, which was "the best in the whole world." The same man created the idea and the philosophy of Pakistan. The word *Pakistan* means "holy land." Naturally he had to create something better than Hindostan. Hindostan was after all just a country, but Pakistan was a holy land. And millions of Hindus and Mohammedans were cut to pieces, killed and butchered. But in my childhood it was not so. Hindus used to go to Mohammedan saints without any difficulty; Mohammedans used to take advice from Hindu saints with no difficulty.

In Muharram, which is a yearly Mohammedan sacred festival, they make these mementos from past memories, fourteen hundred years old. They cannot make Mohammed's image, it is prohibited. We don't know how he looked. We have some idea of Jesus; perhaps it is not very true because photography was not available then. Perhaps it is more imaginative than real, because the people who made the pictures must have tried to do their best, and they must have created the picture to look like a prophet. Whether the man looked like a prophet or not is questionable.

I know of Jewish sources which say that Jesus was only four foot five inches high. Not only that, he was very ugly; not only that, he was a hunchback. Perhaps this is just enmity, perhaps there is some truth in it. Perhaps both are imagination – one of the enemies and one of the friends – and between the two the real is completely lost.

I am absolutely certain that Buddha never looked like his statues because those statues were made five hundred years after him – after Buddha had already been dead for five hundred years. After those five hundred years, Alexander the Great visited India. The image of Buddha is closer to the face of Alexander the Great than Buddha himself, because the face is Greek, the nose is Greek, the eyes are Greek. Buddha's statue does not look like a Hindu statue.

When Hindu sculptors saw Alexander they got the idea he would be a good model. Alexander was really a beautiful man. To make Buddha in Alexander's image was very easy; and there was no proof that he looked otherwise.

If you see the Buddhist monasteries and temples in China, you will see a different Buddha, because the Chinese have their own idea of beauty. It may not appeal to you, but that is your problem; it appeals to them. For example, the nose should not be so pointed and so long, it should be flat. Nobody in the whole world likes a flat nose, but what to do? Chinese have flat noses, and they are one fourth of the whole world: out of every four people one is a Chinese.

I have heard of a man who had three sons, and he said, "Now we have to stop."
His wife said, "Why?"
He said, "The fourth is going to be Chinese. I have read it: out of every four men, the fourth is a Chinese. I have read it from a very reliable source. I am not going to have any more children. Three and we stop – we don't want any Chinese in the house."

If you go to Japan you see a totally different Buddha. If you put a Japanese Buddha and an Indian Buddha together, you cannot believe these two statues are of the same man. You can stretch your imagination as far as possible but there seems to be no possibility that these two statues can be of the same man. The Indian Buddha's belly is in, his chest is out. The Japanese Buddha is just the opposite: his chest is in, his belly is too far out.

Now, no Indian can accept that this is beauty. Alexander was an athletic personality, well-trained, well-polished – and athletes have always liked the belly down and the chest forward, just like a lion. This Japanese Buddha looks like a strange fellow with such a belly: a laughingstock. And his head is also Japanese, his face is also Japanese.

Just a few days ago Sheela brought a picture to me. It was sent from a sannyasin from California. California is just next to Oregon in that way... The sannyasin has been growing a bump on his forehead. It must be a growth of some kind, perhaps some cancer or something. But people love... Even if you have cancer, somebody can say, "This is not cancer, this is a sign of enlightenment" – you will be overjoyed. Ramdas has the same kind of growth. So Ramdas has spread the story in America that when a man becomes a buddha, awakened, this bump grows on the forehead. And he has produced a picture from somewhere of a statue of Buddha with a bump on the head.

I have never seen any statue of Buddha with a bump on his fore-head. That picture was my first experience. And nobody knows whose statue that is. It is only on Ramdas' authority that it is Buddha's statue. It has no similarity to Buddha – Indian, Japanese, Chinese, or Tibetan, all the countries which have been Buddhist. None of them has any statue which has a bump on the forehead.

Now, either it is a photographic trick or somebody may have made a plaster of paris statue of Gautam Buddha with a bump. Then the photograph has been taken, and Ramdas is going around with that photograph, telling people, "Look, it also happened to Buddha." In California you can believe anything. It is the most religious land in the whole world: all the saints are born in California.

Now, this sannyasin sends me the picture because the same bump has grown on his forehead, and he says, "Osho, does it mean that I have become enlightened? – Ramdas says so." The picture is supplied by Ramdas. The sannyasin has the same bump. He sends the pictures of himself from all sides to show his bump clearly: from above, from this side, from that side, so that there is no suspicion about his bump. And he is really exhilarated.

I told Sheela to tell the poor guy to go to a doctor and let it be examined. God forbid that it may have something to do with cancer. Be quick, and don't be befooled by people like Ramdas. And if you can take Ramdas also to the doctor... As far as I am concerned, if I meet Buddha, I will put him into our medical center. His bump has to be removed even at the cost of his enlightenment. If it disappears, let it disappear, but this cancer has to be taken care of first. Enlightenment can happen again. But fools are fools. The sannyasin will be hurt by my answer. He would have loved it if I had said, "Yes, you have become enlightened." It is a strange world! Here people want consoling lies. Nobody is ready for the truth.

But we do have some idea of Jesus' face, at least something close. And of Buddha's, maybe something close. But about Mohammed we have no idea at all because for fifteen centuries Mohamme-dans have persistently destroyed every possible trace of Mohammed's personality.

One of my friends, a Hindu saint, created a temple of all reli-gions. That was his lifelong work. He created a beautiful temple, and it was very difficult for him to collect that much money. It was all made in pure marble, and he made the statues of all the religious people, forgetting completely that you cannot make a statue of Mohammed. He thought he was doing a great work.

He made Buddha, Mahavira, Lao Tzu, Jesus, Moses, Zarathustra. About them there was no problem. Even if no actual photograph exists, some kind of description is available. It just needed a creative artist, imaginative enough to figure it out. If an artist is really imaginative and creative he can come close to a photograph. Artists exist in all great police departments; you have to describe the face of the thief that you saw in the night, disappearing in the darkness. You can't be certain what kind of man he was, but you just describe him, and the artist is capable of figuring out, from your description, the picture of the thief and he draws the picture. I have seen these pictures, and when the thieves are caught, they are so similar to their picture that the artist seems to be simply intuitive: he got the idea from a very meager description.

Even the witness was not certain whether the man had a mustache or not, because in the night when you are in danger – the man is carrying a gun, and your safe is broken – who bothers whether the man has a mustache or not? How long? How small? Whether it is an Adolf Hitler cut...? You are not in a state to think about all these things like what color his eyes are, and in the night... But you give any description, whatsoever comes to your mind and the artist figures it out. And I have seen really impossible things. The artist manages somehow, and through his picture being published in the newspaper the thief is caught.

So there is a possibility... This man had great influence on many people. He managed to get somebody to make Mohammed's statue, but he was not aware that he was going to be in great trouble. His temple was completely burned, broken down, every statue broken, because he had done the most profane act possible according to the Mohammedans. His whole life's work was demolished within hours. There was no temple left at all.

I had seen the temple, and I have also gone to the place after the temple was completely demolished. There were just ruins: statues broken, pillars half standing, the roof burned. Somehow the man who made the temple escaped; otherwise they would have killed him also, because to create the image of Mohammed is one of the greatest crimes against Mohammedanism.

But man after all is man, he needs some substitute. So when

Mohammedans dream a dream of the horse with the flying wings, of course they must be seeing somebody sitting on it but they must not tell anybody. That is dangerous. Mohammedans know only one punishment: to just cut off your head. Beheading is the simplest thing for them to do.

You have a hunger; the dream indicates the hunger, but the dream is not going to fulfill it. It is only indicative. Take the indication, then start getting rid of the dream; its work is fulfilled. Don't follow the dream, don't try to become Christ, Buddha or Zarathustra, no. That was not the meaning of the dream. If you start trying to become a Jesus or a Buddha, the most unfortunate thing is that you may succeed. If you fail there is no harm – most probably you will fail. Two thousand years have passed and nobody has been able to become a Christ again; that's enough proof. But that does not mean that people have not tried.

Millions of people have tried to become replicas, but fortunately failed. But there is a possibility, unfortunately, that you may succeed. That means you have gone insane. It means nothing else; it simply means you have gone insane, you have started believing that you are Christ. Your dream has taken possession of you so much so that now it is no longer a dream, it has become a reality to you.

To go insane is to go farthest from yourself. That's the meaning of insanity to me. Sanity means to be closer to yourself, closer and closer. A day comes when you are just at the very center of your being; then you are the sanest person in the world; when you are just yourself and nobody else, just pure, authentic, with no shadow of anybody else falling on you.

To be at the center of your being is to be sane and to go far away from yourself is to be insane. Now, if you become Christ, you have reached the farthest point from yourself; or if you become a Buddha or you become me, you have reached the farthest point from yourself. It may be very satisfying: you will never see mad people frustrated, you will never see mad people committing suicide. Have you ever heard of it? You will never see a mad person miserable. No, because now his dream has become his reality. He is as happy as you can think a person can be.

The father of Narendra, one of my sannyasins, had phases: for six months he was sane and for six months he was insane. It was a fixed period. The strangest thing to his family, to the doctors, to the whole city, was that when he was insane he was the happiest person in the world, and the healthiest. And when he was sane, he became miserable, unhealthy, with all kinds of sicknesses; everything was wrong, he was complaining and grumpy. His family continually prayed: if he had remained mad the whole year, it would have been the greatest blessing to him and to the family.

But he had his own routine of six months. When he was insane, his whole family regained balance because he was not disturbing anybody, and he was enjoying himself in every possible way. I have seen him doing things – Narendra was very small, but when his father was insane even the smallest child in the house used to watch the shop.

They had a jeweler's shop, so there were costly things – gold, silver, diamonds. And when he was mad he would steal them. It was his shop! Narendra was so small but he would watch and he would shout to his mother, "Come! Come quick, Kaka has opened the safe!" His mother would rush and all the children too. He had many children, I think a dozen, and they all would come running; even the smallest child used to spy on him.

He would be going to the market, and the smallest child, a five-year-old, would be following him. If I came across them I would say to the child, "Where are you going?"

He would say, "After Kaka, because he goes on borrowing things from everywhere and we have to pay."

He would go to the sweet shop and eat as much as he wanted, and he would invite anybody walking past, strangers, to join him: "Come on!"

And the child would be forcing him, "Kaka, you have to come back home, otherwise I will bring mother right now."

The only person that he was afraid of even in insanity was his wife. That proved to me another maxim, that even insanity cannot change the relationship of husband and wife. He would go on giving things to anybody. Somebody had to follow him, so all the children did; there was nobody else, just the twelve children and the wife. He was happy in those six months, and everybody in the town was happy because he was just a joy to be with, always laughing. He immediately started to become fatter, healthier, stronger. And the moment those six months were finished he would become weak, sick. He would be sitting in the shop – there was no need to spy on him – but he was miserable.

Insane people are not miserable. So if you are miserable, be happy! – at least you are not insane. At least you still have some sanity left, hence the misery. What is misery? Misery is the feeling that you are not yourself. It is the gap between you as you are, and you as you feel you should be. The gap is the misery. The bigger the gap, the more miserable you are. Idiots are not miserable, for the simple reason that they do not have the intelligence to see the gap.

The most intelligent people in the world are the most miserable, because they can see the gap so clearly that it is impossible to forget it, to just put it aside. It is always there: whatever they are doing, the gap is in front of them and that gap hurts: "Why can't I be just myself?"

That's why I say if unfortunately you succeed in being a Christ or a Krishna or me, it means that you are no longer part of the sane world, you have become completely mad. Now you cannot distinguish between the dream and the real – and to forget the distinction between the dream and the real is a great loss: it is spiritual suicide.

I would have said to Chuang Tzu, "There is no problem in it, just get up from your bed." I would have gathered his disciples and told them to bring ice-cold water and pour it over the man so he comes to know that he is not a butterfly. And I know perfectly well that before they started pouring he would have jumped out of bed, and he would have said, "Wait! I am Chuang Tzu. I was just playing a joke." Only Chuang Tzu can see the distance between the real and the unreal. The butterfly cannot see it – the butterfly is only a dream.

A dream has no intelligence of its own. A dream is just a cloud around you and because of your sleep you become identified with it. In your waking also; you are not really awake, that's why you get identified with so many things. You become a Hindu; that is an identification. You become a Christian, a Jew; that is an identification – and that shows that your wakefulness is not there. You are just awake in name only. It is such a thin layer of wakefulness that it is disturbed by anything, and you fall asleep immediately. A beautiful woman passes by, and you are asleep. You have gone into a dream of how to get her, of how to possess her. You have completely forgotten that this is not sleep.

One of Dostoevsky's novels, *Crime and Punishment*, has an incident in it:

Raskolnikov is the main character in the novel; he is a student in the university. He lives in a small room in front of a very palatial building in which an old woman lives who is perhaps eighty, or eighty-five or even ninety years old.

In Russia that is not difficult. In Russia you can find people one hundred and fifty years old at least, even more – sometimes one hundred and eighty and still working. Not just one or two, but in thousands, particularly in the Caucasus area, from where Gurdjieff came. A man of one hundred and fifty, sixty, seventy, is still working in the fields, just like any young man.

Raskolnikov is of a very philosophic type of mind, and he goes on watching this old woman from his window. She has so much money, she owns almost half of the buildings of the city. She has nobody else, is alone, and lives in that big palace. She is so miserly that she has not even a servant. Her whole business is lending people money at a high rate of interest.

Raskolnikov, just sitting there, sees poor people bringing things, because she will not give money unless you leave something in her custody. He sees these poor people bringing their things and getting money on interest. They know perfectly well, and Raskolnikov knows, that they will never be able to pay back even the interest, what to say about the original money! And what are they leaving? – they may leave a watch, a clock, some jewelry, something that they had that is then gone. And the woman used to give only half the value of the item that was left in her custody.

Raskolnikov becomes angrier and angrier and angrier, looking at this cheat the whole day. And he starts thinking, "What is the purpose of this woman? She has nothing to live for. She has lived enough and she is still exploiting thousands of people. Why has somebody not killed her?" He starts thinking that there is no crime in killing her, hence the title of Dostoevsky's book, *Crime and Punishment*. He philosophizes about it so much, month by month, year by year, because he is there watching her, that by and by he starts thinking, "Nobody is going to kill her, I have to do it."

Finally, one day he decides, "Now, it is enough, I cannot tolerate it." A necessity has also arisen so he can go to her, because he has to fill in the examination forms and deposit the fee for his final post-graduate class – and he has no money. So, in the evening he goes, taking his wristwatch and waiting till everybody has left, and it is getting dark.

The lady is so miserly she will not even use candles. When it gets dark, she closes the door, locks the door from inside and disappears for the whole night. So before she does that, he enters. She is just coming down the stairs to lock the door as he comes in and says, "I am in great difficulty. You know me, I live in the house just in front of yours. You can keep my wristwatch but you have to give me money right now. Tomorrow morning I have to fill in my examination forms. If I miss tomorrow, my years are wasted."

So she says, "Okay, come along with me."

He goes behind her, ready to kill her. He has imagined so many times how to kill her, because it is not going to take much, she is so old: you just have to press her throat and that will do. He has imagined it, dreamed it, philosophized about it: "It is not a crime, it is not a sin. In fact you are preventing a great criminal from doing so many crimes every day against the whole city. You are a savior! God cannot be so misunderstanding, and when he knows the whole story he will reward you." Raskolnikov has convinced himself that murdering this woman is not a crime. And anyway she is going to die any day. Why let her continue to exploit people any longer?

He gives her his wristwatch. It is getting darker so she goes close to the window to look at the watch to see how much it is worth – because she won't burn a candle. Just by coincidence she has a heart attack, falls there and dies, and because Raskolnikov has lived out this whole idea of killing her so many times, dreamed it so many times, he believes that he has done it.

He escapes, goes to his room but he knows, "The police will be coming soon; it is not right to stay here." He goes to the furthest corner of the city to stay with a friend. But the friend cannot understand: "Why are you so nervous? What has happened?"

And he says, "Nothing has happened, I have not done anything. Don't be suspicious."

Naturally, the friend says, "I am not being suspicious, and I am not saying that you have done anything."

But Raskolnikov says, "Yes, you are not saying anything but your eyes show it. Do you think I am such a stupid guy that I cannot understand what is going on in your mind? Do you think I am a murderer?"

The man says, "You are just crazy! Why should you be a murderer?"

Raskolnikov cannot sleep. He wakes up again and again and says to the friend, "Did you hear something? I just heard a police whistle."

The friend says, "Nobody is here, no police. What would they come here and whistle for?"

Raskolnikov says, "No, perhaps I dreamed it." And again: "Did you hear the knock? I heard boots, police boots coming toward the house."

The man asks, "Are you obsessed by the police?"

Raskolnikov says, "Who is obsessed? You must be obsessed. It is your house, not my house. I have not done anything in the first place. And people die on their own; it does not necessarily mean that somebody has killed them."

By the morning he has driven the friend crazy, and finally he himself begs the friend, "Take me to the police station because they are all around, they are going to catch me. They must have found out by now that that old woman has been murdered by being strangled. And they must have found my wristwatch in her hand, which is a proof enough, because how come that wristwatch was there? Somebody must have seen me going into her house or coming out of her house. There is no point... It is better to surrender."

He goes to the police station. He tries to convince the police. The police say, "You are just mad. The woman has died of a heart attack – the doctor's report has come."

Raskolnikov says, "You are trying to convince *me*? I am the man who has killed her – I confess to you."

This is the meaning of *Crime and Punishment*: guilt arises, he starts punishing himself. Now he cannot figure out whether the dream that he had dreamed so many times is a dream or whether he has really done it. He has not done it but he tortures the police. He goes to the doctor and says, "Your report is wrong. I know perfectly well I have killed her, the wristwatch is proof."

The doctor says, "The wristwatch is not proof. We have examined everything and she died of a heart attack."

But the man needed punishment. Finally the police decide to

put him in the lockup for his satisfaction. What else to do? As he was locked up, he was at ease.

This is insanity: when a dream becomes a reality, when you cannot make the distinction between the dream and reality. And there are millions of people walking, talking, working, and they are not able to make the distinction between the real and the unreal. How many superstitions do you go on carrying? What is God other than a superstition? You have not even dreamed him; it is not even your dream that you are identified with. Perhaps Jesus dreamed him, but he suffered enough for his dream. Now why are you torturing yourself?

But there are people...

I have heard of a man who believed that he was the resurrected Jesus Christ. His family tried to persuade him, "Don't say such a thing to anybody – they will think that you are mad."

He said, "Let them think so, but what I am, I am; and whether I say it or not they are going to find out, so it is better to declare it. It is not a shame, it is a glory. You should all be happy that I am Jesus Christ."

They took him to a psychiatrist, saying, "This poor guy has got the idea that he is Jesus Christ. Something has to be done."

The psychiatrist tried many ways, all the tricks that he knew. Nothing worked. How could they work on a man who is God's messiah? The psychiatrist, just a poor psychiatrist, what can he do? Can he deprogram Jesus Christ? Impossible! Otherwise there would have been no need to crucify him – just deprogram him. Just take him to a deprogrammer for the weekend and Jesus Christ is finished – no messiah, no son of God. He comes back to earth: he knows that he is Joseph's son, not the son of the Holy Ghost, that he is a carpenter, he should go back to his work. What is he doing here? He is not supposed to give sermons on the mountain. He should go to his father's workshop where the poor fellow is still making furniture: "Just cut logs and do things that are needed. Help the old man. What are you doing here?" Only deprogramming was needed, but it is difficult to deprogram people like Jesus Christ.

This man, although he was not Jesus Christ, believed it. Finally the psychiatrist took him before the mirror. He said, "Just look at yourself in the mirror. Do you look like Jesus Christ?"

He looked in the mirror. He said, "Of course. Do you think *you* look like Jesus Christ? You idiot! Anybody can see it. The mirror cannot lie."

Then the psychiatrist tries his final way. He takes his knife, cuts Jesus Christ's finger, blood comes out. He says to him, "Two thousand years have passed since the crucifixion and nothing has been heard of Jesus Christ. He must be dead; this is simple arithmetic. He cannot live two thousand years, nobody has lived that long. The only way is that you may be the dead body of Jesus Christ. But dead bodies don't bleed, and blood is coming out of your body. That proves you are alive."

And this so-called Jesus Christ, laughed and said, "This only proves that dead bodies *do* bleed and you did not hear me right in the first place: I am the resurrected Jesus Christ. I have left death far behind, two thousand years ago."

You cannot convince a madman by cutting his hand and showing him proof that dead men don't bleed. The insane man has his own logic. He says, "That simply proves that dead men do bleed." You cannot argue with a madman. Can you argue with a Christian? – a reborn Christian? Can you argue with Witnesses of Jehovah? – impossible. Can you argue with Hare Krishna people? I have argued with all these kinds of people. It is impossible.

In the first place they don't listen to what you are saying. They go on saying what they want to say; they don't listen at all to what you are saying – they start reading from the Bible. You can see a film covering their eyes. You can see their ears are closed. You can feel that the man is asleep, he is not awake. But all these religious people are asleep and dreaming a thousand and one things. Those dreams their scriptures have given them.

I am not here to give you a dream, just the contrary. I am here to destroy all your dreams. Even if you meet me in your dream, just immediately cut off my head, then and there. And don't ask where to get the sword. If you can get me in your dream, get a sword from the same place. If you can dream of me, you can also dream of a sword.

This is what happened...

A man was looking for a job. He heard that there was a place available on the ship that was just going to leave port. He rushed. The captain asked him, "If the winds are very strong, and the currents are very strong, and you feel that the ship is sinking, what will you do?"

He said, "I will throw the anchor into the water."

The captain said, "That's right." Again he said, "The waves become even stronger and the wind starts becoming even stronger. What will you do then?"

He said, "I will put down another anchor."

And the captain said finally, "Now it is almost impossible to save the boat. The waves are going higher than the boat and the wind has taken the highest speed. Now what will you do?"

He said, "I will put down a bigger anchor."

The captain said, "But from where are you getting these anchors?"

He said, "From the same place from where you are getting these waves, and the wind – from the same place."

So just remember: never ask me from where to get the sword – from the same place. You know perfectly well that if you can create me in your dream it won't be very difficult to find a sword and just cut off my head. And don't be bothered if dead men bleed, because I am going to bleed! But it is only a dream. The sword, me, the blood, is all dream. In the morning you will not find that your bed sheet is full of blood, and a body is lying in your room. Don't freak out! Just throw cold water on your eyes and everything will be okay.

Dreams are indicative. Your innermost self is telling you that you are not yet what you are meant to be, that your destiny is still unfulfilled, that your being is still starved. But that's all that the dream signifies. The dream is not saying, "Come follow me. Become a Christ, become a Buddha, become a Krishna." No, that will be going against yourself.

Just be yourself, utterly yourself. And don't be bothered what kind of flower you turn out to be. It does not matter whether you are a rose or a lotus or a marigold. It does not matter. What matters is flowering.

Let me repeat: the flower does not matter, what matters is flowering, and the flowering is the same whether it is a marigold... The marigold is a poor flower. I don't know about here, but in India the marigold is the poorest flower. Just to give him consolation perhaps, we call him "mari-gold," otherwise it is a poor flower. Roses are rich people, lotuses are just super-rich! But it does not matter.

When the marigold opens up there is the same ecstasy surrounding it as when a rose opens up. There is no difference in the ecstasy, because the ecstasy comes neither from the color nor from the fragrance, nor from the size. No, the ecstasy comes from the phenomenon, the miracle of flowering, opening. The marigold has become a marigold, it was its destiny. The rose has become a rose, it was its destiny. Both are fulfilled. That fulfillment is exactly equal.

The moment you become yourself you will not be me, you will not be Christ, you will not be Krishna; you will be yourself. But the ecstasy that surrounds me will surround you. I cannot say for certain about Jesus, I can only be absolutely certain about myself. I don't know whether he was really fulfilled or just a madman. There is no way for me to decide. I cannot say that about Buddha – he may be awakened, or he may be just a great philosopher philosophizing about awakening, a great dreamer dreaming about awakening.

Have you not sometimes dreamed that you are awake? I think everyone has sometimes dreamed that he is awake, and only when he wakes up does he find, "My God, that was a dream! I thought I was awake." You can dream within a dream, within a dream... For example, you can dream that you are going to your bedroom fully awake. You are going to your bedroom – in a dream – lying down on the bed, pulling your blanket up, falling asleep and dreaming that you have gone to see a movie. And you see the movie. In the movie you can see a man who is asleep and is dreaming – it can go on ad infinitum. You can go on stretching the idea: a dream within a dream within a dream within a dream – there is no problem to it.

You can dream that you are awake – and there are many people who think they are enlightened. They think! I have come across such people.

A man came to see me when I was in Raipur. This man was a very famous Hindu sage, Jagatguru Kripaludasji Maharaj. *Jagatguru* means a world teacher; *Kripaludas*, servant of compassion; and *Maharaj*, the king! He had many, many followers. Particularly in Raipur, he was the most famous teacher, and people believed that he was enlightened.

Somebody told me, "Kripaludas is visiting the town. Wouldn't you like to come?"

I said, "Certainly, because I never miss any opportunity."

I went up to the stage, went close to Kripaludas and gave him the indication that I wanted to say something in his ear. So he gave his ear to me, and I said, "I think you are enlightened."

He said, "Really?"

I said, "Really."

That was all. He inquired about me and the next day he came to visit me, and he said, "How did you find out? – because I also think the same, that I am enlightened."

I said, "There is no problem in it – you *look* enlightened."

He said, "Absolutely right. Many people have said to me, 'You look enlightened.'"

Then I said to him, "Please, enlightenment has no certain way of looking. And you are not enlightened, otherwise you would not have come to me. For what? Just because I said to you, 'I think you are enlightened,' I gave support to your dream. You are dreaming, because you yourself say that you also *think* you are enlightened. Nobody who is enlightened *thinks* that he is enlightened: he simply is enlightened. What business has thinking to do with enlightenment? Thinking can only create imagination. Thinking is part of the imaginative process.

"Thinking is dreaming in words, and dreaming is thinking in pictures. That's the only difference between the two."

Dreaming is a primitive kind of thinking. Because the primitive man has no words, he thinks in pictures. A child does the same, because a child is a primitive man. Look at any children's book: big pictures, strong attractive colors, and few words. *A big mango* – that the child understands immediately. And through that mango – because he knows the mango, he knows the taste of the mango, he knows the smell of the mango – seeing a mango in the picture he is reminded of the taste, the smell; and through that association, the word underneath, *mango*, slowly gets into his mind.

Then as books become of higher grades, the mango goes on becoming smaller and there are more words, with more descriptions of the mango: what kind of fruit the mango is, what kind of taste, where it is found. And the mango goes on disappearing, becoming smaller and smaller. And one day there are no pictures in the book. Now, you have learned a new way of dreaming: that is through words.

But the shift from the mango to the word *mango* is a great jump.

But when you are unconscious, deeply asleep, again you fall back to your primitive language. Then you forget about the language that you have learned.

One of my friends was in Germany. He went to Germany when he was only seven or eight years old. His father was there so he went there, and he lived in Germany for thirty years. He was educated in the German language, but he was born in Maharashtra; Marathi was his mother tongue, but he had completely forgotten it. As seven-year-old child he was not able to understand Marathi at all, and he had never learned to read it. But he had a car accident and became unconscious, and in his unconsciousness he would speak only Marathi.

His brother was called from India because the father had died; the people said, "We cannot understand what he says, and this man has never used any other language than German." But the language that he had learned from his very birth was only in the unconscious mind. That layer of seven years was there, and it was deeper; German was on top of it. But the top layer was now unconscious. So the deeper layer started speaking.

Whenever he would become conscious he would forget that he had been speaking in Marathi, he would speak in German; then he couldn't understand Marathi. His brother would speak in Marathi and he could not understand. And he was continually going in and out of unconsciousness. He would fall back again into unconsciousness, and again he would speak in Marathi; back to consciousness, he would speak German.

In your unconscious you are still primitive, and that's why Sigmund Freud paid more attention to your unconscious – because your unconscious is more innocent, childlike, primitive. It cannot lie, it cannot be deceptive; it will simply say whatever is the truth. But the conscious mind is cunning. It has been made cunning through education, culture, and everything.

One day I was just playing; I must have been four or five years old, not more than that. My father was shaving his beard when somebody knocked on the door; my father said to me, "Just go and tell him, 'My father is not at home.'"

I went out and I said, "My father is shaving and he says to

tell you, 'My father is not at home.'"

The man said, "What? He is inside?"

I said, "Yes, but this is what he has told me. I have told you the whole truth."

The man came in and my father looked at me: "What had happened?"

And the man was very angry, he said, "This is something! You had called me to come at this time, and you send a message with the boy that you have gone out."

My father asked him, "But how did you find out that I was in?"

He said, "This boy has said the whole thing: 'My father is in. He is shaving his beard, and he has told me to tell you that he is out.'"

My father looked at me. I could understand; he was saying, "Just wait! Let this man go, and I will show you."

I told him, "I am going before this man leaves."

He said, "But I have not said anything to you."

I said, "I have understood everything!"

I told the man, "Just stay here. First let me get out, because there is going to be trouble for me." But on departing I said to my father, "You insist with me, 'Be truthful.' So," I said, "this is a chance to be truthful, and to check whether you really mean me to be truthful, or is it just that you're trying to teach me cunningness?"

Of course he understood that it was better to keep quiet, not to quarrel with me then, because when the man was gone, I would have to come home. I came after two or three hours so that he would cool down or other people would be there and no problem would arise. He was alone. I went in, he said, "Don't be worried – I will never tell you anything like that again. You have to forgive me." He was in this way a fair man, otherwise who bothers about a four, five-year old child, and, being a father asks "Forgive me"? And he never said anything like it again his whole life. He knew that with me he had to be different than with other children.

As you grow up, as the society goes on teaching you to be this way, to behave this way, you start becoming a hypocrite, and you become identified with your hypocrisy. My function here is to destroy all hypocrisy in you. To me honesty is not a policy.

Just at supper I was telling Vivek that the man who first made up this maxim, "Honesty is the best policy," must have been a very cunning man. Honesty is not a policy; and if it is a policy, then it is not honesty: you are honest because it pays, you will be dishonest if that pays. Honesty is the best policy if it is paying, but if sometimes it is not paying, then dishonesty of course is the best policy. The question is what is going to pay.

And Vivek told me that just today she had seen in a book, in a single sentence, two words that were very revealing. She had never joined those words together: *policy* and *politics*, *politeness* and *politics*. What is politeness? It is a kind of politics. Both words are derived from the same root. All three words – *policy, politeness, politics* – have the same root, they all mean the same thing. But you think politeness is a nice quality. You would never think of it in terms of politics, but it is politics. To be polite is a defense measure.

In Europe you shake hands. Why do you shake the right hand? Why not the left? It is really part of politics. To shake hands is nothing friendly. It is just a gesture: "My right hand is empty so don't be worried. And let me see that *your* right hand also is empty, that there is not a knife or something in it." When you are shaking right hands you cannot pull your sword out because with the left hand – unless you happen to be a leftist... It is just a way of giving certainty to the other person that you are not going to harm him, and he is giving certainty to you that he is not going to harm you. Slowly, slowly it became a symbol of greeting each other.

In India, you greet with both hands, but that too is simply showing that both hands are empty. It is far better than shaking hands, because who knows about the left hand? Sometimes even the right hand does not know about the left hand, so it is better to show that both hands are empty; that is far better, and far more polite also. But you are saying, "I am completely defenseless. You need not be alert or worried about me. You can relax." These are symbols that people have learned.

In India if you go to a so-called guru, you have to give him a salute which is uniquely Indian. It is called *satsang dandawat*. You have to lie down on the floor with all your limbs touching the floor, because that is the most defenseless position. Even if the other man wants to kill you, he can kill you immediately.

In wartime when prisoners are caught, they are ordered to lie down flat on the ground with their arms spread out. Why? They cannot do anything in that position and then you can search them, and take anything they have. Or else you tell them to stand up with outstretched arms, with their hands up against the wall, which is the same – vertical or horizontal, it is the same.

In war it seems to be perfectly right, but somehow the same war is going on continuously between every individual in the society. So a certain culture develops it as a gesture of tremendous respect. It is not a gesture of respect, it is a gesture of humiliation: "I humiliate myself completely. I am at your disposal. If you want to cut off my head you can. I cannot do anything in such a position." And of course the other person feels great, his ego is satisfied.

Our culture, our education, our religions, all teach us to be hypocrites in such subtle ways that unless you go deep in search, you will never find out what you have been doing. Why do you smile when you meet a friend? What is the need? If you are not feeling like smiling, why do you smile? You have to do it. This is a policy that pays because some day you may need this man's help, and if you have always smiled at him, he cannot refuse. If you have never smiled at him and never even said "Hi," then you need not bother even to approach him; he will throw you out of his house with a "Go to hell!"

One has to understand all these layers and detach oneself from all of them. Become a watcher so that you cannot become identified with any dream.

That's my work; and if you start dreaming about me, you are destroying my whole work. Take the indication, then drop the dream and find real food. Just dreaming of a feast is no good when a real feast is possible. When real joy is available, then why a phony smile? When authentic ecstasy is just close to your hand, perhaps not even that far, then why be satisfied with being miserable, crying and weeping, feeling empty, feeling worthless? Your treasure is within you, and you are becoming a beggar.

My effort is to wake you up. Perhaps it will be hard on you in the beginning because you have been a beggar for so long that you will think I am taking your kingdom. Hence sannyas is difficult. On the surface I have made it so simple because I know that inside it is so difficult; to make it difficult on the outside also would be inhuman. So, on the surface I have made it absolutely simple – it cannot be more simplified – because inside the real work is hard. But it has to be done. Without doing it you lived without knowing what life is. You existed in a way which cannot be called living, it can only be called vegetating.

Don't be vegetables, cabbages, cauliflowers. Yes, these are the two classes of people: cabbages are uneducated people, cauliflowers are college-educated cabbages, but there is not much difference.

The only thing that makes a difference is, wake up!

CHAPTER 4

Jealousy: Society's Device to Divide and Rule

Osho,
What is jealousy? Does our jealousy show that we are very far
from aloneness?

Society has exploited the individual in so many ways that it is
almost impossible to believe. It has created devices so clever
and cunning that it is almost impossible even to detect that they are
devices. These devices are to exploit the individual, to destroy his
integrity, to take away from him all that he has – without even creating
a suspicion in him, even a doubt about what is being done to him.

Jealousy is one of those tremendously powerful devices. From
the very childhood every society, every culture, every religion teaches
everybody comparison. And the child is bound to learn it. He is just a
tabula rasa, a blank paper without any writing; so whatsoever the parents, the teachers, the priests write on him, he starts believing that is
his destiny, his fate.

Man comes into existence with all the doors open, all directions
available; all the dimensions are there for him to choose. But before
he can choose, before he can be, before he can even feel his being,

he is spoiled. And spoiled by those who think they love him: crushed, crippled, conditioned with all the good intentions in the world. But what to do with good intentions? You are poisoning somebody with good intentions. I know that you are not aware that you are poisoning them, because you have been poisoned in your turn and this has been going on since Adam and Eve.

What did God the Father do to Adam and Eve? He deserves to be called "father"; whether he exists or not does not matter, but he deserves to be called father because he fulfilled all the conditions of being a father. His orders to the children, Adam and Eve, his creations were, "You are not to eat from two trees the tree of knowledge and the tree of eternal life." And this man you call father? He is preventing you from having the two most important things! Nothing can be more important than the exploration of your life and its eternity. And without a tremendous inquiry into knowing, into wisdom, you are not going to figure out what life is, where it is moving.

God prohibits Adam and Eve from the most important things that make you an individual, that give you self-respect, that confer on you integrity, authenticity, beinghood. He wants you to remain ignorant forever. He wants you to be unaware of your own life source. Of course this man is your father. And since this great father, all the small fathers have been doing the same.

I cannot forgive God. I can forgive all the other, small fathers; they are poor people. They are doing to you what has been done to them, they are simply transferring their inheritance. What else can they do? But I cannot forgive God. *He* has no father. He cannot find the excuse "Because it has been done to me I am doing it to them. I don't know any other way." No, it is his invention.

Because God does not exist the whole burden falls on the heads of the priests, the priesthood. They have found ways to keep you away from yourself. And if you are away from yourself, many things are absolutely certain. You will remain miserable forever: moving from one misery to another is going to be your life. Yes, you will be hoping that tomorrow things will be different, but tomorrow never comes and things go on getting worse. Yes, they are different, but not better. You are going down the drain every day. But the hope keeps you alive, otherwise there is nothing to support you even in breathing for a single moment. Everything is missing, because you are missing. Even if everything is available, what is the point of it if you are not there?

Jealousy is one of the greatest devices. Look at it very closely: what does it mean? Jealousy means to live in comparison. Somebody is higher than you, somebody is lower than you. You are always somewhere on the middle rung of the ladder. Perhaps the ladder is a circle because nobody finds the end of it. Everybody is stuck somewhere in the middle, *everybody* is in the middle. The ladder seems to be a round wheel.

Somebody is above you – that hurts. That keeps you fighting, struggling, moving by *any* means possible, because if you succeed nobody cares whether you have succeeded rightly or wrongly. Success proves you are right; failure proves that you are wrong. All that matters is success, so any means will do. The end proves the means right. So you need not bother about the means – and nobody does. The whole question is how to climb on up the ladder. But you never come to the end of it. And whosoever is above you creates jealousy in you, that he has succeeded and you have failed.

One would think that spending your whole life passing from one ladder to another ladder, always finding that somebody is still ahead of you – can't you simply jump off the ladder? No, you cannot. Society is very cunning, very clever. It has polished, refined its methods over thousands of years. Why can't you get out of the circle? – because somebody is below you and that gives you tremendous satisfaction. You see the strategy? That somebody is above you creates jealousy, misery, suffering, humiliation, a feeling of worthlessness, that you have not been able to prove your mettle, that you are not man enough. While others go on moving, you are stuck. It makes you feel just worthless, meaningless, useless, a burden on the earth and nothing more.

If *only* this was the case you would have jumped off the ladder and you would have told those people on the ladder to go wherever they want to go. But you cannot jump off because there are people below you: as far as you can see there are rungs below you and rungs below them. That gives a great satisfaction, a great feeling that you have passed so many people; you are not absolutely useless. You have proved that you have some strength of will and you are not a failure; the people under you are enough to prove it.

You are now in a dilemma: whenever you look upward, a great misery descends on you; whenever you look downward, a great satisfaction. Now, how can you jump off the ladder? Because in jumping off it, you will be jumping from both, and nobody will be below you. Nobody will be above you, certainly, but nobody will be below you. And if you jump off, you will be left alone.

Here you are with everybody else, part of the society, culture, civilization; and it is only a question of a little more effort. People go on telling you, "Bravo, go on! Don't be depressed, don't be pessimistic, remain optimistic. The night is not going to last forever." They go on saying, "When the night is darkest, the morning is the closest, so don't be afraid of the darkness, of failure." They will give you a thousand and one examples.

In my middle school I heard for the first time about the Mohammedan conqueror of India, Mahmud Gaznavi. He attacked India nineteen times and he was defeated eighteen times. When he was defeated for the eighteenth time he was hiding in a cave, and saw a spider trying to weave its net in the front of the cave. He was just hiding there with nothing to do, so he started watching the spider and its efforts. It was raining, and the stones were very slippery. The spider went on falling; coincidentally he fell eighteen times but he succeeded on the nineteenth.

Mahmud suddenly became optimistic. He had been thinking to stop this foolish effort. Eighteen times... He had wasted his whole life, thousands of people had been killed to no purpose. He had been defeated again and again by a single man, Prithviraj Chauhan, who was on the border of India. He was the ruler of the frontier of India. Mahmud was never able to enter the country because he was defeated just at the border, and by a single man. It was really too much – he was thinking to commit suicide because "I am no longer able to show my face to my people."

Mahmud was the king of his own kingdom, there was no need to invade India. But nothing satisfies, nothing is enough; it is always less than you want, and there is always much more that is available. He had a small kingdom, and just by its side was this vast country, India. It was immensely rich at that time because the population was very small, only twenty million people – it was called the Golden Bird in those days. Now there must be nearabout eight hundred million.

It is estimated that by the end of this century there will be one billion people; it will be the biggest country in the world. China will be left behind because China is controlling its birthrate very carefully. Right now the Chinese population is ahead of India, but by the end of the century it is going to be left behind. At least in one thing India will be the Olympic winner.

Naturally it was rich when it was a country of only twenty million people. There was no reason for anybody to be poor. So much land, so much gold – there was more of everything than anybody needed. It attracted invaders, obviously. India has been attracting invaders continually for three thousand years. Now nobody is trying to invade India; in fact the last invaders, the British, finally found that they had sucked India totally, there was nothing left. Then it was more of a liability than an empire. You had to take care of so many poor people, otherwise you were blamed; you had to take care of so many criminals, otherwise you were blamed. The empire was blamed for everything that went wrong because it was the enforced slavery that was causing every trouble.

This is not a valid argument. Mahatma Gandhi was very careful to remain always truthful, but about the basics he was not. It was not true to say to India that all the problems were there only because of the British Empire. Because now – after '47 and up to '84 – although there has been no slavery and the country is free, it has fallen far more deeply into misery and suffering.

You will be surprised that since the British left India, the price of things has gone up seven hundred times. Today if you have seven hundred rupees, it is only worth what one rupee was worth in 1947. So today, to earn seven hundred rupees – which is a big salary in India – is just like earning one rupee in 1947. It was not only the British Empire that was responsible for India's problems; for three thousand years so many people had been sucking India dry.

Mahmud gained confidence. He said, "If a small creature like a spider has such tremendous optimism... Am I inferior to this spider? I will try one more time." And what a coincidence! – the nineteenth time, he succeeded. In fact, he succeeded because Prithviraj Chauhan had simply dropped the idea that he would have the courage to invade again. Defeated eighteen times; with what face could he come back again?

So Prithviraj Chauhan simply dropped the idea that there was going to be any invasion. All the preparations that he had continually been making for the eighteen invasions were dropped. It was no longer an emergency. Mahmud was the only enemy at the borders of Prithviraj Chauhan's land, and he was crushed. Prithviraj Chauhan also thought, "In such a situation I would have committed suicide. Any man with just a little bit of self-respect would rather die than be defeated eighteen times." So he simply dropped the idea. The army was dispersed, sent back to work, and Mahmud invaded at a time when he was not expected at all. He won.

This story was told to me in my class by the history teacher. He said, "This is the way one should be. Never be pessimistic. One never knows. If this time you fail, don't be worried; next time perhaps you will succeed, tomorrow or the day after tomorrow. But never lose heart. To the last breath, go on struggling."

I stood up and told my teacher, "Please forgive me. I think this man Mahmud was an idiot. In the first place, to invade somebody for no reason..." Those people had not committed any crime, and in fact they were powerful enough to have invaded *him*: they had defeated him eighteen times. But Prithviraj Chauhan never went beyond his borders. He could have defeated Mahmud, thrown him out and come back. But he never invaded; it would have been the simplest thing to do.

If the enemy is defeated then why leave him his kingdom? Prithviraj Chauhan could have finished this man Mahmud in the first attack. He could have taken over his kingdom and there would have been no chance for Mahmud to attack again. But Prithviraj Chauhan was a man of far superior humanity; Mahmud was never attacked. Prithviraj Chauhan was told again and again by his prime minister and court people, "The best way is to finish this man and take his kingdom. If you leave him, within two or three years he will again gather forces and be back, and again we will have to fight. This is strange – why do you leave him be?"

But Prithviraj Chauhan said, "The people of his kingdom have not done any wrong to us, nor done any harm to us. How can I invade them? My army is not for invading countries, it is only for those rare moments when some fool attacks us. Then it is a defense force." He was a man of a sophisticated mind, a man who could see that this was stupid. He said, "Don't be worried. This man, sooner or later, is going to drop the idea."

I told my teacher, "Don't praise Mahmud in front of me and don't tell me, 'He was such a great optimist and you should be like him.' I can forgive the spider, nobody expects a spider to have any intelligence, and I can certainly say that the spider was not counting the number of times that he had fallen. He may not have even been aware of what was happening."

With spiders, ants, and those kinds of people, you throw them away, and by a strange logic they will immediately run back toward you. The whole room is available, but from wherever you throw them they will run back in exactly the same direction. What stubbornness! If they have some intelligence, at least *that* direction has to be avoided. It is possible for it to escape anywhere. But strange, you go on hitting a spider and it will come back again toward you.

"That spider was not counting, was not optimistic. This was just Mahmud's old ego finding some excuse again, finding some way to go to his people and say, 'Don't be worried, perhaps this time we will win. And one never knows about tomorrow, so let us try once more.' But don't tell me that this Mahmud was an ideal person. To me he is an ugly man, just a spider. I don't count him among human beings. And if this is going to be taught in the history class, then it is not for me. You are teaching us in a clever way to fight, to destroy, to kill, to put others lower than ourselves."

Parents go on teaching from one's very childhood, "Look at our neighbor's boy – he has come first in the school. And what have *you* been doing for the whole year? Don't you have any intelligence?" In the class they will tell you the same. They will give gold medals to those who come first and top the whole school or the whole college or the whole university. My parents and my teachers in the school used to say, "You can easily be always at the top, but you never take any care about the examinations, you don't care about examinations."

This was my routine: I would always go to the examination fifteen minutes late. This I followed for my whole career in school, in college, at university; I would go fifteen minutes late. It was well known. The examiner knew that my seat had to be kept empty; I would be coming, but exactly fifteen minutes late. And I would leave the examination hall fifteen minutes before everybody else, before the end. The time allowed was three hours and I could see that the examination could be managed in two and a half hours; there was no need to waste another half an hour there.

The teacher who was looking after the students to see that they were not copying and not doing some mischief, that somebody was not carrying a book, would say, "There is no hurry; there are fifteen minutes left. Why are you finishing?"

I would say, "I have finished. I began fifteen minutes after the start and I finish fifteen minutes before the end. And it is going to be this way forever because I don't see that it needs three hours; in fact two and a half hours is more than enough. I have far more important things to do."

They all said, "Why don't you care about the examination?"

I said, "For the simple reason that I don't want to be part of a jealous circle. I don't want to be in the game of comparison. It does not matter to me whether I pass or whether I fail; it will not make any difference to me. If I come first, good; if I come last, even better. To be the first seems to me a little violent because you have taken somebody's joy. And to me it is not a joy at all so I am simply wasting the place; somebody else could have been there who is now second to me, and he would have enjoyed it immensely. Perhaps in the rest of his life he may not find anything else to enjoy, and I have destroyed this chance. Anyway I am not enjoying it.

"So it will be better if I am last. At least I will have the solace that I have not spoiled anybody's career, I have not been violent, pushy; I have not tried to invade somebody else's space. Nobody is behind me and because there is nobody behind me, I cannot feel superior."

And there is the logic, simple logic: if you don't feel superior, you can't feel inferior. They come together, they go together. If you drop one, you cannot save the other. If you don't feel superior to anybody, how can you feel inferior to anybody? You simply feel yourself.

But strange as it was, I almost always managed to be the first. My teachers were amazed, my parents were amazed: "This is strange. You never care about the examination. You don't go regularly to school. Even if you go, you are thrown out of class, and stand outside the class the whole day. You disappear from school any time, any moment. You don't ask for permission from any teacher or the principal; you don't even inform them."

My simple way was: "I want to live my life; why should I ask anybody? They can do whatsoever they want to do. They can punish me, they can fine me, they can report me. I will bring the report to you, but that is between you and them; I have nothing to do with it. I simply do what I want to do."

When I felt so much like going to the river, I was not going to listen to a fool talking about some Mahmud who won on the nineteenth try, although he was defeated eighteen times. He was an ugly man. He didn't behave with Prithviraj the same way Prithviraj had behaved with him: Prithviraj never imprisoned him. Prithviraj defeated him eighteen times but never imprisoned him, because he said, "Leave him to his kingdom. Why should we bother to imprison him? It is enough that he was defeated, that his army is finished. It's enough punishment."

But Mahmud was not a man, he was just animalistic. He caught Prithviraj Chauhan; not only that, he took out both his eyes. Prithviraj was a very beautiful man, and Mahmud's revenge for being defeated eighteen times was that he blinded him.

But Prithviraj Chauhan was a great archer. His court poet, a friend, was imprisoned with him, knowingly, to help him. When Chauhan and this poet were brought into the court, Mahmud was sitting in the balcony high above. He was still afraid of this man although he was blind and chained. What fear! But the man had defeated him eighteen times and thrown him out of the country, not even bothering to imprison him. Must have been a lion!

The poet said to Mahmud, "You don't know Prithviraj. I would like to tell you that there is none in the whole world who is such a master of archery as Prithviraj is. Before you kill him, give him a chance to show his art."

But Mahmud said, "Now he is blind, how can he be a great archer? He *may* have been."

The poet said, "Don't be worried. He is such a great archer that just the sound is enough for him to hit the target." All this talk was going on so that Prithviraj could figure out where Mahmud was sitting from the sound of his voice. And Prithviraj killed Mahmud. Mahmud was thinking that he was going to show his art in archery but Prithviraj simply killed him from the sound, with an arrow exactly to the heart.

I was always thinking of all these people – Alexander the Great, Tamerlane, Genghis Khan, Napoleon Bonaparte. Why are you going to teach innocent children about these people? – to create in them the desire to be conquerors, to be rich, to be presidents, to be prime ministers: not to be themselves. Nobody teaches you to be yourself. You can be anybody, but just don't be yourself. And they create jealousy. Alexander the Great – what is great in that man? And why should you go on continuing the names of Nadirshah and Tamerlane and Genghis Khan? Just murderers, the greatest criminals the world has known. You go on putting small criminals to death, and make your history of the big criminals.

I told my history teacher, "Your history is just a history of crime, and you are trying to make everybody a criminal. Can't you find some innocent human beings and talk about them and teach us that these were the real, authentic people?" But no, history is full of all these other people. The history of the whole world needs to be flushed down the toilet, so that we can start from scratch. Then we can be ourselves because no comparison will exist.

When my postgraduate examinations came along in the university, my professor, who loved me immensely, was very concerned that I used to go fifteen minutes late and I used to leave fifteen minutes early: it meant I might miss what was my right. I told him, "It is not my right to come first, to top the university, to have the gold medal. If I get the gold medal, I will throw it into the university well immediately after the convocation, so that everybody, the vice-chancellor and the whole procession of deans and professors and students, can come and see me dropping the gold medal into the well. I simply don't like the idea of people being put into categories: lower and higher, superior and inferior. If it were in my hands people would simply be educated."

There is no need for examinations. What is the need of an examination? What have you been doing for two years – fooling around? What has the teacher been doing for two years? For two years the teacher has been teaching you, for two years you have been learning; that's enough. There is no need for an examination and there is no need to start putting people higher and lower. This is the beginning of comparison; they come from the university and they know where they are standing on the ladder.

So my teacher, Doctor S. K. Saxena, used to come to the hostel to pick me up. It was just a two-minute walk from my hostel to the examination hall, but he would come and pick me up in his car and force me to enter the examination hall exactly at seven. He would wait outside for three hours so that I could not get out fifteen minutes early. But I have my ways. First I would meditate for fifteen minutes, and at the end I would also meditate for fifteen minutes. The examiner said, "That poor fellow, your professor, is standing outside for three hours, and you have still managed…"

I said, "Don't tell him, because he will unnecessarily feel hurt. There is no need to tell him. I will do my thing. What he wanted to do, he has done. I have not refused, I entered. He said, 'Seven,' I said okay. But how can I drop my whole life's way? I meditate for fifteen minutes because this paper is not worth three hours; it is just for two and a half hours. And I have more important things to do. Because I cannot go out, meditation is the best that I can do, so I will do that."

The examiner told Doctor Saxena, "You are unnecessarily trying to force him. He won't do anything that he does not want to do."

Saxena asked, "Then what did he do there?"

The man said, "He meditated for fifteen minutes. He did not even look at the paper for fifteen minutes. He put it upside down and meditated for fifteen minutes. Then he took the paper and looked at it. Exactly fifteen minutes before the end he closed his copy and handed it to me. He said, 'Now this is the time for my meditation.'"

Saxena said to me, "You are impossible! Missing half an hour? You will lose the gold medal."

I said, "Who cares about the gold medal? And if you are so interested you can give me a gold medal. You want me to have a gold medal on my chest? Give me a gold medal! You can manage it, you have enough money."

He said, "You don't understand; it is not just a question of a gold medal, it is a question of topping the whole university. It will make your career."

I said, "My career is going to be made by a gold medal? Do you think your examination is going to make my career?"

He said, "Yes, because I have arranged everything: if you come first then you will get a scholarship for a PhD. If you don't come first, you won't get it."

I said, "Finished! So I will not have the scholarship and I will not have the PhD. Who cares about your PhD? What have you got? You have two PhD's, one DLitt. What have you really got? You cannot deceive me: you live a frustrated life. You wanted to be elected dean of the arts faculty, but you could not win. You have been defeated twice. And I know that you have wept over it, actually wept tears.

"You have fought for election as vice-chancellor, and you could not manage even twenty votes. Out of one thousand professors you got only twenty votes. Who is going to give votes for a professor of philosophy against a man who is a seasoned politician? He has been chief minister of the province. You think you can win against that criminal? – impossible! People are so afraid of him, because there is every possibility that he will again become chief minister and if they don't vote for him, then he will take revenge."

That's exactly what happened. This man, Dwarika Prasad Mishra, was the chief minister of my state, Madhya Pradesh. There was a conspiracy: Morarji Desai was the chief minister of Mumbai state, Dwarika Prasad was the chief minister of Madhya Pradesh, and a few chief ministers of other states joined together to revolt against Jawaharlal's dictatorial regime. Dwarika Prasad was foolish enough to speak first.

Jawaharlal was so angry that he immediately threw him out. It happened so quickly that Morarji and others had second thoughts about whether to then go ahead according to the conspiracy plan or just back out. And they all backed out, so this man alone was caught. But he was of the same quality as Morarji Desai, just a third-rate gutter politician. He managed, for the time being at least, to be the vice-chancellor of a university. And he waited for the right time.

He was clever. He immediately managed to become vice-chancellor, managed to become very closely connected with Indira Gandhi. Indira was not the prime minister at that time but she was the president of the Congress Party, which was the ruling party. He became so close to Indira that she started trusting in him and calling him "uncle." She persuaded her father, Jawaharlal, the prime minister, to forgive him and take him back. He was forgiven and taken back and became the general secretary of the all-India congress committee, and again he was back as the chief minister of Madhya Pradesh.

He took revenge on those twenty people who had voted for S. K. Saxena. He threw them all out of the university, because the chief minister is the chancellor of the university; anybody who is the chief minister becomes the chancellor of the university. So as chief minister he also became the chancellor and threw out all those people.

I asked Doctor Saxena, "What have you gained from all this trying to go higher? Are you teaching me to get into the same trap in which you have suffered? If you really love me, help me not to get into this trap."

He said, "My God! You even want me to go along with you? No! I will fight against him. I will fight again, and you will see that one day I will become the vice-chancellor."

I said, "Even if you become the vice-chancellor, what does it mean? I know you; you will be as miserable as you are now. First you were a lecturer, you were miserable. You became a reader, you were miserable. You became a professor, you were miserable. You have now become head of the philosophy department, you are miserable. I know you. Do you think by your becoming the dean of the faculty of arts your misery will disappear?

"I know the dean of the faculty also. He is far more miserable than you are because he is just one step away from becoming the vice-chancellor. You are two steps back, he is one step back. His misery is more because he is so close. And every time somebody else jumps in from outside, he goes on missing. His misery is really intense; you will not be surprised if he gets a heart attack."

But strangely, because I was not interested in the examinations and I was not interested in the textbooks, but was interested in the whole world of philosophy – my interest was universal – of course my answers were far richer than anybody else's. They could only repeat what was in the textbooks; I could say something which even the examiner was reading for the first time. Otherwise... I know examiners; I have myself been an examiner for nine years. I never read any copy of any examinee.

I just said to one intelligent student who was trustworthy, who wouldn't say anything to anybody, "You will get half the money. Just check all these books, and remember nobody is to be failed, so everybody gets above the thirty-three mark. And nobody gets above sixty percent because I think nobody is that capable. So these are the limits, thirty-three to sixty. Then you can go on doing it howsoever you want." And I knew that when I was a student, my professors' research scholars were examining the papers.

I said to Doctor Saxena, "Sometimes things can work in my way too. Just wait." And certainly they worked in my way; I was so rich in my answers and so original because I had never bothered about the textbooks. I avoided textbooks because they can get stuck in your mind; I never purchased them.

But I have been collecting books from my high school days. You will be surprised that by the time I was a matriculate I had read thousands of books and collected hundreds of books of my own, and great masterpieces. I was finished with Kahlil Gibran, Dostoevsky, Tolstoy, Chekhov, Gorky, Turgenev; the best as far as writing is concerned. When I was finishing my intermediate, I was finished with Socrates, Plato, Aristotle, Bertrand Russell: all the philosophers that I could find in any library, in any bookshop, or borrow from anybody.

In Jabalpur there was a beautiful place where I was an everyday visitor; I would go for at least one or two hours. It was called the Thieves Market. Stolen things were sold there, and I was after stolen books because so many people were stealing books and selling them, that I was getting such beautiful books. I got Gurdjieff's first book from that Thieves Market, and Ouspensky's *In Search of the Miraculous* from that Thieves Market.

The book cost fifty rupees; from there I got it for half a rupee, because in the Thieves Market books are sold by weight. Those people don't bother about whether it is Ouspensky, Plato, or Russell. Everything is all rubbish; whether you purchase old newspapers or you purchase Socrates, it is the same price. I had collected thousands of books in my library from the Thieves Market. Everybody used to ask me, "Are you mad or something? Why do you go continually to the Thieves Market? Because people don't go there, to be associated with the Thieves Market is not good."

I would say, "I don't care. Even if they think that I am a thief, it is okay."

To me the Thieves Market has been the best source – I have even found books which were not in the university library in the Thieves Market. All the shopkeepers were selling stolen books, and every kind of stolen thing. In India, in every big city there is a Thieves Market. In Mumbai there is a Thieves Market where you can find everything at just throw-away prices. But it is risky because it is stolen property.

I once got into trouble because I purchased three hundred books from one shop, simultaneously, in one day, because somebody's whole library had been stolen. Three hundred books for just one hundred and fifty rupees! I could not leave a single one. I had to borrow money. I told the man, "No book should go," and immediately rushed there.

Those books had seals with a certain man's name and address, and finally the police came. I said, "Yes, these are the books, and I have purchased them from the Thieves Market. In the first place this man is almost ninety years old, he will be dying soon."

The police inspector said to me, "What are you arguing about?"

I said, "I am simply making things clear to you. This man is going to die sooner or later; these books will be rotten. I can give you these books, but you have to give somebody one hundred and fifty rupees because I have borrowed the money. In fact, you cannot catch me because that shopkeeper is there; he will be a witness for me that the books were sold to him. Now, he cannot go on remembering who is selling him old newspapers, and old books; he does not know who has brought them. So first you have to go to that man and find the thief. If you find the thief, get one hundred and fifty rupees from him or from anywhere you want. These books are here, and they cannot be in a better situation anywhere else. That ninety-year-old man won't be able to read them again, so what is the fuss?"

The inspector said, "You sound sane, logical, but these are stolen books and I cannot go against the law."

I said, "Go according to the law. Go to the place where I purchased them – and I *have* purchased them, I have not stolen them. That man has also purchased them, he has not stolen them. So find the thief."

He said, "But on the book there is a seal and the name."

I said, "Don't worry; next time you come there will be no seal! First find the thief. I am always here, at your service."

When he went, I tore a page from each book, the first empty page which means nothing, and I signed the books. From that day I started signing my books because it might have come in handy if my books were stolen someday – at least they had my signature and the date. Because I had taken out the first page of those books, I would sign on two or three pages inside also, in case my books were stolen, but they never were.

My professors used to ask me, "You are reading day and night, but why are you so averse to the textbooks?"

I said, "For the simple reason that I don't want the examiner to see that I am a parrot." And fortunately that helped me. I came first in the university and won the gold medal. But I had promised, so I had to drop the gold medal down the well in front of everybody. The whole university was there, and I dropped the gold medal down the well. I said to them, "With this, I drop the idea that I am the first in the university, so that nobody feels inferior to me. I am just nobody."

The vice-chancellor was present. That evening he called me in and said, "This is not right. The gold medal is a prestigious thing; you have topped the whole university. And you have got me in trouble now because I was to give you the scholarship for a PhD.

You have thrown away the gold medal in front of everybody, and they will say, 'That man is strange. Why are you giving him a scholarship for three years?'"

I said, "Don't give it to me."

He said, "Just because you threw away the gold medal and you told the people there, 'Now I am just nobody; don't take me as the first in the university. Please don't be jealous of me, I am not superior to you. It is just chance. Somebody was bound to be first; it is just a coincidence that I happen to be the first. But it makes nobody inferior.' What you said has gone into my heart and I feel that I will take the risk and give you the scholarship."

He certainly gave me the scholarship but no professor was ready to guide me, because I wanted to do research on religion and they each said, "You will create trouble, and as your guide it will be a constant fight between the two of us. I know your ideas and I know that perhaps you are right, but to accept you and to sign the papers that say I have been guiding you means that I am somehow agreeing with you, and your ideas are outrageous! In private I can agree with you, but not in public.

"What about the two other examiners who will be there from some other university? They will just be shocked because you criticize Krishna, you criticize Rama, you criticize Buddha, you criticize Jesus. Is there anybody whom you don't criticize?"

I said, "If I come across somebody I will mention his name, but if I don't come across anybody, what can I do? Of course when Galileo discovered that the earth goes around the sun, he had to criticize everybody without exception – all the scriptures of the world – because nobody had even thought of it. All religions and all scriptures and all books said that the sun goes round the earth, as it appears to. But appearance is not reality, so how can you be certain?

"It may be possible that as far as religion is concerned I am the first man who is right, because if Galileo can be the first man, just three hundred years ago... Before Galileo, thousands of years had passed. If he can be the first man who was right and everybody else before him was wrong, why do you think I cannot be the first man who is right?"

One of the professors said, "This is the problem! Find somebody else. I will suggest a few names; go to these professors."

The philosophy professors were not ready to accept me. They suggested, "It would be good if the research could be done under psychology. You will just have to change the subject to psychology of religion. Do whatsoever you want, just change the title."

I said, "I will try."

The psychologists said, "If your professors, your own professors of philosophy are not ready to accept you, why should we take this unnecessary trouble on our heads? You criticize Sigmund Freud, you criticize Jung and you criticize Adler, and our whole department stands on these three people; we teach them."

I said, "So should I change the subject again? Politics of religion, economics of religion? I am ready to make up any subject."

I told the vice-chancellor, "Find me a guide. *Religion* has to be there. In front of it, he can put anything: mathematics of religion, economics of religion, geography of religion – I will manage any subject." But nobody was ready to accept me so I could not get the scholarship. But I was immensely happy: these are your professors, your topmost intellectuals, who in private are ready to accept a certain thing, but in public are afraid. Are they worth being jealous of? Are these people superior?

I have no desire to feel anybody is inferior. Yes, it is possible that in one thing you may know more, somebody may know less. In one dimension you may be talented, in another dimension somebody else may be talented. That simply shows that people are unique, they have different qualities. But each individual has his own standing, incomparable. I have never thought of anybody as inferior; I have never thought of anybody as superior.

I am myself, you are yourself. Comparison does not arise.

But all children are being forced to compete, compare, and naturally jealousy arises because somebody succeeds and you are not succeeding. Somebody is getting those things that you are not getting.

I have heard...

A Baptist minister and a rabbi lived across the road from each other, and there was great competition continually going on. Naturally, it is a two-thousand-year-old conflict; it started with Jesus, and I don't know with whom it is going to end. I hope it ends with Pope the Polack. But that's just a hope; you cannot be certain about it. For two thousand years they have been in conflict and it has become more and more personal.

If the minister brings roseflowers and plants for his garden, immediately the rabbi will bring double. One year it happened that the Baptist preacher purchased a Lincoln Continental. This was too much for the rabbi. And when he was standing on his porch, the minister came out and poured water on the Lincoln Continental.

The rabbi asked, "What are you doing?"

He said, "I am giving it its baptism, making it Christian."

The rabbi said, "Okay."

The next day the rabbi purchased a Cadillac limousine – far costlier, a six-door. Just standing on his porch he waited for the Baptist to come out. The man came out, and the rabbi went inside, brought out some instruments and started doing something. The minister said, "What are you doing?"

The rabbi said, "Circumcising."

He was cutting the exhaust pipe!

Jealousy, competition, can drive you nuts. If you can baptize, he can circumcise. He is making the Cadillac a Jew. And I think in America the Cadillac is a Jew, because when I told Sheela to have a Cadillac for the Foundation, and the Foundation's president, she said, "No, you don't know: the Cadillac is a Jew." I said, "My God! Cars are also Jews?" She said, "Yes, the Cadillac is a Jew, and I cannot have a Cadillac." Perhaps cars can be converted.

These people, even though they are ministers and rabbis, are just as stupid human beings as anybody else; and the same is true about their God. There is not much in their God either, because it is their projection and a projection is bound to be less than the one who is projecting it.

Another story I am reminded of...

A rabbi and a Christian minister are playing golf and each time the rabbi misses, he says, "Shit!"

The minister says, "This is not good for a religious man, and a rabbi at that, a priest! This is not right. God will get angry."

But what to do with a habit? Again the rabbi missed and he said, "Shit!"

The minister was very angry. He said, "If you say it a third time, I tell you, God will punish you."

And after he missed a third time and said "Shit!" God really did. Lightning came down and from the sky was heard "Shit!" –

because the lightning hit the minister! It is a Jewish God – what else can you expect?

A rabbi and a Jewish God cannot be very different: the same projection, the same mind.

Jealousy is not seeing a simple fact: you have been taught to see yourself as inferior to someone, as superior to someone. And you have become so unconscious of it that you are constantly judging people as inferior, as superior, as good, as bad, right, wrong. Don't judge; everybody is just himself, accept him as he is. But this is possible only if you accept yourself as you are, with no shame, with no feeling of worthlessness.

The questioner is asking if jealousy means that we have gone too far away from ourselves. Yes. In comparing, you have gone far away in both directions. In one direction there is an unending line of people superior to you; in another direction, another line of people inferior to you – and you are in between.

You have no time to see to yourself. You are constantly struggling to take the place of the man who is ahead of you, and at the same time pushing down the man who is behind you because he is trying to take your place. He is pulling on your leg just as you are pulling on somebody else's leg. It is a strange chain in which everybody is pulling on everybody else's legs. All are in trouble, all are being stretched.

When my back started giving me trouble in India, they gave me traction. I asked Devaraj, "Do you know from where the word *traction* comes, and what you are doing to me?"

He said, "No. Traction is a perfectly good medical device and it is used everywhere."

I said, "It was invented by the Christians in the Middle Ages to torture people. It was a Christian device to torture people! You pull on their arms at one end, their legs at the other end, and naturally, if you want any confession they will have to confess. If you want a woman to accept that she is a witch, on traction she is going to accept it because there is a point where she sees, 'Now my arms are going to be pulled off my body, my legs are going to be pulled off my body. It is better to say "Yes, I am a witch," and get finished with this traction.'" But once she has accepted she is a witch she is going to be burned alive.

It was a torture device. It was just by coincidence it was found. A man who was thought to be a heretic was being given traction. He had a back pain, and when he was released from traction he said, "My God! The back pain has disappeared." Just by coincidence it was found that it can help back pain. Since then it has been medical; before that it was part of the church.

But you see your life as a psychological traction; hence you have no time, no energy, no space for yourself. You are always looking at somebody else, either to feel good...

A Christian priest, Stanley Jones, very famous in his time – he is dead, now – was a world-famous Christian teacher, and of course a great orator. Not like the idiot Billy Graham! Stanley Jones was really a great orator, a profound orator; Billy Graham is just an Oregonian. You should look into it; he must have been born in Oregon. His face is typical of that retarded...

No, Stanley Jones was really an impressive personality, and known worldwide. He was wandering around the world giving sermons but he had his headquarters in India: he had made a Christian ashram in the Himalayas. He used to come to Jabalpur also, where I was a professor.

In one of the sermons at which I was present, he told a very beautiful anecdote. Not being aware that a strange person was sitting just in front of him, he said, "There are two kinds of people. One always looks at the high skyscrapers of other people, feels miserable because the lawn is always greener in the neighbor's garden."

It is always greener. From faraway, things look different: your own lawn does not look so green. Your own house looks dirty; the other house looks so beautiful. Your wife, when you go in your house, is continually quarreling. When you go to meet your neighbor, they are both smiling, but you forget one thing: when your neighbor comes to you then you are also both smiling. People go on looking at what other people have and then they start feeling that they are missing it – anything!

Stanley Jones recounted a story. He said, "I have a lifelong friend who is always hopeful, optimistic. He really sees a silver lining in every dark cloud. First I used to think that it was only a philosophy, but the Second World War proved conclusively that he meant what he said. It was not just a philosophy, but his very Christian being.

"I went to see him after the Second World War because he had lost an eye, a hand, and a leg in the war. On the way I was thinking that perhaps he had also lost his positivistic attitude, but to my amazement he was even more positive than ever. I asked him his secret.

"He said, 'It is simple. It is the very fundamental of Christianity. I thank God that at least I have one eye, one hand, and one leg. There are many who have lost both legs, many who have lost both eyes, many who have lost both hands, and millions who have lost their whole lives. I think of them and feel fortunate and blessed.'"

Stanley Jones emphasized through this anecdote that this should be every Christian's approach – that positive philosophy is the greatest contribution of Jesus Christ.

I stood up and said to him, "It is impossible to feel fortunate comparing yourself to those who are in an inferior position, and yet not feel inferior because there are also certainly people who are in a superior position. It is impossible to divide inferior and superior and just choose one; they are aspects of the same coin."

The most amazing part was that the great orator and preacher became very angry, threw down his notes and went inside the house. When he was leaving I told him, "This seems to be the real Christian philosophy. But just being angry and escaping is not an argument; and whenever you come back again to this city, remember, I will be here to remind you of the argument because you are leaving it inconclusive." As it happened, he never came back to Jabalpur.

You will be surprised that comparison is not just to do with money or power, but can be about anything. In my childhood, just as girls in India had earrings rich people's boys used to have earrings also. Now that disease is spreading in the West too. My ears still have the marks of those old holes. I resisted very much but I was too small, and my parents said, "It doesn't look good that every boy in the neighborhood has golden earrings, and you go out without earrings. Everybody is saying to our family, 'What is the matter, can't you afford even two gold rings?' It is insulting!"

Now, what do earrings have to do with...? I said, "It may be insulting to you but to me it simply seems that you are destroying my ears. You will make holes in my ears and I will have to suffer the pain. If God had intended... If he can make so many things, just two holes in the ears are not much craftsmanship. Even the Holy Ghost could have done it."

But they wouldn't listen because it was a constant trouble: relatives would come and they would say, "What! Your boy has no earrings?" Now earrings had become a necessity. That too is part of the competitive society. And they forced me; four people had to keep me down on the bed, and they pierced both my ears.

I said, "Okay, I am small and helpless – you can do any nonsense that you want to do, but remember, I am not going to forgive you for it. It is being done against my will, and I am not going to wear your earrings. Are you going to follow me twenty-four hours a day? Now we will see!" Many times they put earrings on me and I threw them away. Finally they got tired, and it was costly because they were gold earrings and I would throw them away. The moment I got the chance I would throw them away.

Finally they said, "Leave him alone."

I said, "If you had left me alone before, my ears could have been saved. I don't have any hope of being saved in life, but my ears would have been saved."

Competition in everything, strange things... If you are living in a commune or a community of hippies, then the dirtier you are, the greater you are. What I mean to explain to you is that it has nothing to do with money or power or anything in particular. You can use anything to feel superior or inferior. Now the hippie who never takes a bath is certainly superior to the other hippies who are not so seasoned and once in a while need a shower. Certainly he is far superior; he never takes a bath, never cleans his teeth, never uses soap or dirty things like that. He remains completely natural. Perspiring, he remains natural; smelly, he remains natural. He will be thought to be somebody higher: you are not that strong. Once in a while you are weak, you feel like taking a bath. But if a hippie takes a bath he tries to hide it.

In India there are such monks. A Hindu monk used to stay in my home; he was a friend of my father, a childhood friend. My father had a cloth shop, so whenever the monk came, my father would make good clothes for him; if it was winter then winter clothes, woolen clothes. And what would the monk do? First he would make them dirty; he would rub them against the ground, make them old and dusty because a monk is not supposed to have beautiful clothes and be up-to-date.

My father would try to use the best that he had in his shop, and

I told him, "You are just wasting them. That man even makes holes in them and tears them and makes them look old" – because then he was on a higher stage of monkhood. Those who cannot afford such dirty clothes, old clothes, rags are still interested in clothes. They are still attached to material things. There is competition in that too: in who has more rotten rags than you.

There are Hindu monks who will not just eat the food that you give them. First they will dip it in the river to spoil it completely, then mix it all together in their begging bowl so that salty things and sugary things and everything is mixed; and then they will eat it. That is thought to be austerity. And those who do not do it are thought to be still far lower, living still for taste and food – they have to destroy the taste.

Certainly, if you go on in this way, being jealous and competitive of everybody around you, how can you come to yourself? The world is too big, and there are so many people and you are in competition with everybody. And you *are*. Somebody has a beautiful face, somebody has beautiful hair, somebody has a beautiful, proportionate body, somebody has a great intellect, somebody is a painter, somebody is a poet... How are you going to manage? All this, and you alone to compete? You will drive yourself nuts; and that is what all of humanity has done.

Drop competition, drop jealousy. It is absolutely pointless. It is absolutely a cunning device created by the priests so that you can never be yourself – because that is the only thing all the old religions are afraid of.

If you are yourself you have found contentment, fulfillment, ecstasy. Who cares about God then? – you *are* God. You have tasted godliness within yourself. Now you are not even bothered about the emperor; you are not thinking that he is superior to you. How can he be superior to you? You have tasted something of such tremendous dimensions that what can that poor fellow have? You can feel sorry for him, but you will not feel inferior. You will not feel even toward a beggar that he is inferior, because you know that what you have found he is also carrying within himself.

There is no qualitative difference between you, the beggar, and the emperor. The only differences are just on the outside: the clothes, the titles, the elephant on which the king is sitting, and the beggar in his rags. But these are not real differences, not the difference that makes a difference.

Inside yourself you will find a tranquility, a serenity, a silence, a treasure unfathomable. And in finding it you will know everybody has it; whether he knows it or not is a different matter. Knowing and not knowing is the only difference. But as far as existence is concerned, everybody has all the beauty of the world, of the universe; all the ecstasy and dance of the universe. Yes, it will express itself in different ways; there is no need to think that somebody who is expressing it through dance is better than the one who is expressing it through a song or one who is expressing it through his silence. What is being expressed is exactly the same ecstasy.

You will find it only when you have entered your world of aloneness, where there is nobody else. There, you have left the society far behind – because that society has been preventing you. You have left all the priests, all the religions, all the political parties far behind. You are now almost nobody.

I say "almost" because in fact you *are*, for the first time – but on a totally different plane. You have never even thought about it, that this can be your very being, so profound and so full and so eternal. And what are you going to lose by dropping jealousy and competitiveness and comparison? Nothing.

You have nothing to lose but your chains, and you have the whole kingdom of God which is within you to gain.

CHAPTER 5

The Odyssey of Aloneness

Osho,
Our commune is not like any of the traditional ashrams or
monasteries. Would you talk to us more about the function of
your commune?

I t is necessary first to understand the traditional structure of an
ashram, and also of a monastery. It will give you the background
to understand the meaning of my commune.

The ashram is an Eastern concept based on renouncing society,
its comforts, conveniences. An ashram is a group of people living
together in austerity, self-imposed poverty, starvation in the name of
fasting; torturing the body in order to have control over the physical
by the spiritual; doing all kinds of exercises so that they become able
to concentrate on the idea of God if they are Hindus, or on the idea of
the ultimate growth of human consciousness if they are Buddhists
and Jainas.

But the goal is far away for all the three – you can call it God,
you can call it the Buddha, you can call it the Jina. They are different words signifying nothing, but pointing toward a further shore,

so far away that you cannot even conceive it. It remains just a vague idea, a cloudy idea in your mind. For this cloudy idea you have to sacrifice everything that is real, tangible, touchable, which you can see, which you can feel, which you can live. All that is alive has to be sacrificed for something which is nothing but a utopia.

Do you know the exact literal meaning of the word *utopia*? Its literal meaning is that which never happens; the hoped for which never happens. It can keep you engaged for centuries, and it has kept millions of people engaged for centuries. They are still engaged in the same effort: losing *this* for something for which they have no evidence, no proof, not even an argument.

The word *ashram* is very beautiful, but is used in a very wrong context. *Ashram* means a place to relax. Yes, in the very beginning, five thousand years ago, in the times of the Vedas, an ashram was actually a place of relaxation; it was not ascetic. You will be surprised to know this, because for five thousand years asceticism has prevailed so strongly that people have completely forgotten how it used to be in the beginning. It was just the opposite of what it is today.

The *rishis*, the *munis* – these two words you have to understand. *Rishi* means "poet of consciousness." It is only in the East that we have two words for poet: *kavi* and *rishi*. *Kavi* means the poet, but in English there is no equivalent for *rishi*. The *rishi* is the awakened poet. He still sings, but those songs are not composed by him; they filter through him, they come from existence. Just as flowers blossom, poems blossom. The poet is a composer: he plays with the words, with their rhythm, with their sound, and he is capable of creating meaningful, rhythmic songs.

It is good not to meet a poet. Take it as a basic policy never to meet a poet because that will be a disappointment. His poetry is so beautiful but the poet so extra-ordinary. I don't mean extraordinary as one word. I am using the word *extra* to emphasize the word *ordinary*: *extra ordinary*. I don't know who gave this word *extraordinary*, because it simply means the last, the very last – not simply ordinary, but extra ordinary. The people who used this word first must have been thinking of *extraordinary* in the sense of being above the ordinary; but *extraordinary* can mean both. One thing is certain, the poet is not ordinary: he can be above the ordinary, he can be below the ordinary.

There are many words which have this same ambivalence. For example, psychologists use the word *abnormal*. Now, abnormal can mean insane, crackpot, nuts and bolts – anything. But abnormal can also mean one who is above normal: a Buddha, a Jesus, a Moses, a Zarathustra. Both are abnormal in the sense that both are not normal, but there are two sides of not being normal. In the same way, the word *extraordinary* has always been used for those who are above the ordinary. I have tried to find out why it has not been used for those idiots who are below the ordinary. They are also extraordinary. Why this unfairness?

The original ashram, the very word *ashram*, means time to relax, a place to relax. *Shram* means labor, work. The word *ashram* means you have done what was to be done, now it is time to be in a state of nondoing. You have been active your whole life. When are you going to know the strange and extraordinary world of inaction? – so totally silent that nothing moves there. It was a beautiful word and the people who invented it were really doing just that. But it is a five-thousand-year-old story which these five thousand years have been destroying continuously.

You will be shocked to hear that the *rishi* can be translated as the seer. The ordinary poet is blind, he is groping in darkness; the *rishi* is one who has eyes. The blind man can also sing songs of beautiful sunrises, sunsets, flowers, colors, rainbows – yes, the blind man can sing...

In fact blind people are good singers for the simple reason that eighty percent of our body's energy is used by our eyes, and when a man is blind, that eighty percent of his energy starts being distributed to the ears, to the nose, to the mouth – into the other four senses which ordinarily have to share only twenty percent of the energy. With the eyes non-existent, the senses enjoy one hundred percent of the energy amongst themselves. Hence the blind man has a very subtle way of hearing. You cannot hear what he hears. He remembers through hearing.

I was traveling in a train in the middle of the night and I entered the compartment which was reserved for me. It was a small, two-couch compartment. One, the upper one, was already occupied; the lower was reserved for me. As I sat on the lower bunk, gave the money to the porter and gave instructions to the servant about when I would like to have tea in the morning, and when I would like to have my breakfast, I had no idea who was on the upper berth. But the man said, "Is that not you there, Osho?"

I looked up; I could not recognize the man. I said, "Yes, but who are you?"

He said, "Have you forgotten me? I am Sharanananda." He was a very famous Hindu sage; but he was blind. I had met him twelve years earlier. In those twelve years I must have met millions of people; it was impossible to remember him. How could he manage to remember me when he was blind, birthblind?

I said, "Sharnananda, you are doing a miracle! You can't see me, yet you recognize me. And I can see you but I could not recognize you."

He said, "It is because of your eyes. I cannot see – I remember through my ears. Your sound, your way of speaking: those little things become part of my memory. And the meeting with you and the way you talked was so memorable. I could even hear the same way, the same sound, while you were talking to the servant, to the porter. I immediately recognized you. Nobody else talks like you.

"You said to the servant, 'Don't wake me up because my morning begins when I wake, so let the tea wait. When I am awake, I will ring the bell, then you bring the tea.' The moment you said, 'My morning begins when I wake,' I said this man cannot be anybody else. I don't know anybody else in the whole world whose morning begins when he wakes up – the morning begins when it begins – but you can say that, only you can say that!"

A seer is one who is not groping in darkness and just imagining things. Yes, a blind man's imagination becomes very powerful because he cannot see; his whole energy is available inwards. Otherwise, the energy moves outside from the eyes, eyes are the doors opening outwards. When the eyes are closed, the energy moves inwards.

That's why meditators close their eyes. It is a simple strategy: close the eyes and you block the doors; the energy cannot move out, it moves in. So, blind people become very imaginative. They can talk of color although they have never seen it. They can talk of light although they have never seen it. But still, howsoever beautiful their imagination, it is untrue, it is not real.

In India we call these people *kavis*, poets. But don't go to see them, because the poet will be a very ordinary person. It has happened so many times I feel it almost a rule to be followed: just the other day I saw for the first time a film of an Urdu singer, Gulam Ali. He is one of the topmost Urdu singers in the East, he has his own way and style. There are many singers, but Gulam Ali stands far above any of them. But I had always heard Gulam Ali; it had never happened that I had seen him.

We were both moving around the same country but by chance it never happened that we were in the same city. He wanted to meet me. In India a great musician, a great singer, is called *ustad*, maestro. He has disciples just as spiritual masters have disciples, because Eastern music needs a long discipline. It is not like jazz music, that any idiot can start jumping and shouting and it becomes music; it is not the music of the Beatles. It takes twenty or thirty years of training, eight hours or ten hours a day. It is a whole life's work.

Gulam Ali has worked hard and still works hard. It is said that if you don't practice Eastern music for three days, people will recognize something is missing. If you don't practice for two days, only your disciples will recognize something is missing. And if you don't practice for one day, only you are certain to feel that it was not the same thing. Not even a single day has to be missed.

But just the other day somebody from Pakistan sent me a film of Gulam Ali. And what I was expecting, happened. His personality is so poor that it is difficult to connect that beautiful voice with this man who looks like a clerk in a post office, or a ticket collector in a railway company, or a conductor in a bus, that type of man. I had to keep my eyes closed because his face, his eyes, his hands, his gestures – everything was disturbing. I thought that I should send him a suggestion, "You should sing behind a curtain. You are not worth presenting, you destroy your music. The music is almost divine, then you see a donkey standing behind – you cannot connect them."

The same happened a few days ago. I have never seen Mehdi Hasan – another great singer, far more modern than Gulam Ali. Gulam Ali is very orthodox, his training is orthodox. But Mehdi Hasan has a very innovative genius. He is trained in orthodox music but he has not kept himself confined to it. He has improvised new ways, new styles, and he is a really creative man. Gulam Ali is not a creative man; he recites those songs exactly as they have been recited for thousands of years. Listening to him you are listening to thousands of years, the whole tradition behind him.

These singers all have what is called *gharanas* – *gharana* means family. They don't belong to the family of their father and mother, they belong to the family of the master from whom they have learned. That is their *gharana*. They are known by the name of their master, their master is known by his master. Their *gharanas* are thousands of years old, and each generation teaches to the next generation exactly the same tone, the same wavelength.

But Mehdi Hasan is ultra-modern, and he has a creative genius which is far more significant. I have loved him because he has brought a new light, new ways of singing the same old songs. He is so creative that the whole song seems almost new, reborn, fresh, like a just-opened flower with the dewdrops still on it.

But what a misery to see him. He is far worse than Gulam Ali! Gulam Ali at least seems to be a conductor on a bus, but Mehdi Hasan is not even worthy to be conductor. Gulam Ali does not fit with what he is singing, but Mehdi Hasan is exactly *contradicting* what he is singing. Strange that the two persons I have seen on the screen, I have not met. This has been my general practice my whole life in India. I have read poets, heard poets on the radio, but I have not met them because my early experiences of meeting poets were just shipwrecked.

Maitreyaji is sitting there – he knows a great Indian poet, Ramdhari Singh Dinkar. They belong to the same place, Patna, and they were friends. He has written some high-flying songs. He has contributed much to Indian poetry. He was known as the great poet, *mahakavi*; not just *kavi*, a poet, but the great poet. He was the only man known as the great poet.

He used to come to see me, unfortunately. He loved me, I loved him, but I could not *like* him. Love is spiritual, you can love any-body, but liking is far more physical. Whenever he came he would talk of such stupid things that I told him, "Dinkar, one expects some-thing poetic from you."

He said, "But I am not a poet twenty-four hours a day."

I said, "That's right! But come to me when you are! – otherwise don't come, because my acquaintance is with the poet Dinkar, not with you." Whenever he came, he would talk about politics – he was a nominated member of parliament – or he would talk continually about his sickness. He was making me sick! I told him, "Stop talking about your sicknesses, because people come to me to ask some-thing of value, and you come to describe your sicknesses."

But if I prohibited him from talking politics, he would talk of sicknesses. If I prohibited him from talking of sicknesses, then he would talk about his sons: "They are destroying my life. Nobody listens to me. I am going to send them to you."

I told him, "You are too much. And you are spoiling my joy for when your book comes out: I cannot read it without remembering you. In between the lines you are standing there talking about your diabetes, your politics..."

He would talk about diabetes, and he would ask for sweets! "These," he would say, "I cannot leave." He died because he continued to eat things that the doctors were prohibiting. And he knew it; he would tell me everything that the doctors had prohibited and ask me, "Osho, can you tell me some way that I can have diabetes manage to eat all these things?" Maitreyaji knew him perfectly well.

In Jabalpur there was a famous poetess, Shubhadra Kumari Chauhan. I had read her poetry from my very childhood; she was continuously fighting for freedom and revolution. Her songs had become so popular because of the freedom struggle that even small children were reciting them. Even before I was able to read, I knew a few of her songs. When I went to the university I discovered that she had also moved to Jabalpur. It was not her original place; her original place happened to be near my village. That I discovered later on, that she was from just twenty miles away from my village and that she had moved to Jabalpur just two years before I moved there.

But seeing that woman, I said, "My God! Such beautiful poetry, and such an utterly homeless – no, I mean *homely*... I got so distracted by her that I forgot even the word *homely*! Because she was worse than that, and I don't know any other word that is worse than that. *Ugly* does not look right to use for anybody; it seems to be condemning, and I only want to describe, not to condemn, hence homely. *Homely* means you need not pay any attention; let her pass, let her go.

Then there was another poet, of all-India fame, Bhavani Prasad Tiwari, who was in immense love with me. I was very young when I started delivering public discourses; I must have been twenty when I delivered my first public discourse, in 1950 and he was the president there. He could not believe it. He was so overwhelmed that rather than delivering his presidential address he said, "Now I don't want to disturb what this boy has said. I would like you to go home with what he has said, meditating over it. And I don't want to give my presidential address – in fact, *he* should have presided, and

I should have spoken." And he closed the meeting.

Everybody was in a shock because he was an old man and famous. He took me in his car and asked me where he could leave me. That day I became acquainted with him. I said, "It is a shock to me. You are certainly a loving person and also an understanding person. I have read your poems and I have always loved them. They are simple but have the quality of raw diamonds, unpolished. One needs the eye of a jeweler to see the beauty of an uncut, unpolished, raw diamond just coming out from the mine – just born.

"I can also say I have always felt, reading your poetry, like when the rainy season first begins in India, and the clouds start showering, and the earth has a sweet smell of fresh, thirsty earth; and the smell of that earth getting wet gives you a feeling of thirst being satisfied.

"That's how I have always felt reading your poetry. But seeing you I am disillusioned" – because the man had on both sides, inside his mouth, two pans, betel leaves, and the red, blood-like juice of the betel leaves was coming from both sides of his mouth onto his clothes. That was a chain thing, the whole day. All that he was doing was making new pans. He used to carry a small bag with everything in it. And whenever I saw him he was always... This is the way: tobacco in his hand, rubbing the tobacco, preparing it, chewing the pan, and the red juice was all around.

I said, "You have destroyed my whole idea of a poet." Since then I have avoided poets because I came to know that they are blind people; once in a while they have a flight of imagination. But five thousand years ago, in the East, they must have understood that we have to make a distinction between the poet who is blind, and the poet who has eyes.

A *rishi* is one who speaks because he sees. His poetry also has a different name; it is called *richa* because it comes from a *rishi*. *Richa* means poetry coming from the awakened consciousness of a being.

These people were not ascetics. They had wives, they had children, they had beautiful ashrams – so beautiful that even kings used to go there for their holidays. Kings used to send their children to live with the family of a *rishi* in an ashram, because there was nothing more beautiful than an ashram.

Ashrams were deep in the forest, in the mountains, near the great rivers of India, and with an awakened being. He had a wife, he had children. He was just as simple and ordinary as you are – he was not on any power trip. And he was not worried about God, and paradise; he was enjoying life here.

Even kings were jealous, and they used to come for advice because these people were not just spiritual guides, they had eyesight that they could use for anything. They were not averse to riches. All the ashrams were, in the beginning, tremendously rich, because the kings continued to pour in as much money as possible. And it was not only one king coming to one *rishi*, because *rishis* and their ashrams were not part of any kingdom.

That much respect the East knew; that you could not claim the ashram of a *rishi* as part of your kingdom. So a *rishi* was independent; other kings were also coming to him. He was not possessed by any king who could say, "You can only advise me. I have given you the land and I have given you so much money, and so much luxury and so much comfort and protection, so you are to be my adviser only." No, such a thing was inconceivable.

If the *rishi* has accepted all that you have offered, he has obliged you. He could have refused. You were to be thankful to him that he did not refuse you. You were to be obliged to him that he gave you the honor to serve him. He was nobody's possession. His territory was an independent territory, and in his territory anybody could take refuge, even a criminal. Then the criminal was beyond the powers of the rulers from whom he had escaped. You could not catch hold of him or bring the police and the army into the *rishi's* campus. That campus was sacred.

It was literally true that there was no comparison between the ancient Eastern ashram and anything else, even a palace of a king. On each special occasion, the king would go to receive blessings. He would touch the feet of the *rishi*, because he knew he himself was blind, and that it was good to be blessed by someone who had eyes, and to be guided. It happened many times that wars were avoided simply because both kings went to the same *rishi* to ask, "Our armies are standing face to face – what to do?"

The rishi would say, "You ask me what to do? Just take your armies back to your homes! There is not going to be any fight. While I am still alive your armies are not going to face each other again." And that was so. The war was delayed till his death; before, that war could not happen. There was no question of denying him. He had no political power, no army, but they both knew that he had eyes, and if he saw that this was going to be blissful for both, then let it be so. "We are blind. We will step back."

But the birth of Buddhism and Jainism, the two other religions in India, created trouble. They transformed the whole character of the ashram. The first thing to be noted is that Buddhists and Jainas don't have ashrams. To destroy the ashram – because the ashram was the stronghold of brahminism, Hinduism and yet without somebody being a pope, chosen, elected...

You cannot elect a buddha. How can you even think of electing a buddha? What grounds, what criteria will you use? Just think of blind people electing someone who has eyes. Now, how can they determine that he has eyes? They don't have eyes so they can't see. Two persons are standing as candidates, saying "We have eyes, give us votes." Do you see the absurdity? Now, blind people will say, "How can we decide? We don't have any eyes so we don't see whether you are both blind, both have eyes, or one has eyes and one is blind. We cannot determine in any way."

A buddha, an awakened human being, has to declare himself. There is no question of anybody selecting, nominating. Who can select? Who can nominate? Who can elect?

There is a poem sung by this man I referred to, Mehdi Hasan, in which a sentence comes: *I am a man with eyes selling glasses in the city of the blind.* When I heard the line, *I am a man with eyes selling glasses in the city of the blind,* I said, "You cannot have eyes; one thing is certain, you don't have eyes. Otherwise a man with eyes, selling eye-glasses in the city of the blind simply proves that he is far blinder than the people to whom he is selling the glasses! Blind people cannot tell who has eyes and who has not."

So these *rishis* were not popes. The pope is an elected person; two hundred cardinals elect him. All those two hundred cardinals are secretly campaigning for themselves to be elected. It is a secret thing. For twenty-four hours the doors of a particular place in the Vatican are closed. For twenty-four hours those two hundred people are inside, just so that the world does not know how the selection happens, how the person is elected.

They are all campaigning for themselves, each campaigning for himself, or for somebody who will help them. It takes twenty-four hours to find one person; that too is not a unanimous choice. Sometimes there are two candidates, then a vote has to be taken;

sometimes there are three candidates and none are ready to with-draw. By voting, two hundred fallible cardinals can choose one infal-lible pope! This world is really strange.

That was not the case with the *rishis*. But Jainism and Buddhism transformed the whole character of the Eastern way of life. First, to destroy the ashrams they decided that they wouldn't have any ashrams. So Jaina monks, Buddhist monks, are wan-dering monks; they don't have any ashrams – because if you have an ashram there is a possibility that you will start collecting conven-iences, comforts, luxuries. It is very natural.

People will love you, respect you and they will go on giving you things. And you will keep things for certain seasons: the rains will be coming, and you will need an umbrella so you keep the umbrella even in the season when it is not needed. So you will start possessing things. In the rains it will be difficult to go out, so you will collect food, foodstuff. In winter you will need clothes, woolen clothes, so you collect woolen clothes.

You cannot avoid possessions, and both Jainism and Buddhism were determined that the monk should not possess anything – and the Jaina monk, absolutely nothing. He was naked, without even a begging bowl, which had always been accepted. Nobody had even questioned whether a begging bowl was a possession.

But Jainism did not even allow a begging bowl; you had just to eat from your hands. If all the animals can do without begging bowls – you are men, far more intelligent – you can do it. So they drink from the hands, they eat from the hands; that is their begging bowl. They were not allowed to have ashrams because ashrams would become properties, possessions. They had to continually move. A Jaina monk cannot stay more than three days in one place.

Certainly there is some idea behind it, because I have watched: if you stay in a place, it takes some time to get comfortable. For example, the first night you may not be able to sleep at all – a new place, a new house... Nothing is uncomfortable, it's just the new-ness. Perhaps you are accustomed to sleeping in a round bed, and this is a square bed, and that is enough! You are accustomed to sleeping in a square room, and this is a round room; you almost feel as if you have fallen in a well or something. Even in your sleep you will wake up many times.

The first night is very difficult, the second night is easier, and by the third night you are comfortable. This is my experience, because I have been traveling for thirty years, staying in strange places, strange houses. You will not believe it – I have been a guest from the most rotten house you can imagine to the best palace in the world.

It was really a problem because I was continually moving about, not staying for even three days. I am not a Jaina monk; not even three days were available to me. In the morning I was in Kolkata, in the evening I was in Mumbai; by the night I had moved toward Delhi. Mostly I was in trains, planes, cars, but rarely in houses. In fact I have to confess to you, that I became so accustomed to sleeping in air-conditioned trains that in houses I felt uncomfortable. I felt comfortable only on the train, with all the noise, the movement, the hustle and bustle of each station, and the passengers coming in and getting out. All that became part of my comfort.

When I used to sleep in a room, I would wake up a few times, and, "No station?" Because Indian stations are very noisy: all kinds of things are being sold, even in the middle of the night. The whole station is agog, alive, and full of people, because except for the air-conditioned class, all the classes are so cramped. The third class, which is the class for everybody, is always overcrowded. You can see, it is written on the compartment that it is reserved only for thirty people – and you will find sixty, ninety. How they manage…

Once or twice just to have the experience I have traveled third class. And it really is a great experience to travel in the third class in India. A compartment made for thirty people, and ninety or a hundred people are in it, with not even a single inch anywhere can you move. You cannot go to the bathroom – in fact people are also stuck in the bathroom. In the first place there is no way to reach there. Even if you do reach, somehow, treading over people, there is no space in the bathroom; it is already full. People are traveling even on the roof of the train. They are hanging out of the doors, the windows.

Once I traveled third class from Gwalior to Delhi, just to enjoy it. Because I had slept, and there was now no need to sleep – and it was night, a full-moon night – I said to myself, "Enjoy yourself, go third class."

I had an air-conditioned-class ticket. When the ticket collector looked at my air-conditioned-class ticket and then looked at me, he thought I was crazy. I said, "You are right" He handed the ticket back to me.

He said, "This is strange. What are you doing here? Your seat is reserved and it is empty."

I said, "Let it be empty. If I get fed up with this experience I will come along."

He said, "What experience?"

I said, "You don't know what is happening here. If you want, you can stay with me just for one station."

He stayed and he said, "Really, it is an experience."

What was happening was, at the station the lights of the compartment would come on, and as we left the station behind the lights would go out. Ninety people in that small space... And who is pulling whose leg? It was such a joy! I enjoyed it like nothing else in my life.

A Hindu monk was sitting by my side. I was hitting his head, and he would tell me, "Osho, somebody is hitting me."

I said, "In the dark it is very difficult. Remain patient, and if you want to hit, hit anybody! There is no question of who is hitting who."

Somebody pulled the leg of a woman who was sitting in an upper berth and she fell down. And she said, "This is strange – someone is doing this to a woman. Who is this nasty fellow?" In the darkness nobody could be identified as nasty, and as the next station appeared, everybody was sitting perfectly correctly. In the station the lights would come on. If it had been the other way round things would have been simpler. If the compartment lights had gone out at the station, there would have been no problem because there were lights at the station.

The train was going really crazy, and people were shouting in the darkness, "Somebody is pulling on my leg." And, "Who is this fellow?" And, "I will try to find out, but it will be difficult." "Please don't pull my leg!" – but no answer came. In the third class you certainly meet the real India. In the air-conditioned compartment it is not part of India.

In saying three days, the Indian Jaina monks decided very psychologically, because it is my experience too that after the third day you feel at ease. Not to allow you to feel at ease they decided on three days. There must have been somebody among them who had experienced this. It is exactly so because I have told a few of my friends to try it, and they all said, "It is true: after the third day you start feeling relaxed, at home. The new place is no longer new. It takes that much time to be acquainted with it, to have a certain rapport."

Yes, a rapport is needed, even with the walls, the furniture, the people, the food. A certain kind of acquaintance and it takes a little time. What they decided was perfectly right – they measured it perfectly correctly – that the Jaina monk is not to stay more than three days, so no attachment grows. Once you start liking a place, that is the beginning of attachment, desire; then you would like to stay a little longer, then...

I am reminded of a story:

A great master was dying. He called his chief disciple to his side and whispered in his ear, "Remember one thing, never, never allow a cat in the house" – and he died.

"What kind of message...? And for this you called me: 'Never allow a cat in the house?'" The chief disciple inquired with a few old, elderly people, because perhaps there was some meaning in it. "Perhaps it is a code word, otherwise why should he say that? And he died without giving any explanation. I was just going to ask, 'Why are you against cats your whole life? And this is the ultimate conclusion of all your discipline, practices, scriptures, scholarship: don't allow a cat in the house.'"

One old man said, "I know what the matter is. This is the message given to him by his master too, because his master got into trouble because of a cat." The old master had lived outside the village. He had only two... In English it is difficult to translate because nothing like that exists: you have underwear, in India they have *langoti* – they are just strips of cloth. It needs a little practice to put on. It is just a long strip of cloth which you simply wind around yourself and that functions as underwear, or the onlywear. For a monk that is the onlywear.

He had two onlywears – that is my translation for *langoti* – but the trouble was there were a few rats, and they used to destroy his onlywear. He asked somebody from the village, "What to do with these rats? They are very cunning."

The man said, "It is very simple. What we do in the village is just keep a cat. Keep a cat; I will bring you one. She will finish off those rats and your onlywear will be saved."

The old master said, "This is a simple solution." The cat was brought. She really did her job, she finished off the rats, but the problem was the cat was hungry and she needed milk. She was always sitting in front of the monk, hungry. Cats, when they are hungry, look really poor. She had done her job, and without saying it she was saying, "I have done all your business, all the rats are finished, but I am hungry now."

So the old master asked again, "Now what to do? The cat sits in front of me, looking hungrily at me: 'Provide food, otherwise I am going and then the rats will come back.' She does not say all that but I can see in her eyes that she is threatening me, challenging me. I need some milk."

The man said, "You would have to come every day for milk, so I will give you my cow. I have many cows, you can take one."

He took the cow but his problems went on increasing: now the cow needed grass. He again went to the town, and the townspeople said, "You are a strange fellow – problem after problem, problem after problem. Why don't you start growing something around your hut? – there is so much land lying fallow. We will give you seeds; take the seeds and start growing something. It will help you also; you can eat some of it and the cow can eat some."

So he, poor man, started sowing some seeds. But this was great trouble: now the crops had to be cut. And he was a monk; he was not supposed to do all these things. But now one thing was leading to another. He went to the village and he said, "This is difficult. Now those crops have to be cut; I don't have any instruments, and I will need helpers."

The people said, "Listen, we are tired of you. You are worthless; you can't find any solution for anything. Do we have to solve everything? It is simple: a woman has become a widow and she is perfectly capable of taking care of you, your cow, your crops, your kitchen, everything – cat, rats... She is a perfectly experienced woman."

"But," he said, "I am a monk."

They said, "Forget all about that monkhood. What kind of monk are you! You have a cat, you have a cow, you have a field, a crop – and you think you are a monk! Forget about it. And anyway this marriage is just a bogus marriage; you need not have any kind of relationship with the woman. She is poor and in difficulty, you are in difficulty; both of you together will be good."

The man said, "That's right. If it is just a legal thing, there's no harm, because my master never said anything against that. He said, 'Don't get married' but I am not getting married; it is just for show, for the village, so nobody raises any objection that I am living with a woman. I can say that she is my wife, but I don't have to be her husband really, nor does she have to be my wife really."

He talked to the woman. The woman said, "I am not interested in a husband – one was enough – but I am in trouble, you are in trouble; and this is good, we can help each other."

So they got married. Now things went on growing... Sometimes he was sick and the woman would massage his feet. Slowly, slowly, he started liking the woman. A man is, after all, a man; a woman is, after all, a woman. The woman started liking the man. They were both feeling lonely. In the cold winter nights they were both waiting for somebody to say, "It is too cold – why can't we get close?"

Finally the woman said, "It is too cold here."

The monk said, "It is cold here too."

The woman said, "It seems you don't have any guts."

He said, "That's right. You come here – I don't have any guts. I am a poor monk, and you are an experienced woman: you come here. Together it will be warmer."

Of course it was warmer! That's where his whole monkhood went down the drain. When he was dying he told to his disciples, "Don't let any cat stay with you."

And the old man told the chief disciple, "Since then, it is traditional on your path that each master says to the disciple, 'Beware of the cat.'"

It is very difficult to be aware of the cat – the cat comes in somehow or other. Life is so strange.

But Jainas and Buddhists have tried to avoid the cats, all kinds of cats: "Don't stay longer than three days. Don't stay in any family, because the warmth, the coziness of the family, may distract you. Always stay in the temple which is always cold, never warm." Jaina monks are not allowed to burn wood, to have a bonfire in the night as Hindu monks are allowed, because any experience of warmth is dangerous. And it is violent too because you are killing trees, cutting trees, burning wood; and in burning wood you may be burning insects, flies – anything is possible. So they can't have a bonfire, they can't even have a lamp in the temple.

I used to visit Jaina monks sometimes because they invited me, and I would say, "In the day I don't have any time, I can come only at night." And in the night I became aware that they don't have any lamps or any candles – no light. I had to sit with them and to talk with them in darkness. It felt so strange. I told them, "But somebody else can put the switch on; I can put it on, you will not have done anything."

First they went on refusing, telling me, "No, that is not right. There will be light and it is prohibited."

But I was continually hammering on the idea: "If *you* don't do it then there is no harm." Finally one Jaina monk, the head of a big sect, agreed for the simple reason that during the day I had spoken and he had spoken, but he could not use the microphone – electricity! Now, there was no electricity in Mahavira's time. Of course he had not prohibited it, but he had not said that it should be used either. But he was clever enough. He had said, "Things which are not mentioned are not meant to be used. Only things which are mentioned are to be used." So although he had no idea what, he was clever enough to say, "Many things will be coming later on, which I cannot prohibit because I don't know about them."

I told that to the monk but he said, "Mahavira has prohibited it."

When I spoke there were at least twenty thousand people there, and everybody could hear me. They applauded and they were laughing and they enjoyed it. But when he spoke, who could hear? – not more than two or three rows in front. Twenty thousand people were just yawning. I said, "Just look: this is what your Mahavira has done to you. Now allow me." I just took the microphone, put it in front of him and said, "Simply speak. It is none of your business if someone puts something somewhere – who are you to prevent me? Just start!"

He got the idea – he thought the idea was good – and the fool started speaking. I condemned him later on and said, "You fell into the trap. You saw that I was putting the microphone in front of you, you knew what it was and you knew that everybody was able to hear you. You cannot befool anymore. Do you think that you are befooling Mahavira who is omniscient, omnipotent, omnipresent? He was present, watching you doing it. You have fallen."

But the Jainas destroyed the ashrams completely and they created the wandering monks. It is a strange thing about the human mind that it is very much impressed by somebody who goes through austerities. It is a sadistic, masochistic psychology. Why should you be so respectful to a person who is torturing himself? But strangely, everywhere around the world, the martyr is honored. If he is starving, fasting for a great cause, you respect him. You will not respect a man who is feasting for a great cause.

You are not concerned with the cause, remember, otherwise you should respect the feasting also, because he is feasting for a great cause. You are not concerned with the cause; the cause is only an explanation, a rationalization. You are interested in the fasting: the man is capable of having control over his body.

Mahatma Gandhi was the uncrowned king of India for the simple reason that he was able to torture himself more than anybody else could. For any small reason he would go on a fast "unto death." Every fast was "unto death," but within three, four days, it would be broken – there were methods to break it – and soon there would be a breakfast; everything was arranged.

But people can be deceived very easily. He goes on a fast, and the whole country prays to God that he should not die. All the great leaders rush toward his ashram and pray to him to stop but he won't listen unless his conditions are accepted – any conditions, undemocratic, dictatorial, idiotic, any conditions. For example he fasted against Doctor Ambedkar who was the leader of the untouchables. Ambedkar wanted the untouchables to have their own constituencies and their own candidates, otherwise they would never be represented in any parliament anywhere. Who would give votes to a shoemaker? In India a shoemaker is untouchable – who is going to give him the vote?

Ambedkar was absolutely right. One fourth of the country is untouchable. They are not allowed in schools because no other student is ready to sit with them, no teacher is ready to teach them. The government says the schools are open, but in reality no student is willing… If one untouchable enters, all thirty students leave the class, the teacher leaves the class. Then how are these poor people – one fourth of the country – going to be represented? They should be given separate constituencies where only they can stand and only they can vote.

Ambedkar was perfectly logical and perfectly human. But Gandhi went on a fast, saying, "He is trying to create a division within the Hindu society." The division has existed for ten thousand years. That poor Ambedkar was not creating the division; he was simply saying that one fourth of the people of the country had been tortured for thousands of years, now at least give them a chance to

move upward. At least let them voice their problems in the parliament, in the assemblies. But Gandhi said, "I will not allow it while I
am alive. They are part of Hindu society, hence they cannot have a
separate voting system" – and he went on a fast.

For twenty-one days Ambedkar remained reluctant, but every
day the pressure of the whole country was building, and he started
feeling that if this old man dies there is going to be great bloodshed.
It was clear he would be killed immediately, and millions of the
untouchables would be killed everywhere, all over the country: "It is
because of you that Gandhi died." When the whole arithmetic of how
it would work out was explained to him – "Figure it out soon, because
there is not much time, he cannot survive more than three days" –
Ambedkar hesitated.

He was perfectly right; Gandhi was perfectly wrong. But what to
do? Should he take the risk? He was not worried about his life – if he
was killed it was okay – but he was worried about those millions of
poor people who didn't know anything about what was going on.
Their houses would be burned, their women would be raped, their
children would be butchered, and it would be something that had
never happened before.

Finally he had to accept the conditions. He went with breakfast
in his hand to Mahatma Gandhi, "I accept your conditions. We will
not ask for a separate vote or separate candidates. Please accept
this orange juice." And Gandhi accepted the orange juice. But this
orange juice, this one glass of orange juice, contains millions of
people's blood.

I have met Doctor Ambedkar. He was one of the most intelligent
men I have ever met. But I said, "You proved weak."

He said, "You don't understand: the situation was such that I
knew I was right and he was wrong, but what to do with that stubborn old man? He was going to die, and if he died, I would have
been responsible for his death, and the untouchables would
have suffered."

I said, "That is not the point. Even an idiot could have suggested
a simple thing to you. *You* should have gone on a fast unto death.
And you are so overweight" He was a fat man, four or five times
heavier than Gandhi. "If you had asked me I would have said a
simple solution: just put another cot by the side of Mahatma Gandhi,
lie down, and fast unto death. Then let them see! I promise you that

Gandhi would have accepted all your conditions within three days."

Ambedkar said, "But this idea never occurred to me."

I said, "You are a fool if this idea never occurred to you! That was the idea with which that man was controlling the whole country – and it never occurred to you. The only difficulty would have been to go on a fast, particularly for a fat man like you, eating four times a day. Naturally you would not have been able to manage it. Gandhi has practiced his whole life, he is an experienced faster; and you may not have ever missed a single breakfast."

He said, "That is true."

I said, "Otherwise if it had been my problem and he was being so illogical, I would have just lain down, even if I was going to die, and let him be responsible. He would not have allowed that, because my death would have taken away all his mahatmahood, all his aura, all his leadership of the people. He would not have allowed me to die; he would have accepted my conditions.

"But unfortunately I am not an untouchable, and anyway why should I be bothered with you two idiots? To me both of you are idiots. You have one fourth of the country in your hands and you can't do anything; that man has nothing in his hands – but just by fasting... He has learned a womanly trick. Yes, I call his whole philosophy a feminine psychology."

That's what women do every day. Gandhi must have learned it from his wife. In India women do it every day. The wife will fast, she won't eat, she will lie down. And then the husband starts shaking. He may be right, but that is not the point. Now there is no point of right or wrong; now the point is how to persuade her to eat, because she is not eating, the children are not eating – and who is going to cook in the first place? Is he also going to fast? The children are weeping and they want food, and the wife is on a fast – so you agree. She needs a new sari, you bring it. First you bring the sari, then she goes into the kitchen. This is an old strategy of all the women in India. Gandhi must have learned it from his wife, and he used it really very cleverly.

But there is a strange side of the human mind which, for some strange reason, is impressed by anybody who is capable of torturing himself. I know the reason. The reason is your own fear – you cannot do it. You go to the circus to see a man jumping from sixty feet high, pouring spirit on himself, setting fire to the spirit. Burning, he drops from sixty feet; he falls into a small pool of water, and you watch it with your breathing stopped. At that moment nobody breathes.

I have watched it: the people were watching a poor circus fellow, I was watching the people. Was anybody blinking, anybody breathing? No, nobody blinks an eye, they completely forget. Even an unconscious process that goes on automatically – you need not blink, your eye blinks; you need not breathe, your chest breathes. But even the automatic processes of blinking and breathing simply stop, you are in awe.

And there is nothing in it. Those sixty feet are calculated. That man has been practicing continually: it is calculated that within the sixty foot fall, he is not going to be burned. And it is not kerosene, it is not petrol, it is pure spirit. Falling in the water, within seconds the fire is gone, and the man comes up. And he is a hero because you cannot do it. Just a little practice is needed and a calculation of how long it will take for spirit to burn you: the time limit has to be less than that. And you have to be able to jump.

I used to love jumping into the river from the railway bridge, because the railway bridge over my river was the highest place from where to jump. But I slowly worked up from small hills to bigger and bigger hills, until finally I was jumping from the bridge. The bridge was continuously guarded by the army because it was in the days of the British Empire and some revolutionary may have blown up the bridge. So they would catch me, and I would say, "I am not going to blow up the bridge. Just see – I don't have anything. You have nothing to be worried about. I want this bridge to be here, and I am happy that you are guarding it because I need it every day."

Once they said, "For what do you need it?"

I said, "Just see" – and I would jump! And they would be standing there in awe. Once they knew that this boy simply came to jump, they didn't bother. I told the revolutionaries of my town, "If any time you need... I am the best man because the guards don't even look at me now. They say, 'That boy is just crazy. One day he is going to kill himself. But it seems that he is growing more and more accustomed to it. It will be difficult for him to die; this bridge is very small. He needs a bridge at least four times higher – perhaps that may do it.'"

I told the revolutionaries that I knew – they used to visit my house; my uncles were part of their conspiracy. I said, "Any time you need to blow up the bridge, I am the best man. Nobody will ever suspect me, nobody will ever prevent me. I can take your bombs there, leave them wherever you want and simply jump into the river and swim downstream. Then you can do whatsoever you want to do."

They said, "You are not reliable. You may go and give the bombs to the guards; you will show them where we are hiding, and you will certainly jump and swim down the river." They never gave me the bombs. I requested them to again and again. They said, "We don't believe you. We know that you are the best person to reach that bridge because nobody else can reach it; it is continuously guarded."

A guard was continuously moving up and down, and at both ends there were guard rooms. It was an important bridge: all the main trains crossed over it. If you blew it up, you would cut one half of the country from the other. But they never relied on me.

I said, "You can rely on me, even those guards rely on me."

They said, "That's the fear. They rely on you, we rely on you – and what you will do, only you know."

For any austerity you need only a little practice. Fasting is very simple – just the first five days are difficult. I have fasted. The first five days are the most difficult, the fifth is the worst; you are almost ready to break the fast. But if you pass the fifth, you have passed the most dangerous, the most vulnerable period. From the sixth day your body starts functioning in a new way. It starts eating itself. From the sixth day onward things become simple. On the fifteenth day, you are absolutely unconcerned with food; you don't have any hunger. The body is absorbing its own fat, so hunger does not arise.

A man who is perfectly healthy can fast for ninety days without dying. Of course he will become just a skeleton, but for ninety days he can stay alive because a perfectly healthy body goes on accumulating fat for any emergency. This is an emergency situation so the body has an emergency system. If food is not coming from the outside, then the body starts eating from the inside. That's why you go on losing weight every day.

In the beginning you will lose two pounds per day. Then the body becomes aware that perhaps the emergency is going to last longer: then you lose one and a half pounds a day. Strange, the body has its own wisdom. Then you will lose one pound a day, then half a pound a day, because the body will start trying to save as much as possible, and to live on as little as possible; to keep you alive as long as it is in the body's hands.

So it is not something like a miracle, but people get impressed because deep down they feel, "We cannot do this." If somebody is enjoying a feast, you don't have that feeling because you could also enjoy the feast. It is just that you are not invited, that's why you feel angry against that man who is enjoying himself – he is just a glutton; he believes only in the philosophy of eat, drink, and be merry; he is not a spiritual man. This is jealousy, anger because you have not been invited. You are also capable of enjoying the feast, but a fast? You have never tried it.

In the beginning a fast is not a joy. Five days seem like five months. It seems that the clock no longer moves, and the hunger goes on growing. It hurts in the stomach; the intestines feel as if they are shrinking. Your whole body is in turmoil because it is not getting its daily ration. All the parts of the body are in a strange situation; they cannot figure out what has happened, why the ration has been stopped. You have not informed them; you cannot because you don't know their language, they don't know your language.

There is chaos in the body – but only for five days. After that the body automatically moves itself onto the emergency system; then there is no problem. All these mahatmas have learned only that: the strategy of five days. Once you have learned it, then it is not very difficult to last five days.

Jaina and Buddhist monks both impressed the whole of the East so much that the Hindu ashram, which was really a beautiful place, became condemned. Those seers, those sages, became condemned by people: "They are as materialistic as we are. The real mahatmas and sages are the Jainas, the Buddhists. These people are nothing compared to them." Naturally Hinduism had to change its whole structure.

It is a competitive world; to remain in existence, Hinduism changed the whole style of the ashram. The ashram became ascetic but they still retained the old name, they forgot to change the name. It is no longer an ashram because there is no relaxation, no rest, no joy, no blissfulness. Go to an ashram today and you will find self-torturing people, psychologically sick, masochistic, suicidal – but egoistic, because all this torture is bringing them one thing: great respect from the people. The whole country pays tremendous respect for what they are doing. But the beauty of the real ashram has disappeared.

The monastery is the Western equivalent of the modern Hindu ashram, because at the time when the real Hindu ashrams were in existence, the West was absolutely barbarous: it had no religion, no culture, no civilization. Your greatest man was born only two thousand years ago. In India it is difficult to decide this, because Mahavira, who was born twenty-five centuries ago, is the last and the greatest Jaina *tirthankara*, the twenty-fourth. Before him twenty-three *tirthankaras* had passed; and that must have taken at least ten thousand years if in twenty-five centuries there was only one *tirthankara*. And there are relics of cities discovered at Mohanjodaro and at Harappa where Jaina statues have been found.

Now, a Jaina statue can be immediately recognized – the naked statue – because Jainas are the only people with these statues. Romans have made naked statues but they are sensuous, sexual, provocative. They are *Playboy* magazines in marble. You can see that this statue is just a sensuous, sexual statue: all Roman statues are. The Jaina *tirthankara* statue is nude but not naked. Yes, it has no clothes, but it won't give you any idea, any vague idea of sexuality, of sensuality. No, just the contrary.

The whole structure of the Jaina statue is nonsensuous, non-sexual. The eyes are closed, the hands are hanging loose on either side. The body is standing. In the ears birds have made small nests, because the man has been standing for six months in the same position, he has not moved his head. He is not going to scare the bird away saying, "What are you doing? – this is my ear that you are making a nest in." Creepers have started moving up his body. It has a beauty of its own. Creepers, green creepers, have reached up to his neck or up to his head. They have blossomed, their season has come.

Now, this statue is not the Roman type. It has no parallel in the whole world. This kind of statue has been found at Mohanjodaro, which by very strict and orthodox scientific methods was found to have existed at least seven thousand years before Jesus Christ was born. So from today, ten thousand years back is not claiming much.

The Western monastery is a copy of the ashram that exists in the East now. It had been brought to the West by Western travelers, Western philosophers. Jesus himself went to Buddhist universities, Tibetan lamaseries, Ladakh monasteries; Pythagoras traveled deeply in the East – and these people brought all these ideas to the West. The Western monastery is, in a way, nothing but a carbon copy of the Eastern ashram. It has nothing unique to contribute.

My commune is a totally different phenomenon. It is neither an

ashram, modern or ancient, nor a monastery, Christian or Mohammedan. My commune is, in the first place, non-ascetic. It basically
tries to destroy all psychological sicknesses in you – in which sado-
masochist ideas are included. It teaches you to be healthy and not to
feel guilty for being healthy. It teaches you to be human, because my
experience is that people who have been trying to be divine have not
become divine, but have fallen far lower than human. They were
trying to go up beyond humanity – yes, they have gone beyond
humanity, but below it. In the monasteries, people are almost animals, because the more you torture yourself, the more you start
losing your intelligence; intelligence needs comfort.

Intelligence is a very delicate flower. Don't try to grow roses in
the desert. Intelligence is a very delicate flower; it grows in luxury. It
needs a luxurious ground, fertile, creative, full of juice; only then can
it blossom. And without intelligence, what are you?

My effort is first to help your intelligence become a flame, and to
help that flame to consume all that is not your authentic self. You
become a fire and you burn everything that is rubbish, thrown onto
you by others.

So first intelligence, and second meditation.

Meditation comes out of intelligence – burning all crap from
your being. Then you are pure, alone, just the way existence wants
you to be.

The commune is just a place where people who are interested in
this journey, in this odyssey inwards, live together – helping everybody to be himself, allowing everybody enough space, not interfering
in any way, not imposing in any way. If they can support you, good;
if support also becomes a hindrance then they will not even support
you, they will withdraw themselves. They respect your integrity, your
individuality, your freedom. I have chosen the word *commune*
because it is a communion: a communion of rebellious spirits.

It is not another society, it is not a monastery, an ashram. It is
individuals remaining individuals, Still being together; being alone and
still interacting, responding; leaving the other also alone. Aloneness,
to me, is the greatest religious quality.

So we are together but not in any kind of bondage, very loose. No
relationship is binding in my commune. No relationship is really a relationship, it is only a relating, a process. As long as it goes, good, and
when paths divert, change their course, that too is perfectly good

because that's how, perhaps, your being is going to grow. One never knows. We may walk together for a few feet, a few miles, and then depart in gratitude: "It was a joy to be together. Now let us celebrate separation; you helped me, I helped you. Now let us help each other to move in the directions that our beings want us to take."

The commune is a totally new phenomenon. It has nothing to do with anything that has preceded it. The old, ancient ashrams were beautiful but they were part of the society. They propagated the same structure of the society: the four-caste system. The untouchable was untouchable. The untouchable could not enter the ancient Hindu ashram. Only the brahmin could be the seer. That is strange, that only the brahmin could have eyes. That was a brahmin strategy to remain in power, and they *were* powerful. But they were good people, although not revolutionaries; nice, but not rebels.

The rebel is both. He is a sword and also a song. It depends on the situation. He can become a song or he can become a sword.

This is a communion of rebels. We are not supporting any society, any politics, any nation, any race, any religion. We have left all that far behind. We have come alone, to be with those who have also come for the same reason – to be alone.

So remember, aloneness is something sacred. You should not trespass on anybody's aloneness, freedom, individuality. Commune, love, be together, rejoice, but remember always you are alone. You are born alone, you will die alone, you have to live alone. All those who are here are all individuals, alone. They are not following any doctrine, any dogma, they are simply following their own inner voice. Try to hear it and follow it.

Yes, it is a very still small voice, but once heard, you cannot do anything other than what it says for you to do.

CHAPTER 6

Anxiety or Anguish?

Osho,
What is anguish? Is it just another name for anxiety?

Anguish has something of anxiety in it, but it is not just anxiety. It is much more, much more profound.

Anxiety means you are concerned with a particular subject, in a state of indecisiveness. You cannot figure out whether to do a thing or not to do it. What will be the right way to do it? What to choose? – there are so many ways. You are always standing at a crossroad. All the roads seem to be similar; certainly leading somewhere, but do they lead to the goal that you have been aspiring to? Anxiety is that condition of, to do or not to do, to choose this or to choose that. But the *object* of the anxiety is clear: you are indecisive about ways, indecisive about two persons, indecisive about two jobs. Anguish has no particular object.

Anguish happens to very rare people. Anxiety happens to everybody, it is a common experience. Anguish happens to the genius; it is the highest peak of intelligence. It has no particular object; there is nothing for you to choose between, no this or that. There is no question of choice. Then what is the problem with anguish?

You will have to understand a certain phenomenon. There are many things in the world – animals, birds, man – and anxiety happens to all: to the trees, to the animals, to the birds, to man. As far as anxiety is concerned it is a universal experience. But anguish happens only to a very few rare men. They are the very cream, the highest peak of consciousness. Their problem is concerned with the very existence.

For example, there is a rock; it is alive, it grows. The Himalayas are still growing one foot a year. Somebody should say to it, "Now it is meaningless, you are already the highest. Don't take so much trouble." It must be a troublesome thing: thousands of miles, thousands of peaks, the work must be enormous. Even to grow one foot a year is no small thing for the Himalayas. "Now there is no need. Howsoever big you become, you will remain only the highest mountain in the world. You have crossed the borders of all the mountains, you have left them far behind." Mountains don't understand. Man does not understand, what to say about mountains! The Himalayas go on growing, it is a living being.

A rock is born, a tree is born, a lion is born, an eagle is born – but they differ from man. The difference is, their being precedes their existence. It is a little difficult to understand but not impossible. I will try to explain it to you. Their essence precedes their existence: what they are going to be, they are already programmed for. That is their essence. A rose is going to be a rose. Even before the flowers have come, you know those flowers are not going to be marigolds. The bush is that of a rose; the essence of the rose is already there, only its existence has to happen. The basic program is already provided by nature, it has just to be manifest.

It will be good to be reminded of a certain discovery in the past decades that happened in the Soviet Union. A photographer, just an amateur but a very creative genius, was using his cameras, studio, chemicals and photographs, and trying to find different ways to bring something new to photography. Just by chance he happened to discover Kirlian photography, one of the greatest discoveries of human history.

He can take a photograph of a rosebud; he has refined his instruments now so much that you put the rosebud in front of his camera, and he takes a photograph of the flower that the rosebud is going to be. He catches hold of that which is still unmanifest but somehow *is* manifest because the camera catches it. Our eyes are not able to catch it. When the rose blossoms, it is strange, but it is exactly the same as the photograph he has taken.

Somehow the rose energy, which becomes available to our eyes later on, was moving in the same pattern as the flower it was going to be. It was an energy flower, just pure rays of light and color, but in exactly the same shape, preparing the ground for the manifestation. His camera catches those rays and gives you a blueprint of the future rose. Perhaps tomorrow or the day after tomorrow it will be available to your eyes. That means that the rose, before it becomes existent, is already there in essence. Hence the saying: essence precedes existence.

In the Second World War, Kirlian photography worked miracles. It is going to help medicine immensely in the future. It is unfortunate that scientists are also divided according to political lines. What is happening in the Soviet Union is kept secret; what is happening in America is kept secret. This is a sheer wastage of genius, energy, time – and time is very short.

Before the curtain falls and the drama is finished, it would be better if the scientists of the whole world declared: "We are international." And we, our commune, will be supplying them with international passports belonging to no nation. But if the scientists have any courage, they can open up a totally new dimension and carry a passport which is neither Soviet, nor American, nor British, nor Indian – an international passport. Of course many will be caught and imprisoned, but that's nothing to be worried about – how long could it go on?

If all the scientists of the world decide, then all the Nobel Prize winners follow; then all the poets, engineers, doctors, the intelligentsia of the world follow, how can you put all these people in jails? What will you do? What will your idiot politicians do? Without them they will be nothing.

Rajneeshpuram should be the headquarters; we are ready to issue international passports. It will create a revolution. Don't be bothered by national boundaries; at least someone has to begin it. Let all the poets of the world meet, let the scientists of the world meet, and pour their energies into a single pool.

Now, Kirlian photography is still not being used outside the Soviet Union. In the Soviet Union it is doing miracles. It was discovered in the Second World War, and Kirlian was given the job of finding out, if it works on a roseflower, how does it work on human beings? A man's hand has been cut off, because he was damaged in the war. Kirlian takes a photograph, and strangely enough, the photograph shows a faint energy-hand with all the five fingers intact – and the hand is missing from the body. It just shows a little fainter than the rest of the body. The hand is no longer there but the energy that used to move in the hand is still moving. You cannot see it with your eyes, but a sensitive camera catches it.

Now, this gave rise to the idea that if the energy is still moving, there is a possibility of creating a hand through which energy can continue to move; then it will be a real hand. It will not be a wooden hand, or a plastic hand; it will be as real as real hands are – because what is the reality of the hand? Why is it alive? Why is it moving? It is moving because of the energy inside.

When you become paralyzed, what happens? It is not your hand getting paralyzed, it is the energy inside which has stopped flowing. The hand is there, the bones are there, the blood is there – everything is there. What is missing? What is paralysis? The energy is no longer moving, the energy has stopped for some reason. If we can arrange for the energy to move again...

That's what acupuncture in China has been trying to do for five thousand years, to move the energy again. And acupuncture has succeeded in doing great things: a paralyzed man is no longer paralyzed. And what they do *looks* very childish; to the observer it doesn't look like such a great thing. They just go on putting needles in at certain points in the body. The hand is paralyzed, but they may not touch the hand at all. They may be pushing the needle in somewhere else, because they know which part can obstruct the flow of energy in the hand. If that needle removes the blockage, the energy starts flowing: the hand is back, alive.

Another thing that Kirlian photography discovered was that just as a flower can be photographed before it has even opened its petals, when it is just a bud, among the healthy people he was photographing, some parts of their body were not the same as other parts. He was able to say there was some danger coming.

One man said, "There is no problem, I am perfectly healthy." But danger came after six months, at exactly the same spot. The energy was already preparing the ground, perhaps for a cancerous growth. Kirlian photography is the only possibility right now. If we can catch hold of cancer before it materializes, we can get rid of it. There is no need for any surgery; all that you have to do is to stop that energy pattern, change that pattern, change the program, and the cancer will never happen.

In the East it is widely believed that six months before a man dies, he stops seeing the tip of his nose – and I have seen it with my own eyes, so it is not a question of belief for me, I never believe in anything unless I see it. His eyes just won't go down far enough to see the tip of his nose; he cannot see the tip of his own nose. Within exactly six months he is going to die. That is an ancient, perhaps a ten-thousand-year-old discovery of ayurveda. When the ayurvedic physician comes to see if the patient is in the last stage, the first thing he wants to know is, "Please, can you see the tip of your nose?"

Now, any allopathic doctor seeing this will think this is stupid: "What has seeing the tip of the nose to do with his death? He is dying and you are joking, kidding? What are you doing?" The doctor is not aware of a strange phenomenon: that the eyes slowly stop turning downward. When the man dies, they turn completely upward. If you see a dead man you will see his eyes are completely upturned; you will see only the whites of the eyes. That's why in all traditions, all over the world, the dead man's eyes are immediately closed – because he may freak out many people who see his eyes. Just the whites are visible; the black has turned up.

It must have been this experience that gave the idea, ten thousand years ago, that if the eyes ultimately, in death, turn completely upward, they must start turning up some time before that – because life is always a process; nothing happens suddenly. There is nothing like suddenness in existence. So, watching, by and by they discovered that six months before is the time when the eyes start getting less and less flexible, more and more rigid; more and more turning upward, less and less turning downward. And if the man cannot see the tip of his own nose, the physician suggests to the family, "Don't unnecessarily waste time. Prepare him for death. Help him to die peacefully, silently, meditatively, with gratitude."

Only in the East has it been possible to prepare for death. People don't prepare even for life. They come to know that they were alive only when they are dying or perhaps dead. Then suddenly a shock comes to them: "My God! What has happened? I was alive and now I am no longer alive. Those eighty years, ninety years have passed and I have not done anything, not felt for a single moment fulfilled, contented. Not for a single moment could I have said, 'I am blessed.'"

Except for man, everything – every bird, every animal – in existence comes in this way: essence first, then manifestation. They are programmed by nature; their whole life is not an evolution but an unfolding. All that they are going to become is already in the basic program, and they cannot move a single inch from the program. It is not in their power to decide whether to be a rose or to be a marigold. Hence there is no anxiety about it. They are never asked to decide about their essence. They are never on a crossroads; they are always following a single route. There is nothing for them to choose about "being."

Buffaloes, horses, donkeys, elephants don't feel anxiety within their program. Yes, they can feel anger if you obstruct them. They can be destructive, they can be violent if you misbehave with them. They all have a certain code of conduct. If you just keep to yourself without interfering with their territorial imperative... For example, every elephant has its own territory. If you enter his territory you will be in danger. If you just keep out of the territory – and that territory you don't know but the elephant knows. Once you enter his territory you are in danger, you have trespassed.

They can feel anger. They can feel superior, inferior. Just go to a tree in which many monkeys are sitting, and you will be surprised: the boss is sitting on the highest branch, and on the lowest branches are the servants. The boss has all the beautiful ladies. He may be old, he may not be able to reproduce any more, but the boss is after all the boss.

Many times the younger generation kills the old monkey, for the simple reason that he is obstructing them from reaching the ladies, and while he is alive he won't let anybody approach them. He has a harem; he does not bother about whether he is in a state to reproduce or not. His kingdom, his chiefhood, depends on how many ladies he has.

It is from the monkeys that Sigmund Freud got the idea that at some time a younger generation must have killed an old man who possessed all the beautiful ladies. The younger people were of course getting angry: "It is time for this man to die!" But he was not dying, and he was not allowing them either... Sigmund Freud's idea of God is that because the younger people killed the father, they felt guilty; he was their father, their boss, and they had killed him just for the women. Now, two conclusions – Sigmund Freud has drawn only one conclusion... I am surprised how he missed the second, which was more likely to be made by him, but even geniuses are fallible.

Sigmund Freud made one conclusion: that because of killing the father they felt guilty, and to compensate for the guilt – just to get rid of it – they started worshipping the relics of the father, maybe his bones, his dead body that they had buried. They made a small memorial, and they started worshipping, otherwise his spirit may take revenge, his ghost may take revenge. They knew that he was a strict man and very jealous, and that to fool with his ladies... His ghost can create trouble for you. So sacrifice something, worship him, ask his forgiveness, and confess your sin.

Sigmund Freud derived the whole of Christianity, the whole of religion in fact, from the idea that God the father is really father the God. First the father was killed, and just to console his ghost they made him God the father. They said, "You are still our boss; even from here we are under you, we are your servants, your worshippers. Forgive us, it was foolish of us, but young people are foolish. You are experienced, you know everything; we hope you will forgive us." The conclusion of Freud is that this is the way religion must have started. There are no historical facts about it but there is every possibility he is right.

The second thing – and I have always wondered how he missed it – was that they had killed the father for the younger ladies. Now, the second conclusion is so simple: to give solace to the father, all religions went against women. It was the woman for whom they had killed the father! The connection is so clear, and Sigmund Freud completely missed it. Even a blind man would not have missed it. It is so clear that they had killed, for no other reason but to get hold of the young ladies which the dirty old monkey was keeping in his possession. It was because of the ladies.

So, certainly religion should have two sides: one, worship, pray, praise the lord; and two, condemn women. When I first read Freud, I looked in all his books for the second conclusion – which is more Freudian – but he never comes to it. The first is a farfetched philosophical idea, but the second is a very clear-cut Freudian concept. But now Freud is dead, all that we can do is supplement it.

I emphasize the fact that because the killing was for the women, all religions are against women. If it were not for the women, they would not have killed the father. The story of Adam and Eve also says the same thing: it is because of the woman that man's fall happened. Religions can never forgive the woman; they have been condemning her for centuries. Freud could have clearly seen both things: the people who believe in God and worship God disbelieve in the woman and think of her as an agent of the serpent, the Devil, as the original cause of the fall.

You will see in all animals the same hierarchy as you see in the monkeys. But it is programmed, it is not a question of anxiety. Have you seen two dogs barking and jumping and trying to fight, but before the fight starts somehow it is settled? It never comes to the logical end. So what was all that shouting and barking, jumping and showing teeth to each other? It was simply that they were trying to show to each other, "Look how much stronger I am." They are very intelligent people. What is the need to fight? They just show themselves to each other and judge who is the stronger.

Once it is judged which one is stronger, they both agree: the one who comes to understand that he is weaker turns with his tail between his legs. That is a signal, "You are stronger." There is no cowardliness in it; it is a simple fact: "What can I do about it? I am weak, you are stronger; you bark louder, you jump louder, you look bigger: what is the point of fighting? Why unnecessarily shed blood?" He simply gives the signal, turns his tail between his legs, and immediately the other is no longer an enemy. The fight is finished; it is finished before it began.

From my very childhood I have been curious about everything, and in India there are so many dogs. The municipal committees cannot kill them because it is violent and immediately there would be trouble from the people: "You are killing" – so they go on becoming more. Just as people go on becoming more, dogs go on becoming more. Sitting in front of my house in the winter I used to watch the dogs, and it was very striking. Again and again I saw it happen, and I could see the tremendous intelligence of dogs. They are far more intelligent than man.

Even if you understand that you are weaker than the other person, still you will fight because you cannot accept that you are weak. You will try; perhaps by some chance you may defeat him. At least nobody will be able to say to you that you never even tried. You will fight, and you will be beaten. Now, this is absolutely useless on your part and on the other man's part, it is stupid. But you are not programmed, that is the trouble. You cannot be decisive, certain. The other man may look bigger, that is a certainty, but a smaller man may be sharper, cleverer, more cunning, may have known aikido, judo, jujitsu, and who knows what. The stronger man may not know anything, may be just a heavyweight, not a heavyweight champion, and the smaller man may throw him off.

We are not programmed. Dogs are programmed and they can read each other's program easily. They give all the signs of their program: "This is what I can do. These are my teeth, you can see them. This is my bark, this is the way I jump, this is the way I will hit. Show yourself!" They both put their cards on the table. And when you see that one has all the great cards, what is the point? Now it is finished. But man is not made that way; that is the only difference between man and the whole of existence.

In man, existence precedes essence. First he is born, and *then* he starts discovering what he can be. That is anguish. He has no program, no determined guidelines given from nature, no map to follow. He is just left as pure existence. He has to work out everything on his own. Life is every moment a challenge, so every moment he has to choose. Whenever he has to choose there is anxiety – but anxiety is particular.

Anguish is a general state of the human being. He is in anguish from birth to death because he has no way of knowing what his destiny is, where he is going to land. Of course, very few people feel anguish because very few people are so conscious about themselves, their existence, where they are moving, what they are becoming, what is going to happen. They are too concerned with trivia.

So all human beings experience anxiety; trivia creates anxiety. In a certain job you can get a better salary but it is not respectable. In fact that's why a better salary is given, because it is not respectable. In another job which is respectable, the salary is less in the same proportion. Now, anxiety arises – what to do? You would like both the respect and the higher salary, but you can't get both.

Society consists of vested interests, and they are clever. To be a professor in the university is respectable, but the salary is not much. You can earn more just being a pimp than you can earn by being a professor. But a pimp, after all, is a pimp. You cannot manage to be called Professor Pimp. But in fact, linguistically it is not wrong because that is your profession. You can call yourself Professor Pimp! There are people who call themselves professors, magicians particularly, who have nothing to do with professors in the universities. Magicians call themselves professors; they mean by professor, professional magician.

In India there was a very great, world-famous magician, Professor Sarkar, a Bengali gentleman, perhaps the best-known magician in the world. I asked him, "I have no questions about your magic, but I have a question about your professorhood. What is this 'professor'? Where do you teach, in what university? Because I have not heard of a magic department in any university; I have never even heard of any university especially devoted to magic or a college especially devoted to magic – so where do you teach?"

He said, "It has nothing to do with teaching, it is just that traditionally magicians have been using it. It is our profession, and professor simply means a professional."

I said, "That's a great idea. Then anybody can call himself professor; whatever profession he is in, he is a professor."

But one thing is certain: by being a pimp you can earn much more than being a professor. Of course as a professor you will be very respected, but you will remain poor, at the most middle class. So the choice arises. And wherever there is choice, there is anxiety. So everybody, on each step, at every moment of his life is faced with anxiety. Anxiety is a common, everyday affair; anguish is very profound.

Both words come from the same root, hence the question. In anguish there is some anxiety because you are worried, you are concerned. But the concern is not about any job, any thing, anything in particular; no, it is a general vague feeling of: "What am I?"

Gurdjieff stretched the point to its very logical end. I like that man although I may not agree with him on many points. He has a tremendous insight into things, but he is a victim of a particular logical disease; that is, stretching something to its very logical end. The trouble is, whenever you stretch something to its very logical end, you come to something wrong. If you stretch it on one side, you will come to something wrong; if you stretch it on the opposite side, you will again come to something wrong. Extremes are always wrong. Avoid extremes. It is far more probable that you will find the truth somewhere exactly in the middle, between the two opposite extremes.

Gurdjieff stretched this idea of anguish to its extreme: he said man has no soul. This is a simple conclusion. If existence comes first and essence has to be discovered later on, that simply means that man is born without a soul. The soul is your being, your essence. So you are born only an empty box, with nothing in it. Naturally, anguish will be felt: you are empty inside, with nothing in you. Even a roseflower is far richer than you, even a dog is far richer than you. At least he has a program, a certainty of what he is going to be. He is predictable.

I always imagine that among dogs there must be astrologers, palmists, face readers, mind readers and all kinds of esoteric people, because there, everything can be read. The future can be told in detail. But it is a strange fact that all those astrologers, palmists, face readers, mind readers, tarot cards, I Ching – and there are so many areas available – all exist in the world of man. But there is nothing in it to wonder about: what will they do in the world of the dog, the elephant, and the camel?

No camel is at all in anguish. He perfectly naturally follows the program. He is not worried about tomorrow. He knows tomorrow he will be a camel, and the day after he will also be a camel. Just as his forefathers have been camels, he will be a camel. There is no chance to become an elephant or to be worried or to choose, "What do I want to be?" There is never a question of to be or not to be. There are no alternatives open, he has a fixed being. The business of astrologers and palmists is not going to flourish; they will all go bankrupt if they move from the world of man.

But in the world of men, why do these astrologers and palmists go on flourishing? I have seen them so many times but they all are doing the same thing. In Srinagar in Kashmir, a pundit – a very old scholar who was very famous in Kashmir for his predictions – was brought to me as I was having a camp there. Somebody who was attending the camp knew the old man and told him, "Come to see this man and see if you can predict something about him."

I thought he would be looking at my hands so I said, "Okay, you can look."

He said, "No, I never look at the hands, I look at the feet, at the lines on the feet." That was a revelation! I had never heard of it. He said, "This is something special in Kashmir. The lines in the feet are far more certain than the lines in the hand."

And he had a certain reason. He said, "The lines of the hand go on changing, but the lines of the feet remain almost unchanging, for the simple reason that the skin of the feet is harder." It has to be harder, you have to walk on it, your whole weight is on it. Hands don't have that hard a skin, they don't need it. On the softer skin it is easier for lines to change; on the harder skin it is almost like the lines on a stone. He said, "We have a tradition in Kashmir to read the lines of the feet."

I said, "Okay, read the lines of my feet; but one thing you should remember, whatsoever you say I will not allow to happen. Just the opposite will happen."

He said, "It is the first time I have heard this type of statement. People want to know what is going to happen, and you are saying to me that whatever I say, you will try to do just the opposite."

I said, "Certainly, because I want to prove you absolutely wrong."

All palmistry, all astrology, is just an exploitation of man's anguish. Because he is in anguish he wants somehow, some way, somebody to tell him what he is, what he is going to be, what his future is. It is out of anguish that all these sciences have sprung up. And they have exploited man for thousands of years, for the simple reason that man is bound sometime or other to be concerned with what this life is all about: "What am I doing here? Is it really meaningful or meaningless? Is it leading me somewhere or am I moving in a circle? And if it is leading somewhere, am I going in the right direction or in the wrong direction?"

One of my professors, Doctor S. N. L. Shrivastava, used to teach me logic, he was my professor of logic. And he was very angry with me, because in a class of logic he could not tell me not to argue. I had made it clear from the very beginning that in a class of logic you cannot stop me from arguing. "I have really come to learn argument, what else is logic?" So he could not prevent me from arguing. On each point there was trouble. He got so fed up; and the students were praying to me, "Because of you it seems there is not going to be any teaching from the textbooks. From each point it takes weeks to move on; it will take our whole lives to finish this book!"

After two months, S. N. L. Shrivastava got so tired that he asked for a month's leave – he was an old man. He wanted to go to the hill station just to rest from logic, from argument. I had no idea that he was going to the hill station. It was a Saturday and I had gone to a friend's farm. At the farm he had beautiful mangos, but I told him, "These are nothing. If you come to my village, you will know for the first time what a mango should be. These are just wild mangos, small and not so juicy."

So he said, "Why not today?"

I said, "I am always for today," so we dropped everything and rushed toward the station which was not very far away. But the train was just leaving, so I entered and my friend, who was carrying his suitcase and this and that, was left behind. And in the compartment was S. N. L. Shrivastava.

He said, "What! Are you also going to the hill station?"

I was going to my village which was on the way. The hill station was one hundred and fifty miles farther on from my village. But just to joke with him I said, "But this train is not going to the hill station; this is going in the opposite direction. What are you doing here?"

He said, "Help me" – because he had made up his bed and everything in the first class compartment. He just made it, and I somehow managed to push him out with his bag. When he was out my friend came running, and as the train was moving off, he asked Shrivastava, "Why did you get down? I missed the train because I could not catch up with my friend; I was carrying all my load and he went on ahead – he didn't have anything. We are going to his house so he has everything that he needs, but I need clothes and things. But why did you get off?"

S. N. L. Shrivastava said, "This train is not going to the hill station."

The boy said, "What are you saying? This train *is* going to the hill station."

When after two days I came back, I cannot forget the way S. N. L. Shrivastava looked at me; anytime I can close my eyes... He just went on looking. I said, "Will you say something, or will you go on just looking?"

He said, "Is there anything to say? I had taken one month's leave. I had booked a hotel, and with much difficulty I had persuaded my wife to go – and then you appeared in that compartment. I had never expected you there. And it is not good what you did to me.

I said, "What have I done?"

He said, "You said that train was going in the opposite direction."

I said, "That's exactly what I believed, because I had to return from the next station. I also wanted to go to the hill station and that train was certainly going in the wrong direction."

He said, "Now don't try to befool me, because I have inquired from the station master, and your friend himself has told me that the train *was* going to the hill station."

I said, "There seems to be some confusion. Either I was told something wrong – because I asked another passenger and he said, 'This train is not going where you want to go, so get off at this station, and catch the other train which will be coming soon.' Perhaps you are right, perhaps that man was right; but now there is no way to decide."

He said, "You are such a pain in the neck! I used to have so many anxieties before; now I have only anguish. And it is because of you that all my anxieties have disappeared and I have only one anguish, day and night. Even in the night I dream of you, that you are arguing and creating trouble, and I am in difficulty answering you."

That day he used the word *anguish*, that's why I remember him. He said, "You are my anguish."

I said, "That's absolutely wrong." I said, "Here the argument begins again. Anguish is something internal, it cannot be external; if it is external then it is anxiety. If I am your anguish, then you are using the wrong word; I may be your *anxiety*. Anguish is that, Professor S. N. L. Shrivastava, which you have to work out within yourself: Who are you? Do you also think you are Doctor S. N. L. Shrivastava? Do you think you are a Hindu? Do you think you are a man?"

He said, "If I am not a man, if I am not a Hindu, if I am not Doctor S. N. L. Shrivastava, then who am I?"

I said, "*That* is anguish! Meditate over it. If you find out the answer your anguish will disappear."

But before his anguish disappeared he threatened to resign from the college. He said, "Holidays won't help; after all, I have to come back again. Even in the hill station I would have been thinking of this problem that has arisen, and which I don't know how to solve." He was an old man, trained in Aristotelian logic, and I was studying things which were against Aristotle, things of which he had never heard; so he was in continual trouble. He could not say, "I don't know about it" – because to have accepted in front of people "I don't know about it," would have seemed humiliating.

He had to pretend that he knew about it, and then he would get into trouble because he had no idea of what he was getting into – then he was in my hands. I told the principal of the college, "This S. N. L. Shrivastava is a well-known and respected professor, has written many books, has big degrees, honorary degrees, but he is not a man of truth."

The principal said, "How can you say that? I have never felt that he lies or anything. He is a really religious man – not only a professor of philosophy but religious also."

I said, "I have checked it a hundred times: he lies."

He said, "You will have to give me proof."

I said, "I am always ready, but that's the problem: I ask *him* for proof. I am perfectly happy to give you proof. Give me any fictitious name of a book which does not exist."

He said, "What will that do?"

I said, "Just write it down." So he wrote down *Principia Logica*. Yes, there are books called *Principia Mathematica* and *Principia Ethica*, but there is no book like *Principia Logica*. But it sounds perfectly right, on the lines of these famous books – *Principia Ethica, Principia Mathematica* – so there must be a *Principia Logica*. I said, "This will do. I will be back soon."

I went to the class of S. N. L. Shrivastava and I asked him, "I have read this statement in *Principia Logica*; what do you think about it?"

He said, "*Principia Logica*? Yes, I don't exactly remember because I read the book twenty or thirty years ago."

I said, "Just come with me to the principal's office."

He said, "For what?"

I said, "Just come. He has asked me to bring you to his office." I took him there and I said, "Professor S. N. L. Shrivastava says that he read this book *Principia Logica* thirty years ago. He remembers perfectly the name of the book, but he cannot remember the exact quotation that I gave him."

The principal asked him, "Shrivastava, have you read this book?"

He said, "Yes, of course."

The principal said to me, "Forgive me – you are right."

S. N. L. Shrivastava could not understand what was transpiring between me and the principal. He said, "*What* is right? And what is the problem?"

The principal said, "Nothing. This boy was just proving that you are a perfect liar, and you proved to be. This title was coined by me. There exists no such book, there has never existed any such book – how did you read it thirty years ago? You have some nerve to say such a thing – and to these students who have come to study under you. You are blatantly lying."

S. N. L. Shrivastava resigned, because now he was losing face completely. I went to his home to give him solace; he said, "Please, I don't want your solace."

I said, "Once in a while I will be coming, whether you want it or not. I know you need it."

He said, "Is it ever going to end or do I have to commit suicide? Because now I am saying I don't want it, and you say, 'You may not want it but you need it.' Now you will raise the problem: is there is a difference between wanting and needing?"

I told him, "Yes, needing is something different. You may not be aware of your needs. You may know about your wants, and your wants may not be necessarily your needs. Looking at somebody's beautiful hat you may want it. It may not be your *need*; your need may be for better shoes. Want and need are totally different."

He said, "Yes, they are totally different, but please don't come."

But strange coincidences... When I became a professor I was appointed to a university where he was the head of the department of philosophy! As I entered the philosophy department, he said, "What! What are you here for?"

I said, "They have appointed me as your assistant."

He said, "Will you leave me alone or not? It was enough when you were a student. Now you are a professor – and my assistant!" Again he used the word: "It seems you are going to remain my anguish."

I said, "S. N. L. Shrivastava, six years have passed but you have not learned anything. Again, *anguish*? Call it anxiety. Anxiety has an object, a particular situation; anguish is within you, you have to look withinwards."

He said, "Of course, now sitting in the same staff room I have to look withinwards; otherwise I have to look at you, and just looking at you, I lose all my sanity. You drove me out of that college. Now you have come here, and I know we cannot coexist in this staff room.

You are not a person to leave, so I suppose I will have to ask the government to transfer me somewhere else.

"And you have spoiled my wife's mind because she says I am simply afraid of you and I am escaping from every place, wherever you are. She tells me, 'How long can you escape from that man? If he is determined to follow you, he will.'"

I had all the qualifications to follow him anywhere, to any university, wherever he was going. I said, "If I am determined I can follow you, but I don't want to be your anxiety, I want you to feel anguish. Your death is close, you are getting too old; now is not the time for anxiety. Anxieties are for young people who are choosing alternatives, this and that. But for you... Before death comes solve your basic problem."

Anguish is, in short, the quest of who you are.

One of India's greatest seers of this age, Raman Maharishi, had only one message to everyone. He was a simple man, not a scholar. He left his house when he was seventeen years old, not even well educated. He had a simple message. To whoever would come to him – and people were coming to him from all over the world – all that he said was, "Sit down in a corner, anywhere..." He lived on a hill, Arunachal, and he had told his disciples to make caves in the hills; there were many caves. "Go and sit in a cave, and just meditate on 'Who am I?' All else is just explanations, experiences, efforts to translate those experiences into language. The only real thing is this question, 'Who am I?'"

I have come in contact with many people, but I never came in contact with Raman Maharishi; he died when I was too young. I wanted to go, and I would have reached him, but he was really far away from my place, nearabout fifteen hundred miles. I asked my father many times, "That man is getting old and I am so young. He does not know Hindi, my language; I don't know his language, Tamil. Even if somehow I reach there – which is difficult..."

It was almost a three-day journey from my place to Arunachal, changing many trains, and with each change of train, the language changes. As you move from the Hindi language territory, which is the biggest in India, you enter the language of Marathi. As you pass from Marathi, you enter the state of the Nizam of Hyderabad, where Urdu is the language. As you go further you enter Telugu and Malayalam-speaking areas, and finally you reach Raman Maharishi who spoke Tamil.

I said, "For me to travel it will be difficult. And you are not even supporting me with a ticket. I will have to travel without a ticket. For a hundred miles I can manage, I *have* managed. When you don't give me a ticket I simply go to the ticket collector and say, "This is the trouble: my father will not give me a ticket, but I want to go so I will have to travel without a ticket. But I don't want to travel like a thief, so I am informing you."

And it always happened that the man thought, "No person who is traveling without a ticket comes to the ticket collector to inform him." But the ticket collector would say to me, "Okay. Sit down, I will take care. After a hundred miles I will be waiting for you at the gate so I can let you off at the station; otherwise you may be caught there – if you are not caught on the train. I am the ticket collector on the train for the next hundred miles; but you may be caught on the station, so I will be there."

I have traveled many times in my early childhood without a ticket because my father thought that if a ticket was not given to me, how could I go? But soon he learned that I have my ways. He asked me, "Can you tell me how you manage not to be caught?"

I said, "I cannot tell you, it is a secret. But I have told my grandfather; you can ask him."

People around the world are all living in anxiety.

Even if it is told to you – and that's what Raman was telling to people – "Enter the anguish…"

I could not manage to see Raman, but I met many people who had been his disciples, later on when I was traveling. When I went to Arunachal, I met his very intimate disciples who were very old by then, and I did not find a single person who had understood that man's message.

It was not a question of language, because they all knew Tamil; it was a question of a totally different perspective and under-standing. Raman had said, "Look withinwards and find out who you are." And what were these people doing when I went there? They had made it a chant! They would sit down, chanting, "Who am I? Who am I? Who am I?" – just like any other mantra.

There are people who are doing their *japa*, "Rama, Rama, Rama," or "Hari Krishna, Hari Krishna, Hari Krishna." At Arunachal they were using this same technology for a totally different thing, which Raman could not have meant. And I said to his disciples,

"What you are doing is not what he meant. By repeating, 'Who am I?' do you think somebody is going to answer? You will continue to repeat it your whole life and no answer will come."

They said, "On the one hand we are doing what we have understood him to mean. On the other hand we cannot say you are wrong, because we have been wasting our whole life chanting, 'Who am I? Who am I? Who am I?'" – in Tamil of course, in their language – "but nothing has happened."

I said, "You can go on chanting for many more lives; nothing is going to happen. It is not a question of chanting 'Who am I?' You are not to utter a single word, you have simply to be silent and listen. At first you will find, just like flies moving around you, thousands of thoughts, desires, dreams – unrelated, irrelevant, meaningless. You are in a crowd, buzzing. Just keep quiet and sit down in this bazaar of your mind."

Bazaar is a beautiful word. English has taken it over from the East, but perhaps they don't know that it comes from *buzzing*: a bazaar is a place which is continuously buzzing. And your mind is the greatest bazaar there is. In each single mind, in such a small skull, you are carrying such a big bazaar. You will be surprised to know that so many people reside in you: so many ideas, so many thoughts, so many desires, so many dreams. Just go on watching and sitting silently in the middle of the bazaar.

If you start *saying*, "Who am I?" you have become part of the bazaar, you have started buzzing. Don't buzz, don't be a buzzer; simply be silent. Let the whole bazaar continue; remain the center of the cyclone. Yes, it takes a little patience. It is not predictable at what time the buzzing will stop in you, but one thing can be said certainly: that it stops sometime or other. It depends on you, how much of a bazaar you have, for how many years you have carried it, for how many lives you have carried it, how much nourishment you have given to it, and how much patience you have to sit silently in this mad crowd around you – maddening you, pulling you from every side.

Have you ever been in a madhouse? Just sit there and you will have a taste of your mind. One madman may start pulling your hand, another madman may start shaving your beard, somebody may start taking your clothes; they all will become engaged around you. Simply sit silently. For how long can you sit?

One of my sannyasins, Narendra's father, used to become mad for six months every year. And when he was mad he was in such great spirits that he would do strange things. He would go on a journey, a pilgrimage to holy places, anything. One time he went mad and escaped from the house. People searched but could not find him. He was looked for everywhere – as far as it was possible. But he had taken a very fast train going to Agra. Perhaps he was going to see the Taj Mahal or whatever; one never knows with mad people. By the time he reached Agra he was very hungry; he had no money, so he went into a sweet shop.

In India there is a very tasty soft cake – its name is such that it created trouble for poor Narendra's father. It is called *khaja*. *Khaja* has two meanings: one is "softness." The cake is very soft; you just press it a little and it will fall apart into many pieces. But *khaja* has another meaning: "Eat it."

So Narendra's father asked, "What is this?"

The shopkeeper said, "*Khaja*," so he started eating.

The man said, "What are you doing?"

He said, "Eating. *You* said to."

A crowd gathered but he was still eating. And he was a strong man; he said, "When he says, '*Khaja*,' I will finish it – the whole pile that he has in the shop."

The shopkeeper said, "This man seems to be mad! I have been selling *khaja* my whole life, but this is my first experience of a man who takes the meaning of *khaja* as 'to eat.' I have never thought of this possibility."

Narendra's father said, "You said, 'Eat it,' so I am simply eating it." He was brought to the police court and they found that he was mad, so he was put in a madhouse in Lahore for six months. Lahore was so far away – now it is in Pakistan, not even in India – it was the farthest corner of the country. Narendra's family remained concerned; we could not get even a hint as to where he had disappeared, because the court had ordered him to be taken to Lahore. Lahore had one of the biggest madhouses of India.

Narendra's father was very friendly to me because I was perhaps the only one in the whole town who appreciated his madness. We used to talk – Narendra, by and by, became acquainted with me just because of his father – and we used to go to swim together, we used to go to the market. With him it was a joy because I was not needed

for any mischief to happen; he was doing so much mischief that just
to be with him was enough enjoyment.

He told me that up to the fourth month things went perfectly well
in the Lahore madhouse, where there must have been at least three
thousand mad people. "I don't remember those four months," he
said, "they went by just as if I was in paradise. But after four months
an accident happened that created trouble."

He went into the bathroom and found a container which was
filled with some kind of soap to cleanse the toilets and the bathrooms. He was mad, and it looked like milk, so he drank the whole
container. It gave him such diarrhea that for fifteen days doctors
tried everything to stop it. Nothing would work – that chemical was
not meant for the human body. And he had drunk the whole
container – not a small dose of it – which was meant to clean all the
bathrooms of the madhouse. But it cleaned *his* madhouse completely: after fifteen days of continual diarrhea, he became sane. A
certain cleansing happened.

But then came the tragic part: the two months. He would go
again and again and tell the superintendent, "I am no longer mad,
and now this is a torture for me. For these four months it was perfectly okay: they were beating me or I was beating them; it didn't
matter. We were fighting and we were pulling each other and
shouting and screaming and biting. Everything was going on – it
was a free-for-all. But now I am not mad.

"This is the difficulty: I cannot hit them – I feel sad for them that
they are mad. But they are continually hitting me, beating me, pulling
me down from my bed. Somebody comes and sits on my chest...
One man shaved half my head, and four other mad people were
holding me, so I could not escape. I asked them again and again, 'At
least do the full job,' but that was all that they wanted to do; then they
moved on to another person to shave him. That madman must have
been a barber, so he was really practiced, and was still practicing his
old job, his old habit. Those two months..."

But the superintendent said, "I cannot do anything. Court orders
are orders – they are for six months. And moreover, everybody says,
'I am not mad.' Whom am I to believe? What proof have you got
that you aren't mad?"

What proof have *you* got? If someday you are caught in a madhouse and they ask, "What proof do you have that you aren't mad?"

it will be impossible to prove that you aren't mad. If they are determined that you are mad, if they have decided it, whatever proof you give will be a proof of your madness.

"Those two months," Narendra's father said, "I felt the question for the first time: 'Who am I?' Sometimes I am mad, sometimes I am not mad, but these are only phases around me. So who am I? – who gets into madness, who gets out of madness?"

I said to him, "Those two months have given you a taste of anguish. Don't forget those moments. Now you are out, use that anguish for your meditation. Try to find out who you are because you may become mad again and before you become mad at least have something solid figured out: who you are." But it was too much to expect of that poor man, because within a month he was mad again.

But what to say about the whole of humanity? You are aware of anxiety, but you are not aware of anguish yet. In the first place, when you do feel anguish, you will feel in a tremendous turmoil, in a very deep depression; a fathomless abyss opens in front of you, and you fall into it. It is terrible in the beginning, but only in the beginning. If you can be patient, just a little patient, and allow whatever is happening, soon you will be aware of a new quality in your being: All that is happening is *around* you, it is not happening *in* you. It is something without, not within. Even your own mind is something on the outer side.

At the innermost center there is only one thing: that is witnessing, watching, observing, awareness. And that's what I call meditation.

Without anguish you cannot meditate. You have to pass through the fire of anguish. It will burn much rubbish and leave you cleaner, fresher. Your being is not far away. It is there, very close by, but just the buzzing of all the thoughts does not allow you to hear it, to see it, to feel it.

Anguish is the inquiry into one's self, putting the question mark unto oneself. You have asked things like "Who is God?" and "Who created the world?" All those questions are just for retarded minds. A mature mind has only one question. Not even two, just a single question: "Who am I?" That too, you have not to ask verbally, you have just to be in that state of questioning. You are not to repeat, "Who am I?" you have just to be there, watching, looking; not verbally asking, but existentially asking. That existential question is terrible in the beginning, painful in the beginning, but brings all the blessings in the end.

Gautam the Buddha has said, "My path in the beginning is bitter, but in the end, very sweet." What path? He is not talking about the Buddhist religion, although that's how the Buddhist monks will interpret it. He is talking about the path that I am talking to you about – the path that takes you inwards.

Yes, it is bitter in the beginning but sweet in the end. It is deathlike in the beginning and eternal life in the end. All the blessings of the existence are yours; you are so blessed that you can bless the whole of existence. That's the meaning of the word, *Bhagwan*: the blessed one. The blessed one is born out of the birth pangs of anguish.

CHAPTER 7

Enlightened Fragrance of Revolution

Osho,
Is J. Krishnamurti enlightened?

Yes, he is enlightened, but something is missing in his enlightenment. It is like when you arrive after a long journey at an
airport. You have arrived but then suddenly you find your luggage is
missing. With J. Krishnamurti something more serious has happened: the luggage has arrived but he is missing!

It is a little bit complex but it is not unusual. It has happened many
times before but for different reasons. The reason with Krishnamurti
is certainly novel, but the situation is not. There have been people who
were enlightened but they still remained Christians, Hindus, Jainas,
Buddhists. To me it is unbelievable. Once you are enlightened you are
finished with all the conditionings of the mind. Then how can you still
be a Christian? What was your Christianity? It was a coincidence that
you were born in a certain family and those people conditioned your
mind in a certain way. They gave you certain ideologies, gave you a
certain religious outlook, gave you a certain theological jargon; and
you learned it like a parrot.

I know that a child cannot do anything against it, he is helpless; he has to learn whatsoever is taught to him. Even without being taught he picks up things from the environment, parents, friends, the neighborhood. He goes with his parents to the church, to the synagogue, to the temple, and he is continually imbibing. Whether you are directly teaching him or not, he is being indirectly conditioned.

But parents and teachers don't take any chances; they don't leave it just to indirect influences. They make every effort to directly convert the innocent child who comes into the world absolutely unconditioned, a pure mirror capable of reflecting anything. The society, the culture, the religion start painting on the mirror. They can paint a Krishna, they can paint a Christ, they can paint a Moses, they can paint anything. They can paint Karl Marx, they can paint Christianity, Communism, Fascism – anything. And the child is so helplessly dependent he cannot say no. He really has no idea of no.

The child believes and trusts the people who are giving him everything, helping him, supporting him: his mother, his father, his family – the warmth, the coziness… They are providing all the opportunities for his growth; they are not to be distrusted. The question does not arise in the mind of the child, and it is natural that it does not.

But because of this natural situation all the religions have committed the greatest crime in the history of man; that is, making the child a Christian, a Mohammedan, a Jew, a Hindu, a Communist – without the child's acceptance, without the child's readiness, willingness. Of course the child has not said no, but he has not said yes either. If people are sensitive they will wait for the child's yes.

If they really love they will wait till the child asks them, "What is this church all about?" They should make every effort to see that he is not being indirectly influenced; the question of direct influence should not even arise. He should be left clean, pure, as he was born, till the time when he picks up some intelligence.

Growth takes a little time; just a little patience is needed. He will ask questions because everybody is born with a potential for search, inquiry. He *will* come up with questions. Then too, if you are alert, loving, compassionate toward this young fellow traveler… He is not your possession, he has just come through you. You have been only a passage – never forget that. He does not belong to you, he belongs to the whole existence. You have been just a path for him to come into this body.

Don't destroy the child's natural potentialities. Don't divert the child according to your vested interests. Don't be political, at least with your own child. But all over the earth, all the parents, all the teachers, have no idea of what they are doing. In the name of religion they are committing a sin. Ordinarily I don't use that word. To me, in life there may be mistakes, errors – not sins – because man is fallible. Man is not born omniscient, knowing all. He is not a born pope – infallible. He will fall many times, and he will get up again. This is the way he learns to walk; this is the way he learns to see, to inquire.

Yes, many times he will go on the wrong path. Nothing is wrong in that. In going on the wrong path, you are learning that it is wrong, because when you are moving in the wrong direction you cannot feel comfortable: it is a natural indication. You will feel uneasy, your stomach cramped; you will feel tense – because wherever you are going is not the natural way for you. All these are indications to change the route and know forever that this is not right for you.

But about religion I cannot use very ordinary words like *mistake, error* – no. Something really heavy is needed. So I say the so-called religion is the only sin in the world because it commits a crime against somebody who is absolutely helpless and in your hands. It is a crime of tremendous proportions.

So if you become a Christian, if you become a Hindu, if you become a Buddhist, it is understandable. But when a man becomes enlightened what does it mean? It means really undoing what society, culture, religion, the state, the education system, parents have done all together in conspiracy against the small child. To undo it is to be enlightened: to regain your childhood, to regain that freshness, that mirror-like quality of simply reflecting with no judgment.

The mirror simply reflects. When you stand before the mirror, the mirror is not making any judgment about you – good, bad, beautiful, ugly – no judgment at all. The mirror simply reflects. It does not get involved in any way.

I remember my own childhood. The moment I became aware of what was happening – it must have been nearabout the age of four or five – that I was being driven in a certain direction that I had not chosen, I asked my father, "Do you think that just by being born a son to you I have to follow your religion, your politics; that I will have to become a member of the Lions Club, that I will have to do your business? Does it mean that because unfortunately I am born to you, I will have to do all these things?"

He said, "Who said to you that you have to become a member of the Lions Club or that you have to become a member of the political party of which I am a member? Who said this to you?"

I said, "There is no need for anybody to *say* it, for five years continually you have been *doing* it. Why have you been taking me to the Jaina temple? Who are you to decide? Why have you been telling me to bow down before Mahavira's statue, before certain scriptures I know nothing about?" I was not even able to read at that time. The scriptures were just books like any other books, but everybody was bowing down to them.

I said, "You were bowing down and you were encouraging me to bow down, and it looked awkward for me to stand there when everybody else was showing so much respect. But you had not asked me; it was not with my consent that you took me to the temple. Just by the side there is a mosque – my friend is being taken there. Why don't you take me there? Why don't my friend's parents take him to the Jaina temple?

"What else is politics? You are giving me certain ideas, filling me with certain attitudes. And you started so early that I was not even aware of what was happening." I said, "From now onward, stop it; leave me alone. Now I am capable of saying no. And remember, unless I am capable of saying no, how can I be capable of saying yes? The capacity to say one is also the capacity to say the other; they both come together.

"So don't be offended by my no. I *will* say yes, but you will have to wait. Perhaps I may not say yes to this temple, but to some other temple; not to this book, but to some other book. Nothing can be predicted right now; I am not a thing, predictable. Tomorrow the chair will still remain a chair, the table will still remain a table; they are predictable. What to say about the child of a man? – I am not predictable."

A drunkard, completely drunk, went to a sweet shop. He gave the shopkeeper one rupee, purchased sweets for half a rupee and asked for the change. The shopkeeper said, "I don't have any change right now. Tomorrow morning, when you pass by, pick it up. Or you can take your rupee, and tomorrow morning you can give me half rupee – whatever pleases you."

The drunkard said, "Okay, tomorrow morning I will pick up the change." But he thought, "What if the shopkeeper changes his address? The world is so cunning; I should make some arrangement so that he cannot change his address without my knowing." So he looked around and he saw a bull sitting in front of the shop. He said, "That's good. The shopkeeper may not be even aware that bull is sitting there in front of the shop."

The next morning all that the drunkard remembered was that there was a bull sitting in front of the shop, and that he had to collect half a rupee from there. He went in search of the bull, obviously, because that was the only proof that he had. But a bull is not a static thing: the bull was sitting in front of a barber's shop.

The drunkard went in, clutched the man by his neck and said, "You son-of-a-bitch! Just for half a rupee you change your profession, you change your caste; and just overnight the sweet shop has disappeared and you have become a barber!"

The man said, "What are you talking about? Yesterday my shop was closed."

The drunkard said, "Great! You can't deceive me. Look at the bull. Even though I was drunk, I am not that foolish. I knew there would be some trouble so I made a point of remembering the bull; the whole night I had to remember it again and again. The bull is still sitting in exactly the same position, in front of your shop."

The barber said, "Now I understand what the trouble is, because I saw the bull sitting in front of the sweet shop last night. Please go there. A bull is not something that remains in one position, he moves; he *has* moved! What can I do about it?"

But people go on thinking that the child will remain the same as they are making him. Yes, most people remain the same because it is comfortable, convenient. Why bother? When all the answers have been given to you, why be skeptical?

Skepticism is condemned by all the religions. In reality, skepticism is the beginning of a really religious man. Skepticism means inquiry; skepticism means "Whatsoever you have told me I cannot accept unless I experience it." But it is inconvenient. You will have to travel a long way, and you never know whether you will reach the point where you find the answer on your own.

Most people, the greater mass, want convenience, comfort,

ready-made things, ready-made answers. It is understandable. It is an ugly fact about human beings, that even for truth they are not ready to take a little trouble. People want even truth cheap. And because you want truth cheap, there are peddlers who are selling it cheap. Not only cheap, they are selling it without taking anything from you. Not only that, they are rewarding you: if you purchase their truth they are going to reward you. The Christians will call you a saint, the Hindus will call you a mahatma, a sage. Without any effort, without paying anything you gain so much respectability. All that you have to do is to pretend, to be a hypocrite.

The whole human society is pretending. What do you know about Christ's experience? And without having any taste of it, you are a Christian? If this is not hypocrisy, then what is hypocrisy? Knowing nothing about God, you believe in God. If this is not dishonesty, then what else can dishonesty be?

You are not even honest toward God. An honest, sincere person will start from skepticism. He will inquire. He will put a question mark on every conditioning that his parents and his society have burdened him with.

It is understandable about the general masses; they can be forgiven, but how to forgive a man who has attained enlightenment? His enlightenment means he has done away with all conditions, conditionings, all the programs. He is a deprogrammed man, he is a dehypnotized man. But for an enlightened man to say that he is still a Christian is unforgivable, yet this has been happening all through history.

Only very rarely have a few people simply declared their aloneness.

They have taken a small footpath of their own and they have left the super-highway where everybody is moving – of course comfortably. And when you leave the super-highway you will have to create a path just by walking. There is no ready-made path available to you. That's why I say truth is costly. You will have to pay for it.

When you walk without there being any path, your feet will bleed. Your mind will try to persuade you to go back to the highway where everybody else is moving, and say, "Don't be a fool! Here you can get lost. There you were with the crowd; it was warmer. When there were so many people, it was certain that we were moving in the right direction – so many people cannot be wrong."

Alone, what guarantee is there that you are going in the right direction? – you don't have any evidence. There are millions of people ahead, millions of people behind, millions of people with you. What more proof do you need? I can understand that the common man would prefer the super-highway. Whether it is Christian, Hindu, Jaina or Mohammedan doesn't matter – he has to be with a big crowd. As far as you can see there are only crowds and more crowds, and that gives you a deep conviction that you must be on the right path.

I can forgive you. But how can I forgive Saint Francis? He is enlightened and yet he is a Christian and goes to touch the feet of the pope! Now, this is sickening: The pope! – who is not enlightened, who is just an elected person. Anybody who is cunning enough, clever enough to campaign for himself can become the pope.

But why did Saint Francis go there? All over the whole country people had started respecting Francis, loving him, accepting what he was saying, and that news continually going to the pope was shocking. A man who has not been sanctified by the pope as a saint is already being accepted by the people as a saint! The pope was simply bypassed and that could not be tolerated. This man was sabotaging the whole Catholic system, and no bureaucracy can tolerate such sabotage: if he has become enlightened, first he should come to the pope, and if the pope gives him a certificate that says yes, he is enlightened, if he gives him the sanction of enlightenment... That's the Christian meaning of a saint: sanctioned by the pope.

Become anything else, but never become a Christian saint. A Christian saint simply means "sanctioned by the pope." And particularly now, don't become a Christian saint, whatsoever price you have to pay. Sanctioned by a pope! What kind of saint will you be?

But Saint Francis, seeing that the pope was getting angrier and that messages were coming saying, "You have to come first to the pope," went, touched the pope's feet and prayed with folded hands: "Bless me, and tell me how I can serve Christ, his church, Christianity and you." The pope was perfectly happy: Francis was sanctioned as a saint.

I can understand the pope and his stupidity because nobody expects anything else from a pope. But what is Saint Francis doing? Something is missing in his enlightenment. He *is* enlightened but is still imprisoned in the old conditioning. Although now he knows, "I am not the conditioning," he is not brave enough to jump out of his prison. On the contrary, he decides to use the prison itself, the conditioning itself, the language given by the conditioning itself, to bring his message to the people. This is cowardly. And this is why so many saints in the past in all the religions have lost my respect.

I know that they *had* come to understand, but their understanding was not fiery enough, it was very lukewarm. It was not revolutionary, it was orthodox. Perhaps they were common men, and the fears of the common man were still lingering somewhere back in the shadows and influencing their actions. Their language, their behavior, their actions give indications that they were enlightened, but they also show that they were not able to overthrow all their conditioning. Perhaps they thought if they overthrew it, they would not be able to communicate with the people because the people had the same conditioning.

To think in this way is right for a business man, but it is not right for an enlightened person. Who cares whether people understand or not? If they understand, it is good for them; if they don't understand, "Go to hell!" – that is their business. Why should I go on carrying unnecessary luggage, which I know is just crap, for your sake?

In this way many enlightened people of the past have lost my respect. I cannot deny that they were in that space where I would like you all to be: they *were* in that space, but they remained like buds, they never opened up like flowers. They were so afraid that they remained buds. They were afraid to open. Opening is always risky. Who knows what is going to happen when you open up? One thing is certain, your fragrance will be released. And that can create trouble for you. An enlightened person's fragrance is revolution, is rebellion. Perhaps it is better to remain a closed bud like these people who were not brave enough – enlightenment was in the wrong hands.

With J. Krishnamurti the situation is totally new. He is enlightened, and he is not orthodox – but he has gone to the other extreme: he is <u>anti</u>-orthodox. *Anti* should be underlined.

When I was a student in my final post-graduate year there were two girls in my class. We three were the only students of religion. You can understand that the professor was a religious man and as you should expect from a religious man, he was very much infatuated with one of the girls. He was a celibate. He had really been following the Hindu tradition because he wanted to become a monk one day, and he was preparing: practicing Yoga, concentration and visualization exercises, and continually repeating, chanting mantras.

But all these things are on one side; biology is on the other side, and that is far weightier.

Put all your scriptures on the weighing scale – all the scriptures of all your religions – and put biology on the other side. The side of biology will touch the earth and all your scriptures may go to heaven. They don't have any weight. They need idiots to function as paper-weights, to keep them down on the earth.

Now this man was in great trouble. One girl was homely; you would not bother about her. In fact she was a little more than homely. She had a little mustache that she had to shave – what else could she do? She was a Punjabi, and it happens in the Punjab. Punjabi women are strong, hard workers, and work almost like men in the fields. I think that perhaps a mustache and beard start growing with so much work and exertion and strength, because I saw it again in Shri Aurobindo's ashram.

In Aurobindo's ashram everybody had to do certain very arduous exercises. Most of the people in his ashrams were young girls sent by their parents – followers of Aurobindo – to be trained there for a spiritual life. But I was surprised that almost all of them were growing little mustaches. Strange! I said, "If it happens in an ashram, then all ashrams should be destroyed." I inquired about it from the man who was in charge.

He said, "I also feel a little awkward because everybody asks that, and I don't know what is happening."

I said, "Three-hour morning exercises, three-hour evening exercises – these exercises must be doing it." And the exercises were almost like in the army! It has something to do with that. Too much exertion and too much exercise perhaps changes some hormones in the body and the girls start growing beards and mustaches – because I knew that one girl and she was a little more than homely. In fact if you just passed by her, you wouldn't even look at her, and I don't think anybody ever looked back again.

But the other girl was a rare beauty. She was from Kashmir, and Kashmir produces perhaps the most beautiful women on the earth. My celibate professor was wavering and bobbling. And the greatest trouble for him was that the girl was interested in me, not in him. So he was very angry with me, because he would try in every possible way to make the girl interested in him, but she was simply taking no notice of him.

I was not interested in the girl, but the girl was certainly inter-ested in me. She used to come to ask this, to ask that, to take this book... And when she came to me it was natural that whatever she wanted I arranged for her. That man was burning up!

It came to a climax one day because the girl invited me to her house in the city for dinner, and this celibate, religious professor heard that I had been invited by the girl to her house. She was the daughter of the collector of the city and she wanted me to be intro-duced to her parents, her father and mother. Only she knew her pur-pose; I was completely out of it.

I told her also, "I am not interested in any kind of relationship, so you should take note of that first; don't unnecessarily waste a dinner. If you are trying some conspiracy with your parents, I am unaware of it and I am not part of it at all. I can come for dinner – you are inviting me, I will not refuse it – but that's all."

She was shocked. I said, "You can take your invitation back; there is no problem, I will not be hurt. In fact I am hurting you." But this is not the thing that I wanted to emphasize. When the professor heard about the dinner, and that the girl was going to introduce me to her father and her mother and family, he cornered me in the library.

I had my own corner. It was a small room which I had chosen inside the library, allotted to me by special permission from the vice-chancellor so that I need not sit with so many people coming and going but could have my own place. I wanted to be alone, so I used to keep it locked from inside. My interest in books has been immense. I have read perhaps more than anybody else in the whole world, because I was not doing anything else except reading. I used to have three or four hours of sleep, that was all; otherwise I was continually reading.

Somebody knocked on the door. It never used to happen because I had told all my professors that even if the university was burning down I was not concerned; they were not to bother me. I had told the librarian, "If you want to close the library you can – I will remain here the whole night – but don't ever knock on my door. I don't like that kind of familiarity at all."

Somebody knocked; it was the first time. I thought, "Who can it be?" I opened the door.

The celibate, red with anger, closed the door behind him and asked me, "Do you love this girl?"

I said, "I don't even hate her."

He said, "What do you mean?"

I said, "Exactly what I say to you: I don't even hate her; the question of love does not arise. There is not even a hate relationship between me and her – you are unnecessarily getting red and hot. Just get out of the room. As far as the dinner is concerned I have canceled it, so don't be worried. But if you want dinner in the house, I can manage it."

He said, "No, no, I don't want any dinner, and particularly not managed by you." Again he asked, "But what do you mean: 'I don't even hate her?'"

I said, "It is so simple; and you are a professor of religion, can't you understand a simple thing? Because love is a relationship, hate is a relationship. Love can become hate any day, and it does – not any day, *every* day. Vice versa also is true: hate can become love. It is a little rare but it happens, because love and hate are just the same energy arranged in a different way. You have the same sofa, the same chairs, the same table, but you can arrange them in a thousand ways. And people go on doing that. So I simply said, to cut the whole problem from the very root, 'I don't even hate her,' so be completely at ease."

Why did I remember it? I remembered it because of J. Krishnamurti. He hates orthodoxy; he hates all that has passed in the name of religion. Remember the difference: I criticize it but I don't hate it. I don't even hate it! Krishnamurti has a relationship with it; I don't have any relationship with it, and that is where he has missed.

He was brought up in a very strange situation: by Theosophists, to be declared a world teacher. Now, you cannot manufacture a world teacher. World teachers are born, not forced. And world teachers need not declare themselves world teachers: they *are*. It is not a question of declaration, it is a question of recognition on the part of the world; it is none of their business.

Whenever there is a man who has the capacity to attract people from all around the world – intelligent people, people who are seekers, inquirers, people who are ready to risk and gamble – there is no need for him to declare "I am the world teacher." The whole world will laugh at such a man. The world teacher has nothing to do with it; it is for the world to decide.

But what Theosophists were doing was just the opposite: they were trying to create a world teacher. So of course they were disciplining J. Krishnamurti from the age of nine; now he is ninety. He was picked up by the Theosophists while he was bathing naked in a river which flows through Adyar in India, where the headquarters, the world headquarters of the Theosophical movement is. At that time it was a great movement: thousands of people were interested in it. All that was missing was the world teacher.

There were very clever people like Leadbeater, Annie Besant, Colonel Olcott, but none of them had charisma. To be a master, one thing is absolutely essential: the person should have some magical quality, some charisma. Not only his words, but his very being should be capable of pulling you like a magnet. That was not there.

Annie Besant was a nice lady, but what to do with a nice lady? There are millions of nice ladies. Leadbeater was a great writer, but no world teacher has ever been a writer. Not a single world teacher worth the name has ever written, because the spoken word has a magic about it which the written word cannot have. The written word can be written by anybody. Do you think it will make any difference whether Jesus writes it or you write it? Perhaps your handwriting may be better. But it won't have charismatic impact just because Jesus writes it. As far as the spoken word is concerned: the word that Jesus speaks has a certain impact. You can say the same word but it is not going to have the same impact.

All the Christian missionaries are continually repeating the same words. Jesus has not left much; in fact a single sermon, the Sermon on the Mount, contains his whole teaching. And he was not an educated man so he could not use very sophisticated language: it is simple, raw, rough. What else can you expect from a carpenter's son? But its impact must have been tremendous. People are not crucified for nothing.

If the Jews and the Romans both agreed to crucify this man, you can take it for granted that he had something in him which made King Herod tremble on his throne. Listening to Jesus, the high priest of the Jews, who had all the religious power in his hands, understood immediately that no scholarship could defeat the man.

It is not what he is saying, it is the way he is saying it – or even better – it is his presence, the space from which he is speaking that brings a certain fragrance with it, a certain quality of penetration that just goes into your heart. There is no way to prevent it. Later on, perhaps you may find a thousand and one arguments against it, but in the presence of the man – whether he is right or wrong – his impact is absolute. In his presence you cannot doubt him.

Now, you cannot create such a person by giving him lessons in oratory, by teaching him better ways of speaking, expression, language, by making him proficient in every way. But the Theosophists worked hard on J. Krishnamurti until he was twenty-five, and then they thought, "Now is the time to make our declaration – he is ready." But they had really picked a great man.

They had picked a few other boys also because it was just chance who turned out to be the right one. So they were training at least half a dozen boys, but Krishnamurti proved the best to them. And of course he *was* the best – but not for their purposes. For their purposes any one of the other five would have done.

One of them, Raj Gopal, is still alive. He had been personal secretary to J. Krishnamurti his whole life, but just a few years ago he betrayed him – and really betrayed him badly. All power of attorney, all royalties, all book copyrights were in the name of Raj Gopal so that Krishnamurti need not bother about it. When Krishnamurti was eighty, Raj Gopal simply took possession of everything: millions of dollars, all future royalties, books, and all the donations that had come during this fifty-year period. It was a big fortune. He simply denied Krishnamurti, saying, "I am no longer your secretary. Forget about all these things – or if you want to go to court, you can."

This man, Raj Gopal would have proved far better for the Theosophical movement and their purpose. He proved extremely clever, cunning, and of immense patience, really a man of strong will. He waited long enough to betray Krishnamurti: he must have been carrying the idea for fifty years but nobody could detect it in him. Even Krishnamurti was completely unsuspicious. How can you believe that a person who has been serving you for fifty years will suddenly one day cut off your head? – someone who has not even raised a single question, a single doubt, about you. Raj Gopal would have been far better for the Theosophists.

J. Krishnamurti certainly was the best, but not for their purposes. That was proved immediately, and on the very day he was going to declare himself the world teacher. They had prepared every word of the statement he was to give, listened to it again and again so that he could repeat it exactly, because it was going to be a document of historical importance; nobody had done such a thing before.

Six thousand representatives from all over the world had gathered in Holland. One old lady of the royal family had donated her castle and five thousand acres of land so that it could become Krishnamurti's world headquarters. Everything was prepared on a grand scale.

Krishnamurti stood up, and he said, "I am nobody's master and nobody is my disciple. The only declaration I have to make is that I abandon the movement that has been created around me. I dissolve the organization called the Star of the East which has been especially made for my work, and I return the castle and the money, the donations, the land, to their owners."

Annie Besant was crying; she could not believe her eyes. It was such a shock: "What has happened? We have come from all over the world, and the man simply says he is not anybody's master and there is no need for one." But for anybody who could understand how human psychology functions it was very much expected.

The Theosophists were forcing it on him, and this was the first chance that he had to stand up and speak in public: he did not want to lose the chance. Up to then he had been kept in secrecy, and all over the world rumors were being created that he was being initiated into higher and higher degrees of spirituality. "Now he has passed the three-star degree, now he has passed the five-star degree, now seven stars; now he has attained all nine stars and the time has come." That's why the organization specially created for the world teacher was called the Star of the East, because he was the first man who attained to the highest peak of consciousness: nine stars.

It seems like a five-star hotel – a nine-star hotel! And of course when you fall from a nine-star hotel... The whole movement was crushed. Not only was the Star of the East organization dissolved, the shock was so much that Theosophy started falling apart and withering. Now it is just history.

The problem with Krishnamurti is that now sixty-five years have passed and still he goes on continually telling people: "Die to the past; live in the moment." It is an obsession. My understanding is that he has not been able to die to *his* past: those years of discipline, and training, and hypocrisy. Those people who were almost torturing him with Yoga discipline – wake up in the morning at three o'clock, take a cold bath, do all the exercises, repeat all the mantras – have left scars in him.

He says to you, "Die to the past," but he has not been able to forgive those people who are all dead. And he has not been able to forget those early years of torture in the name of training, discipline.

It is a strange coincidence that just for the first time today I have seen J. Krishnamurti on television. Once it happened that I was in Mumbai, he was in Mumbai, and he wanted to meet me. One of his chief disciples in India came to me and said to me – he knew me and he used to listen to me – "J. Krishnamurti wants to see you."

I said, "I have no problem – bring him."

But he said, "That is not the Indian way."

I said, "Krishnamurti does not believe in Indian or European or American ways."

He said, "He may not believe in them but everybody else does."

I said, "I am not going to meet everybody else. You say J. Krishnamurti wants to meet me: bring him. If I wanted to meet him, I would go to him, but I don't see the need."

But again and again his emphasis was: "He is older, you are younger" – I must have been only forty at the time, and Krishnamurti was almost double my age.

I said, "That's perfectly true, but I don't see any need to meet him. What am I going to say to him? I have no questions to ask, I have only answers to give. It will look very awkward if I start answering him when he has not asked anything. He will be expecting a question from me. That is impossible – I have never asked. I have only answers, so what can I do?

"Of course, he is enlightened, so what is the need? At the most we can sit silently together. So why unnecessarily take me ten or twelve miles?" In Mumbai ten or twelve miles sometimes means two hours, sometimes three hours. The roads are continuously blocked with all kinds of vehicles. Mumbai is perhaps the only city which must have every model of cars. The ancientmost, that God used to drive Adam and Eve out of paradise – that too will be in Mumbai. There is no other possibility; it cannot be anywhere else.

I said, "I am not interested in taking three hours, unnecessarily bothering... I have had such experiences before: it is absolutely futile. Go and ask him: if he wants to ask me something perhaps I may think about coming just because of his old age. But I have nothing to ask. If he just wants to see me, then he should take the trouble of coming here." Of course Krishnamurti was very angry when he heard it. He gets angry easily. That anger is due to his past; he is angry with the past.

Just today I saw a BBC interview with Krishnamurti – that was my first acquaintance with how he looks – and I was simply shattered! Again, it was the same story I was telling you yesterday; the same story. He has no charisma at all, no impact. I was sorry to see the interview. I know he is enlightened, but it would have been better if I had not seen his face, his gestures, his eyes, because you cannot find in anything even a shadow of enlightenment. The luggage has reached, the passenger has got lost somewhere on the way.

I still say that he is enlightened because I have read thousands of enlightened people's words – Krishnamurti's words are far more accurate in describing the experience. And the way he revolted is perfectly in tune with enlightenment. But there is a difference between revolt and rebellion, a very delicate difference. Revolt is a reaction. Rebellion is not a reaction, it is an action.

Please try to see the difference: reaction is bound to remain concerned with the situation it was the reaction to. That's what keeps dragging him backward. He cannot drop those shadows – which are nothing but shadows – but he is surrounded by them and he is still reacting to them. While he is speaking to you, it is not *you* that he is speaking to: you are just an excuse to condemn those dead people who have done something wrong to him.

I think he would have become enlightened anyway, if not in this life then in another life. But if he had been on his own then there would have been a totally different quality to it. Then it would have been an action, not a reaction. Then it would have been a rebellion.

I am not reacting to anything. Whatever I am saying, I am saying not as a reaction to something but as my experience. If it goes against something, that is a separate matter; that is a side effect. For Krishnamurti, what he is saying is the side effect; his original concern remains to destroy those people and what they did to him. He is ninety years old but those shadows are around him, and because of those shadows he has not been able to flower into a charismatic being. That's what I saw today: he has no charisma at all.

Ninety years is a long life. And beginning his career at nine – since the age of nine he has been in the spiritual world: for eighty-one years continually. Perhaps nobody ever before has been in the spiritual world that long. But eighty-one years, and that magnet is still missing... He has been speaking all around the world; he must be one of the most prominent speakers in the whole history of man. Jesus was confined to Judea, Buddha was confined to Bihar, but Krishnamurti has been roaming around the world for all these years. He has only special places where he speaks, for example in India: New Delhi, Mumbai, Varanasi and Adyar.

I know about his Mumbai meetings because I lived for four years in Mumbai, and my sannyasins were going to his meetings and reporting to me. One thing: not more than three thousand people listen to him in Mumbai. He has been speaking in Mumbai his whole life, and he comes only once a year, for two or three weeks. In a week he speaks only twice, or at the most thrice; still there are only three thousand people. And the strangest thing is that you will find almost the same people, most of them very old because they have been listening to him for forty years – the same old fogies.

Strange: for forty years you have been listening to this man, and neither does he seem to get anywhere, nor do you seem to get anywhere. It seems that it has become just a habit that he has to come to Mumbai every year and you have to listen to him. By and by old people go on dying and a few new people replace them, but the number has never gone beyond three thousand. The same is the situation in New Delhi; the same is the situation in Varanasi, because I have been speaking at his school in Varanasi.

At his school I asked, "How many people come here?"

They said, "Fifteen hundred at the most, but they are always the same people."

What impact! And this man has made an arduous effort. Jesus, in three years, created the whole of Christianity – almost the biggest religion in the world, rightly or wrongly. But soon after Krishnamurti dies his name will disappear – except from your Krishnamurti Lake! I could see the reason why, today. He is not a man who goes within you, bypassing your intellect so that your intellect may be struggling but he has already captured your heart – and that is where you are. Intellect may try a little fight, doubt this and that, but if the heart is captured, the intellect is poor.

The intellect has to follow the heart. Yes, if the intellect catches hold of something before it reaches your heart, then it can spoil the whole thing. A charismatic personality means a person who can reach directly to your heart without your intellect being even aware of what is happening, what is transpiring. By the time the intellect comes to know that the heart is throbbing with some new joy, it is too late. The intellect cannot undo anything in the heart, it is impossible. The intellect cannot move backward. Just as you cannot move backward in time, the intellect cannot move backward toward the heart: it is just at the gate.

The charismatic personality somehow enters the gate while the watchman is either away or asleep or is lost in some thoughts. The moment it hears bells ringing in the heart, then the watchman wakes up; but it is too late, somebody has gone in. The watchman cannot go in, there is no way – for the intellect, moving backward is not in the nature of things. Yes, if intellect can catch you at the gate, then the heart will never come to know. It is the heart that transforms you, connects you, creates a golden bridge. The intellect is a very superficial thing.

Seeing Krishnamurti's interview today, I could just feel sad for the man. He has been working his whole life, taking immense trouble, but the result is nil. The reason is not hard to find: he has no charismatic vibe, he has no aura. He is surrounded by past shadows, he is overshadowed by them. He is anti-orthodox, anti-tradition, anti-convention; but his whole energy has become involved in this hatred. It is a hate relationship with the past, but it is a relationship all the same. He has not been able to cut himself off totally from the past. Perhaps that would have released his energy; it would have opened his charismatic qualities, but it has not been the case.

The people who become interested in him are mere intellectuals. Remember, I say *mere* intellectuals, who don't know they have a heart too. These intellectuals become interested in him, but they are not the people who are going to be transformed. They are just sophists, arguers, and Krishnamurti is unnecessarily wasting his time with these intellectual people of the world.

Remember, I am not saying intelligent people of the world – that is a different category. I am saying mere intellectuals who love to play with words, logic: it is a kind of gymnastics. And Krishnamurti just goes on feeding their intellect. He thinks that he is destroying their orthodoxy, that he is destroying their tradition, that he is destroying their personality and helping them to discover their individuality. He is wrong, he is not destroying anything. He is just fulfilling their doubts, supporting their skepticism, making them more articulate – they can argue against anything. You may be able to argue against everything in the world, but is your heart *for* anything, just one single thing?

You can be against everything – that won't change you. Are you *for* something too? That something is not coming from him. He just goes on arguing. And the trouble is – this is why I feel sorry for him – that what he is doing could have been of tremendous help, but it has not helped anybody. I have met thousands of Krishnamurti-ites, but not a single one of them is transformed. Yes, they are very vocal. You cannot argue with them, you cannot defeat them as far as argument is concerned. Krishnamurti has sharpened their intellect for years and now they are just parrots repeating him.

This is the paradox of Krishnamurti's whole life. He wanted them to be individuals on their own, and what has he succeeded in doing? They are just parrots, intellectual parrots.

Raosaheb Patvardhan, who wanted me to see Krishnamurti, was one of his old colleagues. He came to know me just in 1965 when I spoke in Pune; he lived in Pune. Now he is no longer alive. I asked Raosaheb Patvardhan, who was a very respected man, "You have been so close to Krishnamurti all your life, but what is the gain? I don't want to hear that tradition is bad, conditioning is bad, and it has to be dropped – I know all that. Put that all aside and just tell me: what have you gained?"

And that old man, who died just six or seven months afterwards, told me, "As far as gaining is concerned, I have never thought about it and nobody ever asked about it."

But I said, "Then what is the point? Whether you are for tradition or you are against tradition, either way you are tethered to tradition. When are you going to open your wings and fly? Somebody is sitting on a tree because he loves the tree; somebody else is sitting on the same tree because he hates the tree, and he will not leave the tree unless he destroys it. One goes on watering it, the other goes on destroying it, but both are confined, tethered, chained to the tree."

I asked him, "When are you going to open your wings and fly? The sky is there. You have both forgotten the sky. And what has the tree to do with it anyway?"

That's why I remembered the incident of my celibate professor and my saying: "I don't even hate her."

I don't hate any religion. I simply state the fact: religions are nothing but crimes against humanity. But I am not saying it with any hate in me. I have no love for them; I have no hate for them. I simply state whatsoever the fact is.

So you will find much similarity between what I am saying and what J. Krishnamurti is saying, but there is a tremendous difference. The difference is that while I am talking to your intellect, I am working somewhere else, hence the gaps. Hence the discourse becomes too long! Any idiot can repeat my discourse in one hour – not me, because I have to do something else too.

So, while you are waiting for my words is the right time. You are engaged in your head, waiting; and I am stealing your heart.

I am a thief.

A Womb for Transformation

Osho,
Please describe an orthodox Rajneeshee.

I t is a contradiction in terms, but I will not dispose of the question
so easily. I will try to squeeze as much juice out of it as possible.
Yes, there is a way to define the orthodox Rajneeshee. It is going to
be a strange definition because two terms which are contradictory
to each other are used together. But still I feel it is significant. The
first quality of an orthodox Rajneeshee will be that he will not be
orthodox – in no possible sense, in no direction.

He will be totally committed to the spirit of rebellion.

He will fight against everything that is dead but that still goes on
burdening human consciousness; things which should have been
thrown away long ago. Because of a strange habit of the human mind,
many dead things go on keeping their grip on you; and the more
ancient they are, the deeper and stronger is their grip on you. The
reason has to be understood.

Before anything like education came into existence, there was
only one way to learn, and that was from the people who were

experienced. Naturally, the older generation would teach the younger generation. The older generation had experience, and experience was the only school; there was no alternative. The younger generation had to accept whatever the older generation was saying; there was no way to bypass them. The older generation was the only source of knowledge; hence the older people became respected. The older they were, the more respected, because their experience was greater, their experience was longer – and it gave them a certain authority.

There was no possible authority to compete with it; the older generation had the whole monopoly. Because of this situation – and this must have prevailed for thousands of years – the mind has the habit, and habits die really hard. Habits which have been accumulated over thousands of years become engrained. They become a kind of program in you.

I was criticizing Mahatma Gandhi my whole life but no Gandhian replied to my arguments. I cannot blame them, because there was no argument on their side: whatsoever they would have said would have looked stupid, and they knew it. To me in private, they accepted, "What you are saying is right, but that you are saying it is not right. Just to say something against a man who is worshipped by millions of people is not right; you are hurting their feelings."

I said, "Do you mean I have to lie not to hurt their feelings? Do you mean I have to stop saying the truth? And Gandhi's whole life can be described as a deep search for truth? He entitled his autobiography, *The Story of My Experiments with Truth*: a man who thinks that his whole life is an experiment with truth. You are his intimate followers, you have lived with him: you have got some nerve to tell me that I should not say it even though it is true."

In public, not a single Gandhian had the courage to accept what I was saying, but they were not able to find any argument against me either. So they found one thing which is tremendously appealing in India: all the Gandhians all over the country started saying that I was too young, inexperienced; that when I became old enough I would not say such things. Even Morarji Desai...

He thinks himself now to be the only living successor of Mahatma Gandhi, and he enjoys one thing very much... Gandhi was called *bapu* all over India. *Bapu* means father, but it is far sweeter than father, closer to daddy or even dad. If it is to be translated exactly I will have to use Jesus' word for father, *abba*. That is

Aramaic, and it has exactly the same meaning as *bapu*. *Bapu* is a
Gujarati term. Morarji Desai is also a Gujarati; and now he is old
enough, ninety, it is time he should be called *bapu* and his followers
have started calling him *bapu*. That is the one thing he enjoys so
much about being called *bapu* – that it is what Gandhi was called by
the whole country.

Morarji Desai was deputy prime minister when he criticized me,
and the only criticism was that I was too young. After a few years,
when he was no longer in the government, he wanted to meet me. He
wanted me to help him overthrow Indira Gandhi from power, and
he wanted my advice about what should be done. When I went to see
him he was standing at the gate to receive me – that was not like him
but now he was in a difficult situation. That was not like him: I had
seen him before, when he was in power.

He took me by my hand into his house and made me comfortable. A few of my hairs had become gray, so he said, "Last time
your hair was not gray."

I said, "What to do? To prove myself right I am making a
tremendous effort to make my hair gray. Unless my hair is gray, I
am wrong."

He could not understand. I said, "Let me remind you. You criticized me when you were the deputy prime minister of the country,
saying that I was too young. Since then I have been trying to
become older. And I still have the same arguments – more strongly,
because now I am more experienced. In a way you were right, but as
far as I can see, the older I become, the sharper my arguments will
be. I don't see any hope that I can ever accept stupidities, whether
they are propounded by Mahatma Gandhi or by God himself."

Morarji Desai was very embarrassed, and I said to him, "If age is
an argument, then have you heard my remark? – 'Morarji Desai has
become senile. If he were a little bit younger he would understand
what I am saying. It needs intelligence, and he is senile. The more
senile he becomes, the more idiotic and stupid will be the ideas that
have a grip over his mind.'"

But strangely enough, Kaka Kalelkar, Morarji Desai, Vinoba
Bhave, Dada Dharmadhikari, Shankar Rao Deo – all great Gandhians
in India – used the same argument, that I was young. As if to be
young is to commit a crime, as if to be young is enough to be wrong,
and nothing else is needed.

I told Shankar Rao Deo, "How old was Jesus Christ when he was crucified? I am older than him – he was only thirty-three. According to your argument, all that he said should be just thrown away, it is just meaningless. What meaning can it have? A man who is just thirty-three, what authority can he have, so inexperienced?

"But," I said, "you may be willing to throw out Jesus Christ because you are not a Christian, so let me remind you how old Shankara, the greatest Hindu philosopher was. He was also thirty-three when he died. If age determines it, then Shankara should never be mentioned again. And Shankara has the greatest hold on the Hindu mind."

No, when it is in your favor – when the young are just following the old without having any skepticism – then their youth is not even mentioned. Their youth comes to be questioned only when they are skeptical, when they start raising doubts against the older people.

In ancient times it was impossible, because young people could not give equal weight to what they were saying; their experience was so small. Now the whole thing has changed, so much so that I can say that it has moved one-hundred-and-eighty degrees. Because of the educational systems, now experience is not the only way to know; in fact it is a very long way to know anything. By education you can know with a shortcut. What a man may be able to know in ninety years of his life, you can know within a year.

Whatever Bertrand Russell has written in a long life of almost one century, you can read within six months. It actually happened: Bertrand Russell's student, Ludwig Wittgenstein, a German, went through all of his books, which is not difficult. Bertrand Russell has written everything that occurred in his mind – he was one of the greatest intellects of any time – but he had to write all that in a long life.

Ludwig Wittgenstein was a young man. He went through all Bertrand Russell's books because Russell was going to be his teacher and he wanted to be absolutely acquainted with what went on in the mind of this man. The day he entered Russell's class he knew much more than Bertrand Russell. Bertrand Russell was ancient; Wittgenstein was very young, but he knew more, because he knew all that Bertrand Russell had written and much more that others had written, much that enemies of Bertrand Russell had written. And he found many fallacies and many loopholes in Bertrand Russell's writings.

Bertrand Russell was simply shocked, but he was an authentic man, an honest man. He accepted: "Ludwig Wittgenstein, although my student, knows far more than I know because he went by a shortcut and I had to go by a long route. He went by a shortcut, became acquainted with everything that I had written, and started arguing against me in such a way that only a tremendously experienced person could."

Bertrand Russell was so impressed in his few days' contact with Ludwig Wittgenstein that he said to Wittgenstein, "Don't waste your time, you have nothing to learn from me. You already know more."

Wittgenstein used to write a few notes in the class. Bertrand Russell just asked him, "I would like to see your notes." And when he saw those notes he said, "These notes are so significant that they should be published."

But Wittgenstein said, "I am not writing for publication, I was just noting down any idea that was coming to me. This book is very raw, it is not a book for publication."

Bertrand Russell said, "Publish it as it is, and I am going to write the introduction for it."

Those notes have been published and they proved revolutionary. They are just fragments, because they were not written as an essay or an article – just any ideas that came to him. But because the book, *Tractatus Logico-Philosophicus*, became so famous – it was only a tract, but it became so famous that no other book in philosophy is as famous in this century – and was so profound, it gave Wittgenstein an idea. He never wrote any books in a different fashion; it became his style just to write notes, fragments.

The fame of the book proved that when you write an essay your idea has to be spread all over the essay and it loses its intensity, its sharpness. It becomes more understandable but less penetrating. When it is just like a maxim, a bare, naked statement with no decorations around it, it simply hits deeper, although it will be understood by only very few people – people who have the capacity to see in the seed the whole tree, which is not yet existent but is only a potentiality.

A man can see in the seed the whole tree.

Wittgenstein's statements are just like seeds. You will have to figure out what potential they have. He does not give you any clue; he simply puts the seed in front of you and goes ahead putting down other seeds. He never tries to connect them; *you* will have to connect them. To read Wittgenstein is really an experience. To read anybody else is like having the food chewed for you and then eating it. With Wittgenstein, it seems he is simply placing the food in front of you: you have to chew it, you have to digest it. You have to find out what it means.

Ordinarily the philosopher tries to convince you of what he means. He tries to prevent you going astray from his meaning, and he gives you the whole package with all the details. But he leaves nothing for you, no homework for you. He is not helping your intelligence; he is, in fact, destroying you. If you start living on liquid food, soon you will be incapable of digesting solid food. The liquid food will destroy your capacity to digest the solid food.

But Bertrand Russell didn't say to Wittgenstein, "You are too young" – no. And that should be the attitude of a genuine thinker.

Education has brought in a new methodology. Just sitting in a university library, within days you can read all that Pythagoras took his whole life to collect; it is all available to you. So when a boy comes back from the university, trouble has arisen in the world. In the past it was always the father who was right, the grandfather was even more right. Now it is not so; it is now the young man who is right, because even if his father had been to university, that was thirty years ago, and in thirty years so much has changed.

When I entered the university to study psychology, my professor was an old man, well-studied, but all that he knew and had studied was half-a-century old. The names that he used to quote had been completely forgotten in the world of psychology. Who bothers about Woodworth? And I told him, "Woodworth? Are you mad or something? It was perfectly okay before the First World War, but two world wars have happened. Have you been asleep or what? – Woodworth is no longer an authority." But when my professor was at university Woodworth was the authority. I told him, "You should read Assagioli."

He said, "Assagioli? Who is this fellow?"

I said, "If you don't know Assagioli, resign! – because psychology has passed from Freud to Adler, to Jung, to Reich; it has come to Assagioli. Assagioli preaches psychosynthesis; Freud was teaching psychoanalysis, it is just the opposite." And I told him, "When I came to study psychology, I did not come here to study some rotten old stuff which is no longer relevant. You died with Woodworth! What are you doing here? You don't know the name of Assagioli? If you don't know about psychosynthesis you are out of date."

I told him, "You remind me of a madman who lives in front of my house. He comes to me early every morning when I am just taking tea, for the newspaper. I go on giving him any newspaper – one month old, two months old – and he takes it joyously and reads it happily. He never bothers about the date.

"I asked the madman, 'You are so interested in newspapers, but one thing is strange about it: you don't bother about the date.' The madman said, 'I am interested in news – who cares *when* it happened? And what does it matter that it happened last year or two years before? It happened, that is enough, and I enjoy it.'"

I told this old professor, "I will come to your house and sort out all the old stuff you are reading."

He said, "No, you should not come to my house, because the way you are talking, you will throw everything away. I was thinking about my reading room, because you will throw away all my books; they all belong to my student days."

I told him, "Then you will have to get up to date, otherwise sit in the class and I will start teaching. If you are not ready to get up to date, then why bother? *You* sit – at least you will be learning something. I don't see that I can learn anything from you. If Woodworth is the end of psychology to you, then…"

He said, "I will try my best." He was a nice man, and he accepted the fact that it was true; many professors would be benefited if they could accept that after they leave university they never read, they never go to the library. In fact I went to the library and checked: "How many professors come to the library?" And I was surprised that the librarian said, "Professors? The library is meant for the students – professors don't come."

I said, "This is something weird. Professors have to be acquainted every day with what is happening, because things are moving so fast, and they are stuck thirty years, forty years back."

In these years so much progress has happened in knowledge that you cannot compare these thirty years with the past three thousand years. What has not happened in three thousand years has happened in thirty years; and what has happened in three years has not happened in the past thirty years.

You can see the fact that now scientific discoveries are not published in book form, they are published in periodicals as papers, for the simple reason that by the time you finish the book it will be already out of date. The book will take time, perhaps a year, to write properly in the old format – giving all the notes, footnotes, appendix. But by that time somebody else may have already published papers which are far more profound than your book. So the scientist today immediately rushes to publish whatsoever he has found, in the smallest paper, in a periodical. One never knows what is going to happen tomorrow.

So now the younger man knows more than the older: the fresher your knowledge, the better. But it was not so in the past. It is not yet so in uneducated countries – for example in India where only two percent of the people are really well educated. They say eight percent of the people are educated; but six percent are "educated" because they can write their signature, nothing else. Even if we count those, then too ninety-two percent of the people in the villages are absolutely uneducated.

In the villages it is still the routine that the father knows; the son has to accept it – and the grandfather knows even more. The older a person is, the more respectable, because he is wiser. It is not strange that all the religions paint God as a very old, ancient man. Have you ever seen God painted as a young man in blue jeans? That will not suit him, it will look insulting, but really today that should be the case.

The way you have been painting God in the past was okay; at that time the older was the wiser – naturally you could not paint God as a young man. But now, the older is simply out of date; the younger, the more up-to-date, is more correct, closer to the truth. If you want God to be closer to the truth, put him in blue jeans. It will look a little odd because he has never been in blue jeans. He may feel a little difficulty, but what to do? Things have changed. But the mind goes on keeping the program somewhere deep inside.

My sannyasin has to be absolutely unorthodox. I will not say anti-orthodox, for the simple reason that if you are anti-orthodox... Perhaps in America I should not say anti-orthodox; here they say "ant-eye-orthodox"! I cannot say that, it is so ludicrous. "Sem-eye-automatic weapons"... These Yankees are doing strange things with a beautiful language. No, I will continue my own way.

I will not call my people anti-orthodox, because if you are *anti*, somehow you are still attached. It is as an enemy, not as a friend, but there is a relationship. It is not of love but of hate, and hate is a far more binding relationship than love.

Have you observed that love is very momentary? It comes and goes just like a breeze. It is here, and you feel so full of love toward someone that you cannot imagine that this love can ever disappear. In such moments people get romantic, start saying things which are only allowed for mad people or poets. But that moment is so overwhelming, they start saying, "I will love you forever!" And it is true – for the moment. They are not lying, that's what they feel in the moment: "If there are other lives I cannot conceive of loving anybody else than you."

Still the person is not lying, he is absolutely honest. He is so full of love that he feels this is how it is going to be, that life is going to be too short to fulfill this love, to share this love. But he is not aware that it is just a breeze which comes from one side, through one door, and moves on to the other side, to the other door, leaving you in the same state as you were before, again back on the earth.

Those wings had suddenly appeared, and you were flying high – "higher and higher, Osho, higher and higher." Those wings... Then you look all around and they are not there. Suddenly you feel lower and lower, lower and lower. You are not even on plain ground, you are falling into a ditch!

Love is momentary, a phase, but hate seems to be far stronger. You fall in love, you fall out of love. But once you fall in hate... It is rarely heard that a man has fallen out of hate. He is stuck, glued. Hate has some force; it keeps you glued to it. Enemies remain enemies for generations.

Neighbors are the worst enemies; where else can you find better enemies than your neighbors? Perhaps it was an afterthought of Jesus Christ's. First he said, "Love your enemies as yourself." Then later on he said, "Love your neighbors as yourself." That is a second thought, because neighbors are really the enemy. You don't have to go far away in search of the enemy, you find them just at your side.

The family that lived at the side of my house had been my family's enemy for generations. I was prohibited from going into their compound, into their garden, and I was not to play with their children as "They are our enemies."

I simply said, "They may be *your* enemies. I have not even been friends of theirs, how can I be their enemy? At least first let me get acquainted."

My father said, "You should not argue about it. We have been fighting in the courts, we have been fighting physically and this has gone on so long, that this enmity is something that has become almost sacred."

I said, "I am no longer a part of it. I am going to play with their children and I am going into their garden, because they have more beautiful mangos than you have. They have such a beautiful well."

There is a special type of well that is made in India. I don't know whether it is made in any other country or not. It is an old type. On one side you can draw water by bucket with a rope, but on the other side it has steps. It is called a *bawdi*. So if by chance you don't have a bucket and a rope, you can go down by the steps and get water.

Particularly in places by the side of the road in a jungle, they will make a *bawdi*, not a well, because sometimes a traveler may be thirsty but may not have the means to reach the water, so both possibilities are made available to him. If he can pull the water out, that is best, that is preferable. The alternative is only for an emergency, because people going close to the water may dirty it, may start drinking just with their hands. So to go down is not encouraged very much. But I enjoyed this way because then I could have a good bath in our neighbor's well.

I said to my father, "Your well is simply a well, and they have a *bawdi*. You take care of your enmity; your forefathers have taken care of it – I am not interested in it. They have nice children and they are good people, why should I be inimical to them? We don't know in what circumstances your forefathers and their forefathers became enemies. And what has that to do with us? *We* have never fought. And whenever I have gone there they have always welcomed me joyously, for the simple reason that they could not believe it: 'It has not happened for centuries between the two families.'" I was the first to break the barrier.

The neighbors were very happy; they said, "We wanted to break the barrier, but who would take the initiative? They would seem weak."

I said, "I am not coming to you out of any weakness. I cannot understand what kind of intelligence you and my family have. You don't even know the names of the people who started this fight." Neither my father knew, nor they knew who was the first. "And you go on fighting. It has become almost a religion to you.

"I am not coming out of any weakness, I am coming from strength. I have come to tell you that it is sheer stupidity to prolong this hatred so long. Nobody prolongs love so long, so why hate? And moreover I am not interested in you, I am interested in the mangos, in your *bawdi*; and I *have* to enter this compound. Whether you are enemies or friends is your business."

I told my father, "Nobody can prevent me from going there. And they have received me, welcomed me, and said, 'We always wanted to break this thing, but who would take the initiative?' I think anybody who has more intelligence should take the initiative, the stupid will lag behind."

Slowly, slowly, because my family could not force me... They knew the more they forced me, the more I would be there. I told my father, "If you insist too much I will start sleeping there, I will start eating there; they have offered me food."

He said, "Okay, I won't insist on anything, but don't eat anything offered by them. They are enemies, they can poison you."

I said, "Forget all about it. They are nice people. I know them more than you do or your forefathers did. I am going there every day, they are so nice. They have not even prevented me from jumping in their well, just for the simple reason that this is the first person from the other family to enter their compound: 'Let him have a bath in the *bawdi*. Don't prevent him – it doesn't look good. After so many generations, the first person has entered, has dared to.'

"Don't be worried about me being poisoned because I have already eaten things from them. I have not told you because I knew this is what you would say. So first I had to eat and see that there was no poison, and there was nobody interested in poisoning anybody. They don't prevent me from taking their mangos and their other fruits, simply for the reason that this is the first person from our family who has come into their compound. I am going to invite their children into our compound, into our garden, and I would expect you to be at least gentlemanly."

And when I started bringing their children, of course my family was nice to them. How can you be against small children who have never done anything, who have just come into the world?

But hate has a very long life; love has a very short life. Perhaps that's the way things are. There are so many roses in the morning,

but by the evening their petals have started falling, they are disappearing. But the rock? It was there in the morning, it will be there in
the evening, it will be there again the next morning. Many roses will
come and go and the rock will remain. Hate is something rocky.
Love is something like a flower.

So I will not say, then, that my people have to be anti-orthodox,
anti-traditional, anti-conventional. No, they have to be unorthodox,
unconventional, untraditional. Unorthodox means you are not
related to orthodoxy in any way, positive or negative. You are indif-
ferent, you couldn't care less. You are not for, you are not against,
you are simply not interested – because "for" and "against" are just
different sides of your interest.

So an orthodox Rajneeshee will be unorthodox in every possible
way. His life will be a life of continuous rebellion. Let me repeat: continuous rebellion.

Rebellion is a continuum.

It is something like a river that goes on flowing. It is not like a
water tank. That's the difference between revolution and rebellion.
Revolution is like a water tank: the French revolution, the Russian
revolution, the Chinese revolution. Just look at what happened. The
Russian revolution happened, but it is not a continuum. It happened
in 1917, then what happened to it? It also died in 1917. Since then
there has been no revolution in Russia.

Since then revolution has become their orthodoxy, since then revolution has become their tradition, since then revolution has become
their status quo. It is not flowing, it is not moving: it is stuck at 1917.
They pay respect to that date every year. They pay homage to the
great revolution that happened in 1917. What kind of revolutionaries
are these, who look backward? Even God is not so much of a reac-
tionary as the Soviet Communist is today.

You can see it clearly: God has not given you two eyes at the
back of your head. A right God – right according to all the ortho-
doxies – should have really given you eyes behind your head, not in
front, because what use are your eyes in front? You have to see
backward, not forward.

It happened in India…

A man was going from Jabalpur to Nagpur with his friend on a
motorbike. It was cold and the winds were blowing against them. So

the man driving the bike had an idea: he turned his coat back-to-front because the winds were so cold, and that way was more protective. But they had an accident, perhaps because of that coat...

Somebody was coming from the opposite direction: a *sardarji*, a Sikh driver. Ninety percent of drivers in India are Sikh *sardar* drivers; I don't know why they have chosen that profession. Seeing a man sitting on a bike backward, in the night, the *sardar* lost his nerve. He could not hold his steering wheel properly and there was an accident. That was not the end of the whole thing, there is still something more – this is just the beginning!

The *sardar* got out to see what happened. He found this motorcyclist and thought, "My God! It seems his head has gone round the other way in the accident." *Sardars* are *sardars*: he forcibly turned the man's head according to the direction of the coat. The man was then still alive, but now no longer. He tried to somehow get out of the hands of the *sardar*, but you can't get out of the hands of a *sardar*. *Sardar's* are strong people and absolute idiots – and he wouldn't listen to the motorcyclist. He said to him, "Keep quiet!" The *sardar* turned the man's head, and he was quiet forever.

I reached there at that point – I was coming from Nagpur – and I saw what had happened. I asked the *sardar*, "What is the matter, *sardarji*?"

He said, "Strange! First, this man was riding backward. That created the accident, because I completely lost my senses; it happened just in a single moment. And then when I got out of my truck to help the people, I saw one man unconscious and this other man... His head must have been turned around."

I went to see. I said, "*Sardarji*, you have killed the man! It was not his head but his coat that was turned around. And it is simple: it is so windy and the wind is blowing in this direction. This poor man must have turned his coat around."

The *sardar* said, "Is that so? Then I should have changed the coat rather than change the direction of his head, because he was alive and I told him to shut up! Then I tried to tell him, 'Now you can open your mouth, you can speak. Say what you want, where I should take you in my truck; I can take you. Forgive me that I told you to shut up' – but he did not speak at all."

I said, "Now he is dead. Don't bother him anymore! Don't tell any of this story to anyone; otherwise you will be caught, because you have done two things: the accident, and the greater accident that you turned his head around."

God has given you eyes to look forward. And the people who are for tradition or against tradition are always looking backward.

J. Krishnamurti is anti-orthodox, anti-traditional, anti-conventional. That's where my differences with him are: I am unorthodox, untraditional, unconventional. So an "orthodox Rajneeshee" – and remember, whenever you write "orthodox Rajneeshee," put it in inverted commas because it is a contradiction in terms – will be a continuous rebellion. Not just a revolution that happens once and is finished: then it itself becomes a tradition.

Jesus was a revolutionary, but Christianity is not. Buddha was a revolutionary, but Buddhism is not, because the revolution happened twenty-five centuries ago. We have left it far behind. Now the Christian is as orthodox as the Jews who crucified Jesus. If Jesus comes again he is sure to be crucified by the Vatican. This time, of course, the scene will not be in Jerusalem, the scene will be in the Vatican, but a crucifixion is certain.

It happened...

I was staying with a Christian family in Hyderabad. The whole day I was engaged in meetings and interviews. In the night when I was just going to sleep, my friend, who was much older than me, said to me, "The whole day I could not find you and I did not want to disturb your appointments, but I have a problem. Forgive me; it is late at night and you are going to rest, but I have to tell you.

"My young son was a Jesus freak. Nobody took it seriously, and there was nothing wrong in it, that he was continually reading the Bible and quoting the Bible. We thought that it was just a phase and it would go, but unfortunately now the Jesus freak is no longer a Jesus freak, he has become Jesus Christ!

"For two months now we have been really concerned. Up to being a Jesus freak it was okay: you read Jesus' sayings – we are Christians – you worship Jesus... That too is okay, although it was getting a little weird because twenty-four hours a day of "Jesus, Jesus..." We are also Christians; on Sunday we go to church for one hour, and that's enough. Jesus is satisfied with one hour every Sunday. You don't have to devote your whole life to him; there are other things also to be done. And we cannot do miracles – turn stones into bread, water into wine, so we have to earn our bread and do other things. One hour is enough, all that we can devote.

"But still we tolerated it, thinking that this phase would pass, it was just the foolishness of a young man who had become obsessed with an idea. But now it is not a phase: he has become Jesus Christ. Now he is no longer quoting Jesus Christ, he simply speaks on his own authority. Now he has become a laughingstock.

"He is standing on the crossroads declaring that he is Jesus Christ, and people laugh and urchins throw stones. Now we are really concerned and sad. His whole career is finished, and you cannot make a career out of being Jesus Christ. Everybody knows what happened to Jesus! – even *he* was not able to make a career out of it, so how can my son make a career out of it? Who is going to give this man a job? He is a postgraduate, a first-class post-graduate; he could get a good job, but for Jesus Christ. Even if he is a first class, the moment anybody hears that he thinks he is Jesus Christ, they will say, 'It will be difficult, because we need an assistant manager, and Jesus Christ as assistant manager? The place is not worthy of him!' So what to do?"

I said, "Tomorrow morning I will have to talk with Jesus Christ – what else to do? Let me meet him."

I knew the young man, I had stayed with the family before. And I knew that he was a freak, but he had never bothered me, although I was staying in the family. He knew that if he was a freak, then I was a double freak! So once and for all I had settled it: "Remember, with me this Bible and this Jesus Christ won't do; you better torture others. Moreover, I am a guest in your house, behave like a host." So he had understood it perfectly well, but that was when he was only a freak – now he was Jesus Christ.

I said to his father, "First let me be acquainted with the situation." So the next morning, rather than his father bringing him to me, I went into his room and I said, "Hello, Jesus Christ."

He said, "You said 'Jesus Christ!'"

I said. "Yes."

He said, "But nobody believes me – not my father, not my mother, even my friends have left me. Since I became Jesus Christ I don't have any friends."

I said, "You can rely upon me. I don't like freaks, but Jesus

Christ... It is a great idea! Come with me. Now we can talk, now we are in the same boat."

He said, "What do you mean?"

I said, "Just come. We *are* in the same boat; you will understand what I mean." I tried in many ways, but he was very defensive and very alert that maybe his father was behind me, working through me and trying to persuade him to come down and just be a Jesus freak: "Now, this is too much. This is the twentieth century, and it will be difficult... Even in Jesus' time is was very difficult, this time it is going to be more difficult."

He wouldn't listen to anything. Then his father came, and I said to his father, "I think he *is* Jesus Christ. Now what he needs is crucifixion."

The young man said, "What!"

I said, "Without crucifixion you won't come to your senses."

He said, "Crucifixion!"

The father also was shocked when I said he needed crucifixion, but I said, "Make arrangements."

And the young man said, "Are you serious?"

I said, "I am always serious; and I told you that if you are a Jesus freak, I am double that. If you are Jesus Christ, I am double that too. I will see that you are crucified; and I am going to remain here until the resurrection."

He just went to his father and he said, "Forgive me, I am just a Jesus freak. I don't want to be crucified because I don't think I will be able to resurrect. That is too much trouble."

For two thousand years Christians have been looking backward; for two thousand five hundred years Buddhists have been looking backward. If you look around the world you will see everybody's eyes are turned backward; and do you know, we are always moving forward. Our legs are going forward and our eyes are focused backward.

Even for a man like J. Krishnamurti it makes no difference: your eyes still remain focused backward. Now you are an enemy; first you were a friend. But to me it makes no difference because your eyes are still looking backward.

Hence I prefer the word *rebellion* – because revolutions have happened but they have always become static, they freeze too quickly. A new orthodoxy is created, a new convention is created: a new God, a new heaven, new hell – everything is new, but soon it starts becoming old.

Now sixty years have passed since the Russian revolution; more than sixty years, now it is a sixty-year-old tradition. Marx, Engels and Lenin are their trinity; *Das Kapital* is their Bible, their Koran, their Gita.

And strangely this similarity is such that one cannot believe it. Neither does the Mohammedan read the Koran: he worships it but does not read it. Who has the time to read the Koran? And it is good in a way that he does not read it, because if he reads it he won't worship it because there is nothing in it worth worshipping.

You can either worship it or you can understand it. Once you understand it, it is finished; there is nothing much in it to understand. So the religious priesthood is not interested in your understanding the Koran, the Bible, the Gita, no: they are interested that you go on worshipping them.

This is fossilized revolution. Yes, those words spoken by Jesus had fire in them. They were words on fire. But do you think you will find fire in the Bible? It would have burned the Bible long ago.

In the Bible you will find a lock of hair your mother has been keeping from the days when your father used to love her and she had cut off a few of his hairs. They are in the Bible – where else to keep them? The Bible is the safest place; even a thief is not going to steal it.

You will find strange things in Bibles. Your daughter or your sister may be keeping her love letters in the Bible, because that is the best place: neither your father opens it, nor your mother opens it; nobody ever opens it. Phone numbers which are very important and secret and which you don't want everybody to know – keep them in the Bible. The Bible is a great safe deposit with no lock. It goes on gathering dust. You can write your name on any Bible just with your finger, because there will be enough dust – no need for any ink or any color.

These are revolutions: once there was fire but now there are only ashes left. My sannyasin has not to look backward. He has not to think of a revolution that happened in the past. No, he has to live the revolution every day. And his revolution is never going to stop. That's why I call it rebellion, just to make the distinction. His rebellion is something alive. It is not an incident in history, it is an explosion in his being. It has nothing to do with time; it has something to do with his inner space. And then it is a continuity: he lives it, he breathes it, it is his heartbeat.

My sannyasin can never become orthodox: how can a constant rebellion be converted into an orthodoxy? That's why you will find my statements so contradictory. The reason is that I have never read any of my books, so I don't know what is in them. It helps me immensely, because then I don't have to bother about whether I am contradicting myself by changing, saying something else. It keeps me free. If you ask me, then whatsoever I am saying right now is the truth. Tomorrow will take care of itself. I cannot guarantee that this will be the truth for tomorrow too, because tomorrow... The whole universe is in a continuous flux.

I am not giving you dead rocks. I am offering you living flowers. What it will be like tomorrow neither I nor anyone else can say. Only tomorrow will bring the revelation.

I have been constantly inconsistent so that you will never be able to make a dogma out of me. You will simply go nuts if you try. I am leaving something really terrible for scholars. They will not be able to make any sense out of it. They will go nuts; and they deserve it, they should go nuts. But nobody can create an orthodoxy out of me, it is impossible.

If with Christianity it is possible, then of course Jesus is responsible. His words may have been fiery but they were too consistent; it was too easy to make a dogma out of them. He was not careful enough. He made such simple statements that anybody could make a catechism out of them.

From my words you can get burned, but you will not be able to find any kind of theology, dogmatism. You can find a way to live but not a dogma to preach. You can find a rebellious quality to be imbibed, but you will not find a revolutionary theme to be organized.

My words are not only on fire. I am putting gunpowder also here and there, which will go on exploding for centuries. I am putting more than needed – I never take any chances. Almost every sentence is going to create trouble for anybody who wants to organize a religion around me.

Yes, you can have a loose community, a commune. Remember the word *loose*: everybody independent, everybody free to live his own way, to interpret me in his own way, to find whatsoever he wants to find. He can find the way he wants to live – and everybody unto himself.

There is no need for somebody to decide what my religion is. I am leaving it open-ended. You can work out a definition for yourself, but it is only for yourself; and that too you will have to continuously change. As you understand me more and more, you will have to change it. You cannot go on holding it like a dead thing in your hand. You will have to change it, and it will go on changing you simultaneously.

A great master, Nan-in, was on his deathbed. He is one of those people who I can say was religious, really religious. His whole life is full of incidents, anecdotes, stories, which give a clear indication of a man of tremendous insight.

He was dying. He had told his disciples, "I would not like my death to be mourned, because it is not death, so you will be unnecessarily wasting your tears and crying and weeping. I will be laughing from the other shore, because I will see: 'These fools! The whole of my life I have wasted, and they have not understood a simple thing.'

"I would like you to dance and sing and laugh and rejoice, because death is *not* death. I am going, leaving this house because it is no longer useful. This body is more of a trouble now than a convenience; I am just changing it. So there is no need to mourn. You should be happy that your master is going into a new life."

They listened to whatever he said, but their faces were showing that they were all ready to burst into tears. They were sad – and who would not be sad when a man like Nan-in leaves the world? But Nan-in had made arrangements. He said, "A few things to be remembered…"

In the East it is a tradition, perhaps in the West also, that before you burn or bury a body you bathe the body and put new clothes on it. I know the reason in the East is that he is going on a faraway journey; maybe there will be a chance to have a bath, or maybe not. And certainly he will need new clothes, so new clothes are given, a bath is given. This is just a way to say good-bye from this shore: "From now onward we cannot help, take care of yourself."

Nan-in said, "Don't give me a bath because I have just taken one. And I don't like baths in such a cold winter; I don't want another bath even if I am dead. I have taken one, which was necessary. I have done it myself because I was concerned that if you give me a bath I won't know how much water you pour in, how cold, and what else you do. I have taken my bath, so that ritual has not to be done.

"And don't change my clothes. You see, I have already changed them, because I don't like clothes which don't fit, which are too loose or too tight. You know I am fussy about that, so I have my clothes ready – you can see they are new." And they saw that he had taken a bath and he did have a new robe.

Nan-in said, "So this is my will: these two things are not to be done, but anything else you want to do, do. Don't weep, don't cry, don't mourn. That would not be the right kind of good-bye for me" And he died.

Although he had said, "Don't cry" – what to do? Tears are not in your hands to stop. To lose such a man, such a tremendously alive man, disappearing into who knows what: "And how much he has given! Now toward whom are we going to look? Questions will be torturing us, doubts will be arising and who is going to say, 'Don't be worried, continue: you are on the right track and the goal is not far away.' His voice was enough to bring courage again, strength again. Now who is going to help?"

They were crying and they were weeping, but they could not manage to do it for long. People like Nan-in are really creative geniuses. When his body was put on the funeral pyre they all started laughing in spite of themselves; tears were coming to their eyes. It was a strange situation: that man had hidden in his clothes many fireworks and small firecrackers!

That's why he had prevented them from changing his clothes, that's why he had taken his bath. His dress was specially made with many pockets inside where he was hiding almost a three-hour celebration. The people were laughing and crying, and the firecrackers were bursting and fireworks were going off – colorful, beautiful, because in Japan they make the best. Nothing can be compared with Japanese firecrackers, they make them in such artful ways.

What Nan-in was continually telling these people appeared in the sky, in writing: "Beware!" A firecracker would go up and burst into small, flower – like pieces and they all would fall together and make the word *beware*.

His disciples were looking at the sky and they completely forgot that it was a funeral; it became a beautiful exhibition of fireworks!

Only as the fire died out and the body was consumed by the fire did they realize that that man had been doing the same thing his whole life. He had even made arrangements before dying so that after death also his work would continue in the same way, uninterrupted. Death made no difference: Nan-in was still doing the same thing.

In the same way, I am putting enough fire, enough explosives in each of my words to go on exploding for centuries.

Nobody can be an "orthodox Rajneeshee" unless you change the whole meaning of "orthodox Rajneeshee" to be according to me, as I described to you: if by "orthodox Rajneeshee" you can mean one who is untraditional, unconventional, unorthodox; rebellious as a continuity, with rebellion as his life; with no tight, regimented, bureaucratic, hierarchical organization, but just an open commune of friends who are only agreed upon one thing – that they love this crazy man.

On everything else they can disagree. Their whole orthodoxy is confined to only one thing: they love this crazy man.

CHAPTER 9

A Conspiracy of the Priests to Manipulate Your Mind

Osho,
What do you have to say about the law of karma?

I have very little to say about it – but it will still take two and a half hours!

The law of karma is, in the first place, not a law. That word gives it an aroma as if it is something scientific, like the law of gravitation. It is merely a hope, not a law at all.

It has been hoped for centuries that if you do good you will attain to good results. It is a human hope in an existence which is absolutely neutral. If you look at nature, there *are* laws – the whole of science is nothing but discovery of those laws – but science has not come even close to detecting anything like the law of karma. Yes, it is certain that any action is going to bring certain reactions, but the law of karma is hoping for much more.

If you simply say any action is bound to produce some reactions, it is possible to have scientific support for it. But man is hoping for much more. He is asking that a good action inevitably brings a good consequence with it, and the same with a bad action.

Now, there are many things implied in this.

First, what is good? Each society defines good according to itself: what is good to a Jew is not good to a Jaina; what is good to a Christian is not good to a Confucian. Not only that, what is good in one culture is bad in another culture. A law has to be universal. For example, if you heat water to one hundred degrees centigrade, it will evaporate – in Tibet, in Russia, in America, even in Oregon. In Oregon it will be a little puzzled, but all the same at one hundred degrees water will evaporate.

A law has to be universal if it is a scientific law. If it is a law created by people themselves, by creating a constitution, a legal system, then it is nothing to do with science and nothing to do with existence. Then it is applicable only within the society that creates it. It is arbitrary, artificial. You can change it – and laws do go on changing. Something that was legal yesterday is illegal today; what is illegal today may become legal tomorrow. These are man-made laws.

Certainly the law of karma is neither a scientific law nor part of any legal system. Then what kind of law is it? It is a hope. A man wandering in immense darkness, groping his way, clings to anything that gives a little hope, a little light – because what you observe in life itself is something totally different from the law of karma. A man who is a well-known criminal may succeed and become the president, the prime minister; or vice versa: he was not a criminal before, but when he becomes the president or prime minister of a country he becomes a criminal.

I have thought about Lord Acton's famous statement from every possible angle, and I have found it always gives some new insight. Acton says: "Power corrupts, and absolute power corrupts absolutely." I don't think so, because I don't see it happening the way Lord Acton is saying. But Lord Acton was speaking from his whole life's experience; he was a politician himself, and what he was saying was not unfounded.

Still, I dare to disagree with him, because my understanding is that power certainly corrupts, but it corrupts only a person who was potentially corruptible. He may not have been known as corrupted before because he had no opportunity, he had no power. But power itself cannot corrupt a man who has no potential for corruptibility. So it is not the *power* that is corrupting the man; in fact the power is simply revealing the man to you. The power is making actual what was only potential; it is exposing the person to you and to himself.

If you look in a mirror and you see an ugly face, are you going to say that the mirror corrupts? The poor mirror simply reflects. If you have an ugly face what can the mirror do about it?

I have heard about a mad woman who, whenever she came across a mirror would immediately destroy it. She was ugly, but her belief was that mirrors were the reason for her ugliness. If there were no mirrors she would not be ugly. Perfect logic! In a certain way she is not being absolutely illogical. If she were alone on the earth – no mirror, no eyes, because eyes are also mirrors – do you think she would be ugly? Alone on the earth without any mirrors, without any eyes to mirror her, she would be just herself: neither beautiful nor ugly. But she would just be the same, the only change would be that now she could not see her reflection. Nothing has changed, only the reflectors have been removed.

The same is true about Lord Acton's famous dictum, "Power corrupts" – it *seems* so. I would like to say that power *mirrors*. If you are potentially ready to be corrupted, power gives you the chance. And if you have an absolute potential – like an Adolf Hitler, a Joseph Stalin, a Mussolini – then what can power do about it?

Power is simply available to you. You can do much with it. If you are a corruptible person you will do what you always wanted to do but did not have the power to do. But if you are not potentially corruptible, then it is impossible for power to corrupt you. You will use the power, but it will not be corruption, it will be creation. It will not be destructive; it will be a blessing to people. And if you have the potential of being a blessing to people, then absolute power will be an absolute blessing in the world.

But man's life has many strange things in it. Only the potentially corruptible person moves toward power. The potentially good person has no desire for power. The will-to-power is the need of a corrupted being, because he knows that without power he will not be able to do what he wants to do.

Adolf Hitler first wanted to be an architect, but all the schools of architecture refused him because he had no potential as an architect. He could not even draw a straight line. He wanted to become an artist – if not an architect, then an artist – but no school would accept him. If the school of architecture was not going to accept him, then... Art, particularly painting, needs an even greater caliber, and he had no talent for art. Disappointed everywhere, rejected from everywhere, he started moving toward power.

Adolf Hitler's will-to-power was really strong. A man who was not able to become an architect or a painter became so powerful that the whole destiny of humanity was in his hands. But you will be surprised to know that the first thing that he did after he became powerful, absolutely powerful, was to make architectural designs for buildings. He made many ugly structures and the government had to build them because, although no architect was ready to accept that those designs were worth even a second look, if they were coming from Adolf Hitler you could not reject them. Their rejection would mean your death, because that was the only language he knew: either you are with me or you are no more.

It is one of the blessings of the Second World War that all Adolf Hitler's great buildings were destroyed; otherwise he would have left those ugly structures behind. But his designs have been found, and they are enough proof that this man simply had no qualities to conceive buildings.

The moment Adolf Hitler became powerful, in his spare moments he was painting; and of course, then, everybody had to appreciate his paintings. None of his paintings were worth calling a painting; they were just a waste of canvas and color, without any significance. Not only that, they were ugly, nauseating. If you had kept his painting in your bedroom, in the night you would have suffered nightmares.

Power brings into actuality what is hidden in you. But strangely, the good man has no need to be powerful, because good can manifest without power. There is no need for good to have power; it has its own intrinsic power. Evil needs some outside power to support it.

Kahlil Gibran has written a beautiful story. This single man has written so many beautiful stories that there seems to be no comparison to him in the whole history of man. This story is a very small, and that is where Kahlil Gibran's beauty is. He does not write big stories that can be made into films; his stories are only of a few lines, but they penetrate to the very depths of man.

The story is:

God created the world, and he created everything else that was needed. He looked around and he felt that two things were missing: beauty and ugliness. So the last things he created were beauty and ugliness. Naturally, he gave beauty, beautiful clothes and to ugliness, ugly clothes; and he dropped them from heaven to come to the earth.

It is a long journey, and by the time they reached the earth they were feeling tired and dusty, so the first thing they decided to do was to take a bath. It was early morning, the sun was just rising, and they went to a lake, dropped their clothes on the bank and both jumped in. It was really refreshing and cool, and they enjoyed it.

Beauty went swimming far into the lake, and when she looked back, she was surprised; ugliness was missing. She came back and she found that her clothes were missing too. Then beauty understood what had happened: ugliness has taken her clothes and run away.

The story ends: since then ugliness is hidden in the clothes of beauty, and beauty is compulsorily wearing the clothes of ugliness. Beauty is running after ugliness, searching for her, but she has not yet been able to find her.

It is a beautiful story. Ugliness needs something to hide itself behind, to help it pretend: to have a false mask. Beauty had not thought about it at all; the idea had not even occurred to her, that it was possible that ugliness would steal her clothes and run away.

The man who has a heart throbbing with goodness, with blessings, feels no need to be the president or the prime minister. He has no time to waste in this ugly game of power politics. He has enough energy. Good brings energy with itself. He will create music, he will compose poetry, he will sculpt beauty in marble; he will do something for which power is not needed. All that is needed is already provided for him. That's the beauty of good, that it is intrinsically powerful.

Let it be very clearly understood: you can be certain that anything that needs power from outside is not good. It is something intrinsically impotent; it will live on borrowed life. So in life this strange situation happens: bad people reach good positions, become respectable or honored, not only in their time but throughout history. It is full of their names.

In history you will not find people like Gautam Buddha, Mahavira, Kanad, Gautam, Lao Tzu, Chuang Tzu, Lieh Tzu, even in the footnotes. And Alexander the Great, Genghis Khan, Tamerlane, Nadirshah, Napoleon Bonaparte, Adolf Hitler, make up the major portion of history. In fact, we have to write the whole of history again because all these people have to be completely erased. Even the memory of them should not be carried on, because even their memory may have evil effects on people.

A better humanity will not give these names even a place in the footnotes; there is no need. They were nightmares; it is better they are completely forgotten so they don't follow you like shadows. We have to discover people who have lived on this earth and made it in every way beautiful; shared their joy, their dance, their music, shared their ecstasies – but lived anonymously. People have completely forgotten even their names.

People don't have any idea how many religious people have lived on this earth and are not known. The reason that you know those few names that *are* known, is not simply that they were religious – there are some extra reasons. Just think: if Jesus hadn't been crucified, would you have ever heard his name? So it is not Jesus – not his qualities, not his goodness – but crucifixion which makes him a historical figure.

You know of Gautam the Buddha, not because he was an enlightened man but because he was the son of a very great king. And when the son of such a great king renounces his kingdom, of course the whole country far and wide buzzes with his name. It is not because he is religious but because he has renounced such a big kingdom – the same kingdom that you have been aspiring to and dreaming of perhaps for many lives. This man has some guts: he just drops the whole kingdom without ever looking back.

That's why you remember Gautam Buddha. Somewhere they have to mention his name because he was a king who renounced his kingdom. If he had been a poor man's son then nobody would have even heard about him. And there have been many whose names are not known at all. Even while they were alive only a few people came to feel that they had a different kind of presence. Goodness has its own intrinsic power, and it has its own benefit, blessing. It is not somewhere else in some other life: if you do good now, you will get paid for it in your other life. That is a strange kind of law; and that's what the law of karma is.

If you are living a poor, miserable, suffering life, the law of karma says it is because in a past life you committed evil acts – this is the result of them. If somebody is enjoying good health, money, power, all the joys of life, you need not be jealous of him: he has done good deeds in a past life and now he is reaping the crop. He has sown the seeds in his past life.

But why so much distance between sowing the seeds and reaping the crop? Is it that always in one life you do good or bad, and in another life the result comes? To me there seems to be some conspiracy in it. It is not a law, it is a conspiracy, because the priest cannot manage to explain why somebody is rich when everybody knows that what he is doing is evil – and still he goes on becoming richer. And we know that somebody is good, but he is starving. So what good is good?

Now, the priesthood is in a difficulty to explain this situation which is occurring everywhere. Good people will be found in every corner of the earth, poor, starving, suffering. Bad people will be successful. The cunning – who are ready to cut anybody's throat, who have cut many people's throats, who have been stepping on people's heads toward power and riches, who have used people as if they were things – have all that should really belong to the good people.

How is the priest going to explain it away? He has found a way: the law of karma. He cannot explain it herenow so he shifts the whole scene. He makes death come in between your actions and their results; the results will be after death, in the next life. But why? You put your hand in the fire and you will be burned in the next life? If you put your hand in the fire now, you will be burned now.

So, take any priest, any monk, anybody coming from the East talking about the law of karma to the fireplace. Tell him, "Put your hand in the fire so we can see whether the law of karma works herenow. Or does it take so much time that it is necessary for death to happen first, and then the result will follow? Action – death – result? Death has to intervene absolutely?" I know he will not be ready to put his arm into the fire.

That's why I said I don't have much to say about the law of karma, only very little, just two words: *boo boo*.

Now I will have to explain to you – it is an Oregonian story...

If I am not mistaken, Senator Fatfield had gone to visit his constituency. The particular place that he was visiting was a reservation for Red Indians. He used to go there only once in five years, just when the election was coming closer. The Red Indians had become perfectly aware that he only came once every five years, promises great things and then disappears – and the things never happen.

Again he appeared after five years, and again the same game. Red Indians are simple people... Their chief gathered them all into one place that used to serve as their common meeting place. Senator Fatfield started the same promises: "Forgive me for last time. There were so many difficulties, so many problems, a financial depression, and so many wars, that I could not manage to make the bridge over the river, the road to your reservation, or good houses for you."

And each time he said something – "a bridge" – they would say, "*Boo boo!*" and they would rejoice and almost start dancing. Fatfield was feeling very good, seeing how they appreciate him. They would clap and shout and scream, "*Boo boo!*" and that gave him more incentive and more inspiration.

He gave free rein to his imagination: "I will make a hospital, a college, a university..." When you are simply going to promise something and never fulfill it, it does not matter what you promise; you can promise paradise, you can promise anything. And that is what he did; "Within five years you will see this place will be a paradise on earth" – and they all shouted, "*Boo boo!*"

Senator Fatfield was very happy, so happy that he said to the chief, "I would like to go around the reservation to see if anything else is needed."

The chief said, "That is okay; just one thing. We Red Indians are absolutely childlike: we use the whole field like it is an open toilet. So if you are going around – I have no objection – just be careful not to step in the *boo boo*."

Now Fatfield understood the meaning of *boo boo*, but it was too late.

The law of karma is nothing but *boo boo*. And you understand the meaning now, so there is no problem.

To me, certainly each action has its result, but not somewhere far away in a future life. An action and a result are continuous, they are part of one process. Do you think sowing the seed and reaping the crop are separate? It is one process. What begins in sowing the seed, grows, and one day that one seed has become thousands of seeds. That's what you call your crop. It is the same seed which has exploded into thousands of seeds. No death is intervening, no afterlife is needed; it is a continuum.

So the one thing to be remembered is, yes, in my vision of life every action is bound to have some consequences, but they will not be somewhere else, you will have them here and now. Most probably you will get them almost simultaneously. When you are kind to someone, don't you feel a certain joy? A certain peace? A certain meaningfulness? Don't you feel that you are contented with what you have done? There is a kind of deep satisfaction. Have you ever felt that same thing when you are angry, when you are boiling with anger, when you hurt somebody, when you are mad with rage? Have you ever felt contentment or anything similar to it? Have you ever felt a peace, a silence descending in you? No, it is impossible.

You will certainly feel something, but it will be a sadness that you again acted like a fool, that again you have done the same stupid thing that you decided again and again not to do. You will feel a tremendous unworthiness in yourself. You will feel that you are not a man but a machine, because you don't respond, you react. A man may have done something, and you reacted. That man had the key in his hands, and you just danced according to his desire; he had power over you. When somebody abuses you and you start fighting, what does it mean? It means that you don't have any capacity not to react.

Gurdjieff's father was dying. His last words to Gurdjieff were immensely significant: perhaps no father has ever advised a son with such a great insight. Gurdjieff was only nine years old, so his father said, "I know you may not be able to understand right now what I am saying, but I have no more time, I have to say it now. You have time – just remember the words. Whenever you have enough maturity to understand what these words mean, then act on them. But don't forget. Remember, it is a simple sentence."

He told Gurdjieff to repeat the sentence three times, so he could die peacefully. And he said, "Forgive me because I am not leaving any inheritance to you except this sentence." And what was the sentence? – a very simple one. Remember, if somebody creates anger in you, tell the person you will come back after twenty-four hours to answer him. For twenty-four hours, wait; and after twenty-four hours, whatever comes to you, go and do."

Strange advice, but not strange if you understand it. This simple advice changed Gurdjieff's whole life. This single sentence made a man like George Gurdjieff – and that kind of man is created only after centuries.

But the old man must have been a man of great insight. He left nothing else; he said to his son, "Now you will have to look after yourself. Your mother is dead, I am dying. You will have to earn your bread. You will have to learn things on your own." A nine-year-old child...

But this became a great opportunity for Gurdjieff because he started moving around with nomads. Gurdjieff was born near the Caucasus in the Soviet Union; still there are nomads, wandering tribes. Even sixty years of Communist torture has not been able to settle those nomads, because they consider this to be man's birthright, and perhaps they are right.

Nomads all over the world believe that it is the woman who has created the house. Man has *made* it, but it is the woman who has tethered the man to the house; otherwise, man is basically a wanderer, he would have liked to move. A tent was enough; a tent, a horse, a bullock cart – that's enough. And who bothers to live in the same place year after year? The nomads go on moving – a few days here, a few days there.

This nine-year-old child, having nothing else to do, joined a nomad group. Then he started moving from one group to another. He learned many nomadic languages, he learned many nomadic arts. He learned many exercises which are not available to civilized people any more, but nomads need them.

For example: it may be very cold and the snow is falling, and to live in a tent... Nomads know certain exercises of breathing that change the rhythm of the breath, the temperature of your body increases. Or if it is too hot, if you are passing through a desert, then change again to a different rhythm, and your body has an automatic, inbuilt, air-conditioning system.

Gurdjieff learned his first lessons in hypnosis with these nomadic groups. If the wife and the husband are both going to the market in the village to sell things, what are they to do with the children, the small children? These nomads have used hypnotism for centuries. They will just draw a circle around the child and tell him, "Till we return you cannot get out of this circle." Now, this has been told for centuries to every child. From the moment he could understand, he has heard it. He is hypnotized by it. The moment it is uttered, the moment he sees the line being drawn around him, he simply relaxes inside: there is no way to get out, he can't get out.

Gurdjieff was very puzzled, because he was ten or twelve years old then: "What nonsense is this?" Each child in every nomad camp is just surrounded by a line, and that's all. The father and mother disappear for the whole day to work in the town. By the evening when they come the child is still inside the circle.

Gurdjieff started wondering how it happened, why it happened, and soon he was able to figure out that it is just a question of your unconscious accepting the idea. Once your unconscious accepts the idea, then your body and your conscious mind have no power to go against it.

In his own exercises that he developed later on when he became a master, Gurdjieff used all these nomad techniques that he had learned from those strange people – uncivilized, with no language, no written alphabet, but who knew very primitive methods. He was surprised to see that hypnotism works not only on children but on men, because those children become young adults, then too it worked. Then they become old, then too it worked. It did not change with age.

Gurdjieff used to play with the old people, drawing a circle around them, and the old person would shout, "Don't do that, don't do that," and before the circle was complete he would jump out. If the circle was complete then it was impossible, you were caught. And this boy – who could know whether he would be coming back again or not? When the circle was half completed, something was open: you could escape. Then you were saved, otherwise you were caught in it. And many times Gurdjieff succeeded in making the circle complete. Then even an old man would simply sit down, just like a small child, and would pray to him, "Break your circle."

Gurdjieff used that technique in many ways – and many other techniques that he learned from those people. He used to have an exercise called the "stop exercise," and he exhibited it all over the world, particularly in America and Europe. He would teach dances, strange dances because nobody knew those dances that the Caucasian nomads dance: strange instruments and strange dances.

They had strange foods that Gurdjieff learned to make. His ashram near Paris was something just absolutely out of this world. His kitchen was full of strange things, strange spices that nobody had ever heard of, and he himself would prepare outlandish foods. He had learned it all from those nomads. And those foods had a certain effect. Certain foods have certain effects; certain dances have certain effects; certain drums, instruments, have certain effects.

Gurdjieff had seen that if certain music is played and people are dancing a particular dance, then it is possible for them to dance on red-hot, burning coals and still not be burned. The dance is creating a certain kind of energy in them, the music is creating a kind of energy in them, so that they can escape the law of fire – which is a lower law. Certainly, if consciousness knows something higher it can escape from lower laws.

All the stories about miracles are nothing but stories about people who have come to know certain higher laws; naturally then the lower laws don't function. Gurdjieff had seen all these things, he had experienced them when he was a child, and children are very curious. There was no father, no mother to prevent him from doing anything, so he was experimenting with everything, in every possible way. And once he was finished with one nomad group, he would simply move to another because from other groups he had other things to learn. He developed all his exercises from these nomadic people.

The stop exercise was tremendously significant, perhaps one of the greatest contributions to the modern world – and the modern world is not even aware of it. Gurdjieff would tell his disciples to be engaged in all kinds of activities: somebody is digging in the garden, somebody is cutting wood, somebody is preparing food, somebody is cleaning the floor. All kinds of activities are going on, with the one condition that when he says "Stop!" then wherever you are, in whatsoever posture you are, you stop dead. You are not to be cunning, because then the whole point of the exercise is lost.

For example, if your mouth is open and you see that Gurdjieff is not there to notice, and you just close your mouth and rest, you have missed the point. One of your legs was up – you were just moving – and one leg was down; now suddenly the "Stop!" call comes. You have to stop, knowing perfectly well that soon you will fall down; you cannot stand on one foot for long. But that is the whole point of it: whatever the consequence you simply stop as you are, you become just a statue.

You will be surprised that such a simple exercise gives you such a release of awareness. Neither Buddha, nor Patanjali, nor Mahavira was aware of it, that such a simple exercise... It is not complex at all.

When you become just a statue you are not even allowed to blink an eye; you stay exactly as you are at the moment you hear the word "Stop!" It simply means stop and nothing else. You will be surprised that you suddenly become a frozen statue – and in that state you can see yourself transparently.

You are constantly engaged in activity, and the mind's activity is associated with the activity of the body. You cannot separate them, so when the body completely stops, of course, immediately the mind also stops then and there. You can see the body, frozen, as if it is somebody else's body; you can see the mind, suddenly unmoving, because it has lost its association.

It is a simple psychological law of association that was discovered by another Russian, Pavlov. Gurdjieff knew it long before Pavlov, but he was not interested in psychology so he never worked it out that way. Pavlov also got the idea from the same nomads, but he moved in a different direction; he was a psychologist. He started working on the lines of the law of association.

Pavlov would give food to his dog, and while he was giving the food, he would go on ringing a bell. Now the bell and the bread had nothing to do with each other, but to the dog they were becoming associated. Whenever Pavlov gave the dog some bread, he would ring the bell. After fifteen days he would simply ring the bell and the dog's tongue would start hanging out, ready for the bread. Now, somewhere in the dog's mind, the bell and the bread were no longer two separate things.

Gurdjieff was doing far higher work. He found a simple way of stopping the mind. In the East people have been trying for centuries to concentrate the mind, to visualize it, to stop it – and Gurdjieff found a way through physiology. But it was not his discovery, he had just found out what those nomads had been doing all the time.

Gurdjieff would shout "Stop!" and everybody would freeze. When the body suddenly freezes, the mind feels a little weird: "What happened?" – because the mind has no association with the frozen body, it is just shocked. They are in cooperation, in a deep harmony, moving together. Now the body has completely frozen, what is the mind supposed to do? Where can it go?

For a moment there is a complete silence; and even a single

moment of complete silence is enough to give you the taste of meditation.

Gurdjieff had developed dances, and during those dances he would suddenly say "Stop!" Now, while dancing you never know in what posture you are going to be. People would simply fall on the floor. But even if you fall, the exercise continues. If your hand is in an uncomfortable position under your body, you are not to make it comfortable because that means you have not given a chance for the mind to stop. You are still listening to the mind. The mind says, "It is uncomfortable, make it comfortable." No, you are not to do anything.

When he was giving his demonstration of the dance in New York, Gurdjieff chose a very strange situation. All the dancers were standing in a line, and at a certain stage in the dance when they came dancing forward and were standing in a line with the first person just at the edge of the stage, Gurdjieff said "Stop!" The first person fell, the second fell, the third fell – the whole line fell on each other. But there was dead silence, no movement.

One man in the audience got his first experience of meditation just seeing this. He was not doing it, he just *saw* it. But seeing so many people suddenly stop and then fall, but falling as if frozen, with no effort on their own to change their position or anything... It was as if suddenly they had all become paralyzed.

The man was just sitting in the front row, and without knowing he just stopped, froze in the position he was in: his eyes stopped blinking, his breath stopped. Seeing this scene – he had come to see the dance, but what kind of dance was this? – suddenly he felt a new kind of energy arising within him. And it was so silent and he was so full of awareness, that he became a disciple. That very night he reached Gurdjieff and said, "I can't wait."

It was very difficult to be a disciple of Gurdjieff; he made it almost impossible. He was really a hard taskmaster. One can tolerate things if one can see some meaning in them, but with Gurdjieff the problem was that there was no obvious meaning.

This man's name was Nicoll. Gurdjieff said, "It is not so easy to become my disciple."

Nicoll said, "It is not so easy to refuse me either. I have come to become a disciple, and I *will* become a disciple. You may be a hard master, I know; I am a hard disciple!" Both men looked into each other's eyes and understood that they belonged to the same tribe. This man was not going to leave.

Nicoll said, "I am not going. I will just sit here my whole life until you accept me as a disciple" and Nicoll's case is the only case in which Gurdjieff accepted him without bitching; otherwise, he used to be so difficult. Even for a man like P. D. Ouspensky, who made Gurdjieff world-famous – even with him Gurdjieff was difficult.

Ouspensky remembers that they were traveling from New York to San Francisco in a train, and Gurdjieff started making a nuisance of himself in the middle of the night. He was not drunk, he had not even drunk water, but he was behaving like a drunkard – moving from one compartment to another compartment, waking people and throwing people's things about. Ouspensky just followed him and asked, "What are you doing?" but Gurdjieff wouldn't listen.

Somebody pulled the train's emergency chain, "This man seems to be mad!" So the ticket-checker came in and the guard came in. Ouspensky apologized and said, "He is not mad and he is not drunk, but what to do? It is very difficult for me to explain what he is doing because I don't know myself." And right in front of the guard and ticket-checker, Gurdjieff threw somebody's suitcase out of the window.

The guard and the ticket-checker said, "This is too much. Keep him in your compartment and we will give you the key. Lock it from within, otherwise we will have to throw you both out at the next station."

Naturally Ouspensky was feeling embarrassed on the one hand and enraged on the other hand that this man was creating such a nuisance. He thought, "I know he is not mad, I know he is not drunk, but..." Gurdjieff was behaving wildly, shouting in Russian, screaming in Russian, Caucasian – he knew so many languages. The moment the door was locked, he sat silently and smiled. He asked Ouspensky, "How are you?"

Ouspensky said, "You are asking *me*, 'How are you?'! You would have forced them to put you in jail, and me too – because I couldn't leave you in such a condition. What was the purpose of all this?"

Gurdjieff said, "That is for you to understand. I am doing everything for you, and you are asking me the purpose? The purpose is not to react, not to be embarrassed, not to be enraged. What is the point of feeling embarrassed? What are you going to get out of it?

You are simply losing your cool and gaining nothing."

"But," Ouspensky said, "you threw that suitcase out of the window. Now what about the man whose suitcase it is?"

Gurdjieff said, "Don't be worried – it was yours!"

Ouspensky looked down and saw that his was missing. What to do with this master!

Ouspensky wrote: "I felt like getting down at the next station and going back to Europe. What else would Gurdjieff do?"

Gurdjieff said, "I know what you are thinking, you are thinking of getting down at the next station. Keep cool!"

"But," Ouspensky asked, "how can I keep cool now that my suitcase is gone and my clothes are gone?"

Gurdjieff said, "Don't be worried. Your suitcase was empty; I've put your clothes in my suitcase. Now, just cool down."

But later, when he was in the Caucasus and Ouspensky was in London, Gurdjieff sent Ouspensky a telegram: "Come immediately!" When Gurdjieff says "Immediately," it means *immediately*! Ouspensky was involved in some work, but he had to leave his job, pack immediately, finish everything and go to the Caucasus. In those days Russia was in revolution, so to go to the Caucasus was dangerous, absolutely dangerous. People were rushing out of Russia to save their lives, so to enter Russia and for a well-known person like Ouspensky, well-known as a mathematician, world famous... It was also well-known that he was anti-Communist, and he was not for the revolution. Now, to call him back into Russia, and that too, to the faraway Caucasus...

He would have to pass through the whole of Russia to reach Gurdjieff, but if Gurdjieff called... Ouspensky went. When he arrived there he was really boiling, because he had passed by burning trains, stations, butchered people and corpses on the platforms. He himself could not believe how he had managed, that he was going to reach Gurdjieff, but somehow he managed to. And what did Gurdjieff say? He said, "You have come, now you can go: the purpose is fulfilled. I will see you later on in London."

Now this kind of man... He has his purpose – there is no doubt about it – but has strange ways of working. Ouspensky, even Ouspensky, missed. He got so angry that he dropped all his connections with Gurdjieff after this incident, because: "This man had pulled me into the very mouth of death for nothing!" But Ouspensky missed the point. If he had gone back as silently as he had come, he may have become enlightened by the time he reached London – but he missed the point. A man like Gurdjieff may not always do something which is *apparently* meaningful, but it is always meaningful.

Nicoll became his disciple, and he had to make it through so many strange tasks, strange in every possible way. No master before Gurdjieff had tried such strange ways. For example, he would force you to eat, to go on eating; he would go on forcing you, "Eat!" and you could not say no to the master. While tears were coming to you he was saying "Eat!"…and those spices, Caucasian spices – Indian spices are nothing! Your whole throat was burning, you could feel the fire even in your stomach, in your intestines, and he was saying "Eat! Go on eating until I say stop."

But he had some hidden meaning in it. There is a point for the body… I said to you just the other day that a point comes for the body, if you fast, when after five days it changes its system. It starts absorbing its own fat, and then there is no more hunger. That is one method which has been used. This is also a similar method – in the opposite direction. There is a point beyond which you cannot eat, but the master says, "Go on." He is trying to bring you to the brink of the capacity of your whole physiology, and you have never touched it. We are always in the middle. Neither are we fasting, nor are we feasting like Gurdjieff: we are always in the middle. The body is in a settled routine; hence, the mind is also settled in its way of movement. Fasting destroys that.

That's why fasting became so important in all religions; it brings you to a moment after fifteen days when you simply start forgetting thoughts. Bigger gaps start appearing: for hours there is not a single thought, and after twenty-one days your mind is empty. It's strange that when the stomach is totally empty it creates a synchronicity in the mind – the mind becomes totally empty.

Fasting is not a goal in itself. Only idiots have followed it as a goal in itself. It is simply a technique to bring you to a stage where you can experience a state of no-mind. Once that is experienced, you can go back to food. Then there is no problem, you know the track. And then you can also go into that state any time you want, eating normally.

Gurdjieff was doing just the opposite because that's what he had learned from the nomads. Those are a totally different kind of people. They don't have any scriptures. They don't have any people like Buddha, Mahavira, or any others, but they have passed on by word of mouth, from generation to generation, certain techniques that were given by the father to the son. This technique Gurdjieff learned from the nomads. They eat too much, and go on eating, and go on eating, and go on eating. A moment comes when it is not possible to eat anymore – and that is the point when Gurdjieff would force you to eat.

If you say yes even then, suddenly there is an immediate state of no-mind because you have broken the whole rhythm of body and mind. Now it is inconceivable for the mind to grasp what is happening. It cannot work any longer in this situation. It has not known it before because – always remember – mind is exactly like a computer. It is a bio-computer, it functions according to its program. You may be aware of it, you may not be aware of it, but it functions according to a program. Break the program somewhere... And you can break the program only at the ends, only at the boundary, where you are facing an abyss.

Gurdjieff would force people to drink so much alcohol – and all kinds of alcoholic beverages – that they would go almost crazy; so drunk that they would forget completely who they were. And he would go on giving it to them. If they fell he would shake them, sit them up and pour them some more, because there is a moment when the person has come to a point where his whole body, his whole consciousness is completely overtaken by the intoxicant. In that moment his unconscious starts speaking.

Freud took three years, four years, five years of psychoanalysis to do this. Gurdjieff did it in a single night! Your unconscious would start speaking, would give all the clues about you of which you have not even been aware. You would not know that you had given those clues to Gurdjieff but he would know. And then he would work according to those clues: what exercises would be right for you, what dances would be suitable for you, what music was needed for you.

All the clues have been given by your unconscious. You were not aware of it because you were completely intoxicated. You were not present when he worked on the unconscious and persuaded it to give all the clues about you. Those were the secrets about you – then he had the keys in his hands. So if somebody refused, "Now I cannot drink any more," he would throw him out. He would say, "Then this is not the place for you."

The law of karma is something psychological: neither legal, nor social, nor moral, but something psychological. It has not been worked out that way up to now.

Whatever you do contains in itself its consequence.

It does not matter whether you call it good or bad, because what you call it – good or bad – will depend upon your conditioning. If you are eating meat, and you are a Mohammedan, or a Christian, or a Jew, there is no question of "bad." Others may be doing the same act, but their moral interpretation may be different. If you are a Jaina or a Buddhist or a brahmin – in the first place you cannot eat meat, and if you are eating it, you are doing the same act but your interpretation is that you are doing a bad act, a bad action.

Now, a Jaina eating meat, and a Christian eating meat – the acts are the same, but to the Christian conscience it is good, to the Jaina conscience it is bad. The action is exactly the same but the consequence will be different, because it is a question of psychology, it is not a question of nature. Otherwise, the consequences would have been the same.

Their psychologies are different: they have different minds, different conditionings. The Jaina will immediately feel guilty and will feel great fear. He will fall into self-condemnation and feel that he is absolutely unworthy, that he has fallen from grace. Now, this is the consequence, but this is not the consequence of the *act*; it is only the consequence of the act through his psychology.

The Christian feels nothing bad about it, in fact he is very happy: it was a good treat and he enjoyed it. Now he is sitting in his armchair with his cigar in his hand, enjoying, really relishing how tasty it was. Now do you think it was a consequence of the act? No, it is not. It is just a different psychology.

If you really want to know what the act brings, then you have to drop your psychology; then you will know the law of karma, not before. Before that you will know only that law working through your psychology, and your psychology will change it completely.

To a Jaina, it is a sin and he is going to hell; to the Christian there is no problem. Jesus was eating meat, Moses was eating meat, and I guess God also must be eating meat, particularly the Jewish, the Christian and the Mohammedan Gods. You cannot deprive God of such nourishing, delicious food. Or do you think you are going to keep him vegetarian?

In front of me once lived a doctor, a Bengali doctor, Doctor

Datta. Bengalis are not vegetarian. Once in a while, if I was sick or something – he was very friendly to me and he would come to see me. My aunt, who used to live with me, would ask him, "Doctor Datta, is there anything about food – what he should eat, what he should not eat?"

And Datta would say, "No need to worry. You are just grass-eaters. What can be cut from your diet? You are dieting continuously. Now, I cannot give you any suggestions. We can diet; we can become grass-eaters just as you are; that will be dieting for us. But for you, if you diet then you will be finished; there is nothing else to eat – so don't bother about it."

To a Jaina it would be a sheer impossibility to conceive that Jesus can be enlightened: he eats meat, he drinks wine. And most amazing, he not only drinks wine, he turns water into wine. Now, to a Jaina the real miracle will be somebody turning all the wine of the world into water. That will be a real miracle, a religious miracle. You call this a miracle? – turning water into wine? This is a crime!

Unless you drop your psychologies... For example, to me who has no psychology: in between me and my life there is no mind. I am in direct and immediate touch with my life. If I eat meat, it is not that it is going to throw me into hell. No, that is stupid. In the first place there is no hell. In the second place, there is no law of nature that by eating meat you will go to hell, because if that is the case then all the animals and almost all men will be going to hell; heaven will be absolutely empty. And because all the animals are eating meat, there is no possibility for animals to grow toward higher consciousness.

I used to say to Jaina monks, "You are preaching a stupid thing. You say that animals go on growing, moving upward; finally they become man. How can they become man? If eating meat throws people into hell, then how can meat-eating animals grow in consciousness and become men? If animals grow and become man by eating meat, then man by eating meat will grow and become God. There is no problem, growth is not prevented."

Those Jainas would say to me, "With you, argument is just impossible. From where do you get these ideas? We have been reading the scriptures our whole life, and we have been reading that animals grow and become man, but this idea never occurred to us. Yes, it is true: if they are eating meat and growing in consciousness, then what is wrong in eating meat?"

"And particularly," I said, "eating the meat of animals who are growing upward will be a great help for evolution." In fact that's what Mohammedans say. They have a very strange idea – it's this idea that I am telling you. They say that you have to eat animals because only by eating them do you transform them and make them capable of moving upward. Because you absorb their body and their soul, it goes upward, so release as many animals as you can. God has made it clear in the Koran that he made the animals for man to eat. What else, what other authority, is needed?

I am not a Jaina or a Jew or a Mohammedan because I don't have any psychology. These are all psychologies created by different religions for their own purposes. I have dropped all psychology.

I don't eat meat because to me the act itself is ugly. It is not a question that I will suffer in a future life. No, the very act, even the idea that you have to destroy life just for your taste buds, which are not many – just at the back of your tongue, perhaps two inches... If your tongue is cleaned a little deeply with a razor, all your taste will disappear.

It happened in the Second World War that a man got shot in his neck. He was saved by medical science, but his food pipe had to be closed. Now there was trouble, so they made a small hole into his stomach through his side and fixed a pipe there. He used to put food in it, and it was working perfectly well, but he was very unhappy because there was no taste. You could put anything in his pipe, no problem, but he was very angry: "This is not a solution; there is no taste. Life is meaningless. Without food, more than half your life is finished."

So finally the doctor decided, "Do one thing: first chew the food so you have the taste and then drop it into your pipe" – because his tongue was perfectly okay; only his food pipe was closed so he could not directly swallow food. And the idea worked. That man lived almost twelve years after this, chewing food. He enjoyed it more than you do, because he chewed for longer. That was his only joy, so why chew and just swallow?

Because your swallowing is so close to chewing, you never chew perfectly. If you want to chew perfectly, you have to chew forty-two times. I have tried, but by twenty, twenty-one, twenty-two... It becomes so boring; forget about the scientific law – I just swallow it. But if you chew exactly forty-two times then you have chewed your food perfectly well. That man may have been chewing even eighty-four times – there was no problem – and then dropping the food into his pipe. We are also doing that, but our pipe is joined; his pipe was separate. He lived for twelve years, joyously eating all kinds of delicious food.

But killing, just for those small buds on your tongue, taking any-body's life is simply unaesthetic. It is not a question of morality, it is not a question of religion, it is a question of aesthetics: your sense of beauty, your sense of respect for life. And by not eating meat, you are not going to heaven – because there is no heaven either.

But to me, just to attain to this aesthetic sensibility is to be in heaven. The man who has no aesthetic sensibility is below human. He is still an animal: walking on two legs of course, but just walking on two legs instead of four can't make much difference. Or do you think it can make much difference? If that is the only difference between human beings and animals, that they walk on four and you walk on two, that they are horizontal and you are vertical... Do you think geometry is the difference between you and animals?

You were certainly horizontal once, like those other animals. That's why when you sleep you feel so restful, because you come back to your primitive state, horizontal; and the mind moves into the collective unconscious, far back when you were also moving on four feet.

If you look at the faces of animals you will find them graceful. Have you seen any animal in the same kind of states as you see in man's changing faces? No, because there is no emotion, no sensi-bility, their faces remain the same. But your face is continuously changing; you have sensibility. Your sensibility is the basic quality that differentiates you from animals.

To me, if your aesthetic sense allows you an act, you will imme-diately feel immensely fulfilled.

I don't issue any promissory notes to you. All the religions have done that. I am absolutely for cash! I don't believe in promissory notes, I believe in cash. My religion is a cash religion: you act, and out of your action you get the result immediately, connected to it as a continuation. There is no discontinuity. This is *my* law of karma. This is absolutely different from all the philosophies of the law of karma that have been preached in the past, particularly in the East. But my law of karma has a different dimension: it is aesthetic. The more your senses become alive, the more you become full of reverence for life; it is bound to happen. With sensitivity, you will become so respectful that even to pluck a flower from a plant will be an ugly act.

A very great painter not much known in the West, although he was a Western man, lived in the Himalayas. He was a Russian, Nicholas Roerich, and he belonged to the czar's family. When the revolution happened and nineteen members of the czar's family were slaughtered, even a six-month-old child – sometimes these revolutions can be so ugly – Nicholas Roerich escaped; he was just a boy at that time.

He lived in the Himalayas. He was a painter, but not a painter for art galleries and marketplaces. He never sold any of his paintings – not because people were not ready to purchase them, but because he was not willing to sell. He said, "It is not a commodity, it is me spread on the canvas. How can I sell it?" He died with all his paintings in his house.

I have been to his house – he was very old at that time – and seeing that he was vegetarian, I asked, "You are a Russian, why should you be vegetarian?"

He said, "Because of my paintings. I cannot even destroy a painting, which is not alive. How can I destroy a living being for my food? And if I can destroy a lion or a tiger, then why not destroy a man?"

...Because human meat will be more digestible, more in tune with you. What is wrong with the cannibal? Why is everybody against the cannibals just because they eat human beings? Cannibals say human meat is very delicious. They say there is nothing as delicious on earth as human meat, particularly the meat of small children. If deliciousness and taste are decisive... Perhaps they may be right, because they have eaten other foods also, and they are saying it: all cannibals agree. But *you* can't think of eating a man. How can you think of eating a tiger? How can you think of eating a deer? If there was no mind given to you by the past, or if you can put it aside and see directly, you will be simply amazed at what people have been doing.

Vegetarianism should not be anything moral or religious. It is a question of aesthetics: one's sensitivity, one's respect, reverence for life. To me this is the law of karma. All other interpretations of it are absolutely wrong, just *boo boo*.

CHAPTER 10

An Outsider, Just a Guest

Osho,
You say Christ was the last Christian. Are you the last Rajneeshee?
Please explain.

I t was not me who said that Christ was the last Christian. I was
simply quoting Friedrich Nietzsche; it was Nietzsche who made
that statement. In a certain sense Nietzsche is absolutely right,
because in this world no individual is ever repeated.

The uniqueness of the individual is absolute.

Not only is nobody like you in contemporary times; in the whole of
eternity there is never going to be a person like you again. There has
never been a person like you before. You are simply you, incomparable.

Hence I support Nietzsche's statement in this sense, that the last
Christian was crucified two thousand years ago. But I would like to
add something more to it. First: Jesus was not only the last Christian,
he was also the first Christian – the first and the last Christian.

But this is only one sense of the statement. In other ways I am
not in agreement with it because as far as the word *Christian* is
concerned, Jesus never even heard the word. He was born a Jew, he

lived as a Jew; he tried his whole life to prove himself to be a real Jew. In fact he was crucified *because* he was trying to prove himself to be a Jewish messiah. He had never heard the word *Christ* or *Christian* because he knew no Greek, no Latin; he knew only Aramaic and a little bit of Hebrew. Both languages have the word *messiah*, but *Christ* is a Greek translation of the word *messiah*.

The word *Christ* came into existence after Jesus, after three hundred years had passed; and out of the word *Christ*, came *Christian*. Slowly people completely forgot that poor Christ had no idea that he would be called Christ and his followers, Christians.

You will be surprised to know that in India the Hindi word for *messiah* is *masiha*, and the word for Christian is *masihi*. *Masihi* is far closer to the Aramaic and Hebrew than what the Christians all over the world go on calling themselves. Perhaps the Hindi words *masiha* and *masihi* came into existence because Jesus, after escaping from the crucifixion – it was not a resurrection, it was an escape – lived in India for a long time, to the age of one hundred and twelve. His most beloved disciple, Thomas, followed him.

Indian Christianity is the oldest in the whole world; the Vatican is a later development. Jesus remained in Kashmir, completely tired, perhaps finished with humanity and the hope for a better future for it, because if this was the result – that you crucify a person who works for you and for your redemption, your salvation... Of course he was not an idiot: he learned the lesson.

Jesus stayed silent for the remaining time. Yes, a few people came to him on their own, but it was not a problem because in India there have been so many incarnations of God, and it is an accepted fact that it is nobody else's business: if somebody feels he is an incarnation of God, let him be. What is wrong in it? Somewhere else the same person will be crucified, will be imprisoned; he will be psychoanalyzed, deprogrammed. All kinds of stupid things will be done to the person because he thinks he is an incarnation of God, but in India he will be worshipped.

Nobody will object to it. There is no question of objecting, because one thing is certain: you cannot judge whether he is or he is not; there are no criteria, no methods to measure. And India has seen so many people like Jesus that it has come to realize that each one of them was so unique that you cannot derive any criteria from one which can be applied to another.

Buddha was just himself. No similarity between Buddha and Krishna can be found; everything in them is just opposite to each other. But India has lived thousands of years of religious philosophizing, teaching, arguing. It has attained to a certain liberality of mind as far as religion is concerned.

India knows that a Krishna can be an incarnation of God although he lives in a palace with every luxury; Buddha can be an incarnation of God although he renounces his kingdom, luxuries, comforts; Mahavira can be an incarnation of God although he discards even his clothes and lives naked.

India has seen the ways of so many people like Jesus that it has come to one conclusion: leave the person alone. If you can learn something from him, good; otherwise there is no harm in paying him respect. Perhaps he is right; if he is wrong, what are you losing? Giving respect, even to a wrong person, is not bad.

So in Kashmir Jesus was not troubled by anybody. He was not news there. In India it is not news. He sent Thomas to the south of India for a special reason. Northern India is very sophisticated, and all these great teachers, Buddha, Mahavira, Krishna, Patanjali, Gorakh, Kabir – it is an unending line – were all born and lived in northern India, for the simple reason that northern India is Aryan.

South India is non-Aryan, it has Negroid blood. Once South India was just part of South Africa; South Africa has drifted away. It is a late discovery in geography that continents go on drifting, they are still drifting. The drift is very small, a foot in a year, so you cannot feel it. But continents are continuously drifting, they are not fixed: in thousands of years, of course, much change happens.

It was a great insight of Jesus to send Thomas to South India where it was possible to preach and spread Jesus' word. In northern India nobody would have bothered about it. Northern India was so full of philosophical reasoning, argumentation, was so sophisticated that who was going to listen to Thomas, a poor, uneducated man?

But perhaps South India would be receptive; and it was. The whole state of Kerala is eighty percent Christian; and it is not a new phenomenon, it was Thomas' work. Goa is completely Christian – Thomas' body is still in Goa.

It reminds me to tell you of one thing: Thomas' is the only body, outside Tibet, which is still the same as it was on the day the person died. It has not been preserved by any chemicals, or by any scientific methods. It is one of the rarest phenomena on the earth. Every year the body is brought out of the inner chambers of the church for the public to see.

I have seen the body, and you can see it is as if the man has just gone to sleep, and not even died. Yes, he is not breathing, but in two thousand years the body has not deteriorated. Scientists have tried to find out how it is preserved. There is nothing to find because it is not preserved by any preservatives; it is through a long training in Yoga and certain breathing exercises that have the capacity to change the inner workings of biochemistry.

Thomas practiced Yoga for thirty years and lived like a Hindu brahmin. If you see a picture of Thomas you will be surprised. What kind of Christian is this? – his head shaved like a Hindu brahmin monk, with a small piece of hair on the top of his head left uncut, the *choti*. He even wore the thread, *yagyopavit*, that is only worn by born brahmins. He used just a small piece of cloth just to cover the lower part of his body, the loincloth as it is called.

If you have seen Mahatma Gandhi's picture you know the cloth that covers him from his waist to his knees – that's enough. And in the south they use it just as a wraparound; Thomas used just the wraparound *lungi*, only down to the knee. And he used wooden sandals. He looked a perfect Hindu.

He became vegetarian when he was in India. He tried to learn as much Yoga as possible and he really performed a miracle. He said, "After my death don't bury my body and don't make a grave for me. I have managed to change its inner workings." It was predicted by Thomas – and that prediction may come true – that his body would remain preserved till the very end of the world. Two thousand years have passed and the body is preserved. Only last year, for the first time, a little sign of deterioration was detected. Perhaps the end of the world is close. If the man was right about his body, saying not to destroy it, that it is going to remain till the very end of the world – and according to many sources the end of the world is coming closer – his prediction may also be true.

Only last year, for the first time, a little deterioration has been seen. Perhaps by the end of this century the body may have deteriorated completely. Thomas' prediction is that the day his body deteriorates completely, that is the end of this world.

Thomas and Jesus both brought to India the word *messiah* which became *masiha*. When a word changes from one language to another language, it has to be adapted to the whims of the other language. *Messiah* will not fit in Hindi; *masiha* fits. *Messiah* would have remained something foreign, but *masiha* is transformed, is no longer foreign; and the Christians have been called *masiha* for two thousand years.

What I want to point to is that Jesus had no idea, not at all, what a Christian is, what a Christ is. He had never heard those words. In that sense Nietzsche's statement is not right. In the same reference I would like to say to you: although I have heard the word *Rajneeshee*, I am neither the first nor the last. I don't belong to any group, any religion, any organization. Even in your commune I am an outsider, just a guest – a guest of the Rajneeshees. I am not a Rajneeshee.

A Christian is comparable to a Hindu, to a Jew, to a Buddhist, to a Jaina, to a Communist even, because they all believe in tight organizations. They all believe in one leader, one prophet, one messiah, one God, one holy book. Nietzsche's statement cannot be applied to me because as far as Rajneeshism is concerned there is no God, there is no holy book, there is no messiah.

I am not a messiah. To be a messiah, first a God is needed. I have cut the legs off by declaring that there is no God. Now I cannot declare myself a messiah; that possibility is closed. It is God who sends messiahs and messengers and now there is nobody. There is nobody above me and there is nobody below me.

There are only two ways to be superior. Either you are sent from high above, from the great boss, as Jesus is sent, as Mohammed is sent: they come from the great boss, with all the powers invested in them. That is one way to declare yourself superior to others. Not all are begotten sons of God, it is only Jesus. Not all are messiahs, it is only Jesus. Jesus is declaring his superiority: you are just sheep, he is the shepherd. He is the only shepherd; amongst millions of sheep, the only shepherd. I don't like such company. Millions of sheep and I am the only shepherd? What kind of company is this? And you are judged by your company; even if you are a shepherd it is not much to brag about, but it is a way to prove yourself superior.

The other way is followed by the Buddhists and the Jainas, because neither of them believes in God, so that possibility is closed. They have found another possibility, and that is the *tirthankara* – the Jaina equivalent to the messiah – who is not sent by God, because there is no God, but who attains to the same state of cosmic consciousness through millions of lives' effort. You are millions of lives behind him, below him. It will take millions of lives for you to be able to reach that state.

That is the other way of declaring superiority – perhaps a far better way, because it is so arduous. To become a messiah all that you need is a retarded mind, stupid, stubborn – and you can declare yourself. To declare yourself the only begotten son of God, what do you need? Just no sense of shame, that's all; otherwise such a stupid thing... Any intelligent person, even if he *is* the only begotten son of God, will try to hide the fact: if somebody hears, what are people going to think about it?

Even if he knows that he is a messenger from God he will not tell anybody. He will deliver the message and escape because it looks so foolish that you are the son of a poor carpenter, uneducated, and you have been chosen to be the messenger of God. God could not find an educated, sophisticated rabbi? And there were thousands! In fact rabbis are some of the most scholarly people in the world. God seems to be crazy: He should have chosen somebody refined, cultured, who knew all the scriptures, but Jesus was not even able to read. And there were people whose whole life was devoted to study, to thinking, to contemplation – it was a traditional thing.

Judaism and Hinduism are the only two basic religions in the world. Other religions are offshoots either of Hinduism or of Judaism, but Judaism and Hinduism remain separate. There is no connection between them, no communication has happened between them; and both are tremendously scholarly.

If God chooses Krishna as an incarnation it can be understood. Krishna has that understanding, wisdom, education. The best that was available was available to him; the most famous teachers were his teachers. He was trained to be a wise man, and he was a wise man.

And there were so many rabbis commenting on the Torah, and such intelligent commentaries that if you look at those commentaries even today you will find them immensely contemporary. Perhaps they are three thousand years old but so insightful and so beautiful. Small statements in the Torah or the Talmud have been made so significant in the rabbis' commentaries, that when you see the statement itself you think there is not much in it.

But when you see the commentaries and commentaries upon the commentaries, you become aware of the immense dimensions opening from that stale statement. There was nothing in it – you could not have found anything in it – but these commentators have some third eye. They go on looking – something like an X ray – and they go to the very depth. Perhaps they create the depth: they are so creative that they bring something significant out of an absolutely insignificant statement. God should have chosen these people, not a carpenter's son.

But Jesus proclaimed himself to be the messenger of God. He must have looked like a buffoon. I can't help saying it. He used to travel on a donkey declaring himself the only begotten son of God. The messiah that you have been waiting for for centuries is coming on a donkey? People must have laughed. In the beginning he was just a laughingstock – yes, it was funny – but this man went on and on. Soon people started realizing that it was no longer funny, it was becoming a serious business because Jesus was gathering a few idiots around him who were saying that he was the messiah.

And there was, as there has always been, a class of people who are rejected by the society: thieves, prostitutes, gamblers, tax collectors. These people are rejected people; and these were the people who Jesus collected. It was easy to collect them because they were rejected by society and Jesus was rejected by society. They had found a great messiah: "So let's just follow him." Not a single rabbi went with Jesus. This is strange; this has never happened anywhere else.

Buddha was speaking against brahmins, against Hindus, but all his great disciples were brahmins. It seems sensible because he was appealing to the best in the society. Although he was against brahmins, the brahmins were the topmost, and out of the brahmins came the greater part of intelligentsia.

Sariputta was a brahmin, Moggalayan was a brahmin, Mahakashyapa was a brahmin. They had all come to Buddha, not because they were illiterate idiots, the rejected – gamblers, prostitutes, tax collectors, thieves – no, but because they were great scholars and they could understand that what Buddha was saying was right. They were not nobodies.

When Sariputta came to Buddha, he himself had five hundred disciples of his own coming with him, all great scholars. He had come first to have a discussion and Buddha was very happy: what could be more welcome? But Buddha asked, "Have you experienced the truth or are you only a great scholar? – I have heard your name."

Looking at Buddha for a moment in silence, as if looking in a mirror, utterly naked, Sariputta said, "I am a great scholar, but as far as knowing the truth is concerned, I have not known it."

Buddha said, "Then it will be very difficult to argue. Argument is possible between two people who don't know truth. They can argue till eternity because neither knows. Both are ignorant so they can go on playing with words and logic and quotations and scriptures, but because neither knows, there is no possibility of their coming to a conclusion. At the most what can happen is whoever is more clever and cunning and tricky may defeat the other, and the other will become the follower of the more cunning or more sophisticated. But is this any decision about truth?

"Or there is a possibility of a meeting of two people who have both realized the truth, but then there is no way to argue. What is there to argue about? They will sit silently, perhaps they may smile, or hold each other's hands, but what is there to say? Looking into each other's eyes they will see that there is nothing to say: "We both know the same things, we are in the same space," so there will be only silence.

"Or the third possibility is that one knows and one does not know. Then it is going to be very troublesome because the one who knows cannot translate what he knows into the language of the ignorant one. And the one who does not know will be unnecessarily wasting his time, his mind, because he cannot convince the one who knows. The whole world cannot convince the person who knows, because he knows and you don't know."

Buddha said, "You have come with your five hundred disciples. You don't know, and it is absolutely certain that in these five hundred disciples no one knows; otherwise he would not be your disciple, he would be your master. You are more scholarly, they are less scholarly. You are older, they are younger. They are your disciples.

"How are we going to discuss anything? I am ready, but I know. One thing is certain: you cannot convert me. The only possibility is that you will be converted, so think twice." But Sariputta was already converted. Seeing this man… And Sariputta was intelligent enough, he had defeated many great scholars.

It was a tradition in India in those days that scholars would move all over the country, defeating other scholars. Unless a person had defeated all the scholars, he would not be recognized by the scholarly mob as a wise man. But to stand before a Buddha, before one who knows, it is not a question of your scholarship and how many scholars you have defeated.

Buddha simply said, "I am ready. If you want to argue I am ready, but what argument is possible? I have eyes, you don't have eyes; I cannot explain to you what light is. You cannot have any idea what light is. You will only hear the word *light* but the word will not have any meaning for you. It will be contentless; heard, but not understood.

"So if you are really interested in truth and not in getting defeated or being victorious... That is not my interest. I have arrived; who cares to defeat anybody? For what? If you are really interested in truth then just be here and do what I say. You can argue later on when you have come to know something substantial, existential. Then you can argue."

But Sariputta was a tremendously intelligent man. He said, "I know that neither can I argue now, nor will I be able to argue then. You have finished my argumentation. Now I cannot argue because I don't have eyes; then I will not be able to argue because I will have eyes. But I am going to stay."

He stayed with his five hundred disciples. He said to the disciples, "Now I am no longer your master. Here is the man; I will be sitting by his side as his disciple. Please forget me as your master. If you want to be here, he is your master."

Now, if a man like Buddha had said, "I am a messenger of God," he would not have been laughed at. But he didn't say that. He and Mahavira were contemporaries and both had an absolute trust in their experience that there is no God. But they found another way.

To me it is the same. Whether you descend from above; then you are special... They ascend from below and go on above you, so far away. You will have to work millions of lives and then you will be able to reach that state – it is almost impossible.

I cannot declare myself a messiah because there is no God. I cannot declare myself a *tirthankara* or an *avatara*, because to me truth is not attained by arduous effort in millions of lives. It can be attained instantly, immediately, herenow, because you have it already. So it is not a question of achieving it; you have not to go somewhere to find it.

You are carrying truth within you all the time.

It is just that you are not awake. But awakening does not need millions of lives. Just a good hit on your head and you will be awake – more than awake.

So I don't see myself superior to you. I don't see anybody inferior to me; I don't see anybody superior to me either – neither Jesus, nor Buddha, nor Mahavira. I don't see them as superior to me, because it is such a simple human experience. Why make so much ado about nothing? Somehow even in Mahavira and Buddha some shadow of the ego still persists. They have arrived but they are not whole. Perhaps a leg is missing, a hand is missing; something is missing, something is left behind.

Pakhtoonistan is a very small country between Pakistan and Afghanistan, almost a part of Afghanistan. Once it was a part of India; now legally it is part of Pakistan. But the Pakhtoons don't want to be part of Pakistan, they want to be part of India; and if that is not possible they want... Because now Pakistan is in between: they are Mohammedans but a different race.

The Pakhtoon is a really beautiful man, perhaps the tallest in the whole world, the strongest in the whole world, and lives longest in the whole world. You will not find a single Pakhtoon who is fat: they are so proportionate and so tall and so beautiful, as if sculptured by someone like Leonardo da Vinci. They don't want to mix with Pakistan, they would rather be together with Afghanistan.

These tribal people have a strange idea. I am reminded of it because I said that it is as if Buddha has left something behind, as if Mahavira has left something behind. Pakhtoons believe that when a man dies he should die with his body complete. No part should be missing because God will ask, "Where is your hand? When I sent you into the world you were whole." So they never allow any operation, any amputation. They would rather die than have their kidneys taken out, because they are simple people, primitive people, and their logic is simple: when God asks, "Where are your kidneys?"...

A beautiful story happened. In the First World War in Lahore, a Pakhtoon got shot in the hand. The situation was such that if his hand was not cut off, then his whole body would be poisoned. The decision had to be taken immediately, because even a few moments delay would be too late. The Pakhtoon himself was unconscious, in a coma. His family was somewhere in Pakhtoonistan and difficult to find, because Pakhtoonistan still has no postal system, no telegraph, no telegrams, no telephones, no roads.

Only one road passes from Pakistan to Afghanistan, and even to pass through that road is very difficult because Pakhtoon children go on practicing shooting – shooting drivers, shooting passengers in the buses! They are very primitive and simple people. Where to learn? They don't think of making a target – and what is the point when there are so many targets?

When I was traveling in Pakhtoonistan, my driver said, "I won't allow you to drive here."

I said, "Why? It is such a beautiful country."

He said, "You don't know: drivers are just targets! I won't allow you. Sit in the other seat, the passenger's seat; I will have to drive. I have driven on this road so I know where the danger is and how to avoid it and what to do. They are just children and continually shooting; from the very childhood all that they want is a gun."

So where to find his family to get their consent to cut his hand off? And he is a Pakhtoon: when he comes back to consciousness and finds that his hand is missing, he is going to create trouble. But there was no other way. The doctor, who was an Englishman, said, "I take the responsibility. I know the man and I will convince him somehow. Cut off his hand."

When the man came back to consciousness he was really furious. The doctor listened to his anger, then explained to him that the situation was this: "I have taken the whole responsibility, and look, I have preserved your hand." He had kept the hand in a big jar full of spirit. He said, "I have preserved it, so when you die we will put your hand with you."

They are simple people; he understood the logic. He said, "That's right. What else could you have done? That's perfectly good. So you keep it, because we Pakhtoons are continually traveling."

They used to travel all over India because from Pakhtoonistan they used to bring dry fruits – the best fruits grow in Pakhtoonistan – and woolen clothes: blankets, sweaters. These things they would carry from Pakhtoonistan to India to sell.

Really, since Pakistan has been divided you don't see Pakhtoons coming into India. You don't get that quality of dried fruits that they used to bring. It was the most superior you could get anywhere.

So he said, "I am continually traveling. Now, to carry this hand everywhere will look odd. Secondly, I may forget it. It may get dropped somewhere. It is in a glass jar – it may be broken. You keep it, and I will tell my family that when I die they should get the hand from you."

The doctor said, "That's perfectly okay."

But an accident happened: the hospital was burned down, and with it, the hand of the Pakhtoon. The doctor was not very worried about it because he was retiring and going back to England, so far away from Pakhtoonistan that those people could not bother him in any possible way. Who was the doctor and where had he gone? Where were they going to find him? And they could not go to England, they were poor people.

But he was afraid that even in England… "Who knows? Those people are dangerous. They may find a way. So it is better to keep a hand ready, in case." But he forgot that he had cut off the left hand. He got a right hand from a hospital and kept it preserved in his bedroom so that if some time somebody came…

The story is that one night somebody knocked on the door. The doctor opened the door and the Pakhtoon was standing there, furious. The doctor could not believe his eyes. The Pakhtoon didn't say anything, he simply showed him his left arm and asked, "Where is my hand?" – not verbally; he just showed him his arm: "Give me my hand."

The doctor almost had a nervous breakdown. He just got hold of the flask and took it out. At that moment he realized the mistake, that it was the right hand! The Pakhtoon seeing it, kicked the flask over, took the hand and threw it into the room. He said, "Tomorrow night I will come again. Find my hand!" And this became a nightmare every night…

Perhaps the second part of the story is psychological. The doctor gets into this insane idea that the Pakhtoon has died. Perhaps somebody from Lahore – a colleague, another doctor – has informed him that the Pakhtoon has died, and to be aware. Perhaps it is only his own imagination, but he thinks he sees the ghost of the Pakhtoon. Whatever the case – I don't believe in ghosts, but you can imagine… If you can imagine God, why not a ghost? – just a very small creature. If you can see Jesus and Krishna and Buddha, then there is no problem: you can hallucinate a poor Pakhtoon. And there was enough cause – the doctor had broken his word.

Pakhtoons are very truthful. If they give a promise they will fulfill it whatsoever the cost. They will risk their lives even for a small thing; if they have promised, they will do it. So he was perhaps afraid because of that. The doctor had lived amongst Pakhtoons in Lahore and he knew what kind of people they are. And particularly in England, ghosts appear more than anywhere else.

England is somehow very attractive to ghosts. There are proportionately more houses in England than in any country which are haunted by ghosts. Britain has a certain magnetism for ghosts. Perhaps that is why British people look so serious, afraid.

Don't start a conversation with sannyasin Proper Sagar unless you have been properly introduced. Perhaps there is also a fear of getting into conversation with a ghost: you don't know who he is. If somebody you know introduces you, then it is okay; otherwise who knows who is who? This doctor must have been a "Proper Sagar."

The story is that he died because of this continual nightmare. One morning he was found dead. He must have thought that the Pakhtoon had pressed on his neck and throat, but actually he was pressing on his own throat; and in the morning, when he was found, he had killed himself. But he must have thought, hallucinated, got into the idea and killed himself. He must have died thinking that the Pakhtoon was killing him.

But the idea of the Pakhtoon, that you should be whole when you go back, is significant.

Buddha *has* left something behind: he is still somehow saying to you that he is higher. He declares that he has attained the highest cosmic consciousness, which nobody had ever attained before. Now, this is the same game, played more sophisticatedly. But what he is trying to do is the same as what Jesus is trying to do in saying, "I am the only begotten son of God. Nobody was before, nobody is going to be afterwards; I am the only son." He is making his place superior forever. Buddha is doing the same; of course he says that he is coming from millions of lives.

In one life he was an elephant – but then too he was superior. He tells the story that when he was an elephant the jungle caught fire. The fire was spreading so fast, and the wind was so strong, that all the animals were running out of the jungle. He was also running, but finding a big shady tree he stood there just to rest a little in the coolness of the shadow.

He was just going to move and had lifted up one of his feet, when a small rabbit, running in the same fear of the fire, also came under the shadow of the tree, and rested there just where the elephant was going to put his foot. Now, to put his foot down would kill the rabbit, but not to put his foot... For how long could he stand on three feet? And you should understand: an elephant standing on three feet is a really heavy job, just the one foot up is enough.

But Buddha said, "I kept my foot up and saved the life of the rabbit, although because of keeping up that great a load I tumbled and fell sideways and died. But because I had done that good deed, I was born as a man."

Now, even while he was an elephant he was a superior elephant, not an ordinary elephant; otherwise I don't think any elephant is going to be bothered by a rabbit. In the first place he won't even see if the rabbit is there. Elephants are big but their eyes are very small. Have you seen that strange combination? – such small eyes in such a big animal. Who is creating these designs? A little proportion is needed. Or do you think the elephant can see the rabbit who is sitting just underneath his feet? I think it will take long Yoga practice for the elephant to look down; it is not easy for an elephant to look that far down. Just draw a picture of an elephant – I have drawn one and I have tried in every possible way to imagine myself as the elephant, but I couldn't see the rabbit. The foot is there, and the rabbit is underneath the foot – but such small eyes in such a big body, it is just not possible.

Even in his elephant life Buddha was so nonviolent, non-hurting, that he preferred his own death rather than killing a rabbit. He tells many stories of his past lives, and in every life he is superior. That superiority continues even into this last life: now he is the suprememost enlightened man.

For you it will take millions of lives – you may not yet be at the stage of the elephant. Would you be ready to die to save a rabbit? You won't be even ready to save your wife – particularly your wife, because in married life people say to each other...

A lover was saying to his beloved, "Without you I will die, I can't breathe. Without you I can't see any meaning in life. Without seeing you, my whole day becomes dark and dismal, but on the days I see you I am so full of joy that I can even see stars in the daytime."

Women are more practical; they don't listen to all this garbage. She knew that he must have learned the dialogue that he was speaking from some film or somewhere. She said, "What about tomorrow? Are you coming tomorrow?"

He said, "If it does not rain – because I havn't had my umbrella repaired yet."

Poetry is one thing, but when things come to reality then it is a totally different world.

Buddha is not only trying to prove himself only higher than you. He tells the story, "When I became enlightened all three Hindu gods…" Just like the Christian trinity, Hinduism has the trimurti, the three faces of God – one body but three faces. It looks more logical than the Christian trinity – God the Father, the Holy Ghost, and Jesus Christ the Son.

That trinity looks a very incomplete family: there is no mother, no brothers, no sisters. And the story is so old that it must have been a joint family. In those days such a nuclear family – only one son, and that too without a wife! Great birth control – even the wife is dropped. It doesn't look as if it can be real.

The Hindu God seems to have some logic about it: one body, three faces. Brahma is the creative face who creates the world; Vishnu is the sustainer who sustains the world; and Shiva is the destructive part who destroys the world. This seems to be more logical, perhaps more scientific too.

It is a strange thing: science goes on dividing and dividing – molecules have been divided into atoms and atoms themselves have been divided – and the ultimate division that they have come to is of three. One is positive, that can be the creative part; the other is neutral, that can be the sustainer part; the third is destructive, negative, that can be the third face of the Hindu God.

Sooner or later Hindus are going to brag that this is what their three faces mean – electron, neutron, proton – that this is the new way of saying the same thing; but it is one body, it is the same electricity, the same force. What does Buddha manage to do with this? He says, "When I became enlightened all three Hindu gods, Brahma, Vishnu, Shiva came to touch my feet."

Now, this is even better than Jesus. Jesus after all is just a son. Buddha manages to have all the three Hindu gods touch his feet, because those three gods say, "The enlightened being is far higher than a god. We also desire, in some life, to gain the same state of being."

In Hinduism, gods are not permanent beings. They have a certain period of time in heaven that they have earned through being good in the world, a certain bank balance of virtue. They will live in heaven till that bank balance is finished. Once it is finished they are thrown back into the world, again on the road, in the wheel of life and death. The enlightened being does not go to heaven, he goes to *moksha*.

Moksha is above heaven, from where no fall is possible, because it doesn't happen through virtue or good deeds, it happens through awareness, total awareness. And once you are totally aware, how can you fall? So Buddha uses a far more clever strategy to prove himself superior. Mahavira uses it in the same way. A *tirthankara* becomes a *tirthankara* through millions of lives of arduous austerities; and there are only twenty-four *tirthankaras* in one cycle of creation.

Only recently has Western physics become aware of such immensely large numbers of time, but Hinduism, Jainism and Buddhism have been aware of them for a long time. In English you cannot find the equivalent to many numbers which are available in Indian languages. One cycle is not a small thing but millions and millions of years. Creation does not begin like Christians say – which looks very childish – four thousand and four years before Jesus Christ.

Now, the Eastern people will laugh and say, "Whom are you kidding? Creation happened four thousand and four years before Christ?" China has existed for at least ten thousand years. India has been, according to Indian scholars, for at least ninety thousand years.

If you don't believe them it is difficult to argue against their argument because in the Rig Veda the Hindus have a description of stars in a certain combination which happened – according to scientific astronomers – ninety thousand years ago. If that particular combination of stars was known to the people who were writing the Rig Veda, it is proof enough that the Rig Veda is far older than ninety thousand years.

Even if the Rig Veda was written later on, that particular combination of stars was kept in mind, at least in the memory of the people – and the Rig Veda says it happened exactly ninety thousand years ago. Their book is ninety thousand years old; your creation is only six thousand years old – from today. So it is very difficult to argue that it is not so. Hindus will laugh and say, "What are you talking about?"

Jainas are even more mathematical. In the Rig Veda, their first *tirthankara's* name is mentioned. That becomes even more compli- cated a problem because their first *tirthankara*, Rishabhdeva, is mentioned by name with great respect.

It is very logical: to show so much respect to a person who is against your religion makes one thing certain: he can't be contem- porary. These are simple, logical ways to think. In the first place, if somebody is your contemporary, you are full of contempt toward the man. Perhaps that is the meaning of *contemporary* – you cannot believe in him.

That's why they could not believe in Jesus Christ. They couldn't believe in him. When Buddha was contemporary, Hindus did not recognize him. But five hundred years after he died they had to rec- ognize him as one of the Hindu incarnations of God because his influence had grown so much. Now to reject him meant to reject all the Buddhists. That would have been a great loss to the Hindu priesthood. It was better to absorb them, to keep them under the Hindu fold so that you could go on exploiting them; otherwise they would move apart.

So for five hundred years Hindus were continually criticizing Buddha, but after five hundred years they changed their tactics, their strategy. Up to that time they had only ten incarnations of God, and there was no place to adjust for Buddha, but Buddhists wouldn't agree for any lesser position than that. So they had to increase the quota! Five hundred years after Buddha, the Hindus changed and started saying, "If we have twenty-four *avataras*... Just as Jainas have twenty-four *tirthankaras* and Buddhists have twenty-four bud- dhas, we also have twenty-four *avataras*."

Gautam Buddha was born into a Hindu family, obviously – just like Jesus was born into a Jewish family – so he was a Hindu, and he died as a Hindu. They reclaimed him and declared him one of the incarnations of the Hindu God. But for the contemporary Buddha there was nothing but contempt.

It is so common a practice all over the world that you can respect a man who is dead, and the longer he is dead, the better. If he is outside the scope of your history then you can respect him very easily, then there is no problem at all. He is so distant from you, it does not hurt.

But somebody sitting by your side declaring himself the only begotten son of God...! You cannot believe this guy – perspiring, stinking – is the only begotten son of God. You feel like kicking him! The only son of God? You feel angry at him, at God, at everything that this man... But after two thousand years have passed nobody is worried; nobody seems to be concerned whether Jesus was really the son of God.

Christians have accepted it but Jews don't talk about him. Mohammedans have accepted him because they have no problem about him. Hindus, Jainas, Buddhists, have no trouble with Jesus. You cannot convert a single Jaina to Christianity, or a single Buddhist to Christianity, because Christianity is a far more primitive religion. Those people are far superior in their arguments and their logic.

Many Christians have become Buddhists; not a single Buddhist becomes Christian. There is nothing in it to appeal to them. Do you think a Buddhist will be impressed by the fact that Jesus is the son of the virgin, Mary? He will simply laugh; he will say, "You are joking!" What has Christianity got?

A Christian missionary went with his Bible to see a Zen master. He started reading the Sermon on the Mount. Of course, that is the best part. In fact that's all that Christianity is about.

He had read only one or two sentences when the Zen monk said, "Stop. Whoever the guy was, he was a bodhisattva." – *bodhisattva* means in some future life he will become a buddha – "Be finished! These sentences are proof enough that in some future life this guy is going to become a buddha. But don't be bothered with him, he is not a buddha right now – only a bodhisattva."

Bodhisattva means essentially a buddha, but everybody is a bodhisattva essentially. You may take lives to make your essence actual; that depends on you, but you are a buddha. Not only you, the trees, the birds, even the dogs are essentially bodhisattvas. They may take a little longer, or maybe some intelligent dog rushes ahead and leaves you behind. It is happening: all the intelligent dogs have come to Oregon. They have made a party: 1000 Friends of Oregon. They are known as watchdogs!

I was thinking about why they are called watchdogs. Finally the revelation came to me that they are dogs, but very intelligent. Most of them are in the legal profession; they have changed themselves into watchdogs. Even dogs, even the watchdogs of Oregon are bodhisattvas. So that Zen master was not saying much, but the missionary was overjoyed. The story was being told all over in Christian churches that a Zen master had accepted Jesus; but the missionary did not understand the meaning of bodhisattva.

Bodhisattva does not mean buddha. *Sattva* means essence, potentially; but potentiality may always remain a potentiality – there is no necessity for a seed to become a tree. A seed may remain just a seed forever. There are types of seed; some seed may choose to sit upon a rock. You can go on meditating sitting on a rock, but you are not going to become a buddha. On a rock a seed will remain a seed.

To become a tree the seed has to die into the earth, dissolve himself completely: on his death is the birth of the tree. His death is absolutely essential. Here he dies, and on the other side the tree is born, a small sprout, but alive. The seed was almost dead. I say "almost" because he had the potential of life. But a seed can remain a seed – and millions of seed remain seeds.

So it was nothing much; that Zen master really joked with the missionary. He said, "Stop, enough! Those two lines are enough. Whosoever said it..." He did not even bother to ask who had said it. He said, "Whosoever has said it is a bodhisattva. Close the book – now talk business."

I am not the first Rajneeshee or the last Rajneeshee. I am not a Rajneeshee at all; I am just an outsider. You may be Rajneeshees, but don't drag me into your Big Muddy Ranch. Enjoy the Big Muddy Ranch and leave me outside.

I am just a guest, because in the first place I don't want to be crucified – no interest in it at all. I don't want to be deified – no interest in it at all, because whatever I am is so fulfilling that I don't see any need to be something else. I don't see anybody superior to me, I don't see anybody inferior to me.

In fact both those things exist together. Anybody who thinks somebody is superior must think somebody else inferior, and vice versa: if you think somebody is inferior to you, you are bound to think of somebody as superior. It is the same mind; and those two dimensions are not two dimensions but two polarities of the same thing.

I am simply out of it. I am just not playing that game of being superior and inferior.

If you are really interested in what I am doing and saying and being, then never let Rajneeshee become something like Christian, Hindu, Mohammedan, no. Never get serious about it. It is just a word to demarcate. It is not a creed, a cult, a dogma that you have to fight for, that you have to go on a crusade for. No, you need not become Don Quixotes, you are not to convert anybody.

Rajneeshee is simply a name. Some name is needed; *XYZ*, anything will do, just to give you a demarcation. You are not Hindus, you are not Mohammedans, you are not Christians. People are going to ask, "Then who are you?"

I have never voted. My name is not even on the census reports in India because whenever the census people came there was a clause which had to be filled out: to which religion do you belong? I said, "This is difficult – I don't belong to any religion." But they insisted the form had to be filled out completely, only then was it acceptable. I said, "Forget about it. Don't accept it – I don't care about it. Your form is your business. Just get lost! I am not going to fill in that clause because that would be a lie: I don't belong to any religion."

Those poor people insisted, "You must belong to something. If you are an atheist you can say, 'I am an atheist.'"

But I am not an atheist. I am not obsessed with the idea that there is no God, and I am not after him. If there is no God why should I be after him? And why should I call myself an atheist when there is no God? Theism is belief in God; atheism is disbelief in God. My God! – disbelief in God?

I told these people, "I don't believe, I don't disbelieve: I simply have nothing to do with God."

They said then, "But you must be saying some prayers."

I said, "Never. I have never said any prayers. Why should I say any prayers?" They were almost angry at this. Once it happened that they had come to my house and went away very angry. Then they came to the university, but they did not recognize me because in the house I had been simply sitting with a *lungi* on, my body half-naked, and in the college I had on a robe. So they could not figure out that I was the same person: again they brought out the form.

I said, "Listen, if you show me this form again I am going to hit you really hard."

They said, "Again? But we have never met."

I said, "You have forgotten. That guy who was…"

Then they looked again and they said, "Yes, that's true. Now we will be continually aware of beards. We may come across you again somewhere."

I was at that time really strong – one hundred and ninety pounds – and I was running eight miles every day, morning and evening, whenever I could find time. So when I said to anybody, "I will hit you hard," they understood it would be hard.

I had enjoyed jumping, running, swimming so much that my family was always worried: "Will you do anything else in life or not? And you create such a nuisance for other people."

I said, "But I simply do my thing. I don't get in anybody's way." But they had something at hand – a report had arrived.

So they said, "This is not true. What business did you have that you were running backward this morning at four o'clock? We know there are people who go running, but *backward*?"

In India there is a belief that ghosts walk backward. The place where I lived was in the most beautiful area with big, tall trees and a long row of bamboos, so it was always shadowy near the bamboos. It was a full-moon night, and I was just doing my exercises by the side of the bamboos. It is more joyous to run backward because you are moving into the unknown; you can't see what might happen. And at four o'clock the street was almost empty. But there is an Indian belief that ghosts walk backward.

There was a man who used to live at the corner of the road who had a small tea shop. He used to get very afraid, but only in the beginning. Then I went to him and told him, "You need not be afraid. I am a man, I am not a ghost, and you see me every morning; so once and for all be settled about it and go on sleeping. Don't get disturbed."

But what happened that day was that the milk man… They come early in the morning because they bring milk from nearby villages with two big drums full of milk on a bicycle. The milkman was coming along the road when suddenly he saw me. He lost his balance and fell from the bicycle. Because the drums fell and made so much noise, I turned back: "What is the matter?" I saw the bicycle, the drums and the milk all over the road. And the man, far away, running!

I simply forgot that it was not good to follow him. I just wanted to help him and tell him that I was not a ghost, so I followed him. And because I was always running he could not escape me. When he saw me coming behind him, he simply fell down, unconscious.

By that time the man who lived at the corner came and said, "Look, this is what used to happen to me. And if he fell from his bicycle, what business was it of yours to follow him?"

I said, "I was simply trying to help, to make him sure that I am a man."

He said, "Now have you made sure? Now *he* is close to becoming a ghost!"

That report had reached my family and that was why they were saying: "This is not right. You should not get in people's way."

Those census officers said, "Sir" – because there they were respectful to a university professor. At my house I was in the garden, digging a hole. There they were very angry with me, thinking me a gardener or somebody who was just talking absurdities in saying that he could not fill in this line. In the university they said, "Sir, please remember one thing: if we come across you again, remind us and we will simply leave. We will not say anything."

So my name does not exist on the Indian voters list. I have not voted in my whole life because my name never appeared on the voters list. It was not even in the census list, for the simple reason that I could not say what my religion was.

You are fortunate, you can say Rajneeshee. But it is not to be taken seriously. You are not to fight for it; you are not to die for it.

You have to *live* it, enjoy it, relish it. And please, leave me out of it!

About the Author

Osho defies categorization. His thousands of talks cover everything from the individual quest for meaning to the most urgent social and political issues facing society today. Osho's books are not written but are transcribed from audio and video recordings of his extemporaneous talks to international audiences. As he puts it, "So remember: whatever I am saying is not just for you... I am talking also for the future generations."

Osho has been described by *The Sunday Times* in London as one of the "1000 Makers of the 20th Century" and by American author Tom Robbins as "the most dangerous man since Jesus Christ." *Sunday Mid-Day* (India) has selected Osho as one of ten people – along with Gandhi, Nehru and Buddha – who have changed the destiny of India.

About his own work Osho has said that he is helping to create the conditions for the birth of a new kind of human being. He often characterizes this new human being as "Zorba the Buddha" – capable both of enjoying the earthy pleasures of a Zorba the Greek and the silent serenity of a Gautama the Buddha.

Running like a thread through all aspects of Osho's talks and meditations is a vision that encompasses both the timeless wisdom of all ages past and the highest potential of today's (and tomorrow's) science and technology.

Osho is known for his revolutionary contribution to the science of inner transformation, with an approach to meditation that acknowledges the accelerated pace of contemporary life. His unique OSHO Active Meditations are designed to first release the accumulated stresses of body and mind, so that it is then easier to take an experience of stillness and thought-free relaxation into daily life.

Two autobiographical works by the author are available:
Autobiography of a Spiritually Incorrect Mystic,
St Martins Press, New York (book and eBook)
Glimpses of a Golden Childhood,
OSHO Media International, Pune, India

OSHO International Meditation Resort

Location

Located 100 miles southeast of Mumbai in the thriving modern city of Pune, India, the OSHO International Meditation Resort is a holiday destination with a difference. The Meditation Resort is spread over 28 acres of spectacular gardens in a beautiful tree-lined residential area.

Uniqueness

Each year the Meditation Resort welcomes thousands of people from more than 100 countries. The unique campus provides an opportunity for a direct personal experience of a new way of living – with more awareness, relaxation, celebration and creativity. A great variety of around-the-clock and around-the-year program options are available. Doing nothing and just relaxing is one of them!

All programs are based on the OSHO vision of "Zorba the Buddha" – a qualitatively new kind of human being who is able *both* to participate creatively in everyday life *and* to relax into silence and meditation.

THE DETAILS

OSHO Meditations

A full daily schedule of meditations for every type of person includes methods that are active and passive, traditional and revolutionary, and in particular the OSHO Active Meditations™. The meditations take place in what must be the world's largest meditation hall, the OSHO Auditorium.

OSHO Multiversity

Individual sessions, courses and workshops cover everything from creative arts to holistic health, personal transformation, relationship and life transition, work-as-meditation, esoteric sciences, and the "Zen" approach to sports and recreation. The secret of the OSHO Multiversity's success lies in the fact that all its programs are combined with meditation, supporting the understanding that as human beings we are far more than the sum of our parts.

OSHO Basho Spa

The luxurious Basho Spa provides for leisurely open-air swimming surrounded by trees and tropical green. The uniquely styled, spacious Jacuzzi, the saunas, gym, tennis courts...all these are enhanced by their stunningly beautiful setting.

Cuisine

A variety of different eating areas serve delicious Western, Asian and Indian vegetarian food – most of it organically grown especially for the Meditation Resort. Breads and cakes are baked in the resort's own bakery.

Night life

There are many evening events to choose from – dancing being at the top of the list! Other activities include full-moon meditations beneath the stars, variety shows, music performances and meditations for daily life.

Or you can just enjoy meeting people at the Plaza Café, or walking in the nighttime serenity of the gardens of this fairytale environment.

Facilities

You can buy all your basic necessities and toiletries in the Galleria. The Multimedia Gallery sells a large range of OSHO media products. There is also a bank, a travel agency and a Cyber Café on-campus. For those who enjoy shopping, Pune provides all the options, ranging from traditional and ethnic Indian products to all of the global brand-name stores.

Accommodation

'ı can choose to stay in the elegant rooms of the OSHO 'ouse, or for longer stays opt for one of the OSHO Living-In ackages. Additionally there is a plentiful variety of nearby 'iced apartments.

meditationresort
guesthouse
/livingin

For More Information

Thanks for buying this OSHO book.

You can find more OSHO unique content in multiple languages and formats at the following websites online:

The official website of OSHO International is www.OSHO.com and a comprehensive inventory of OSHO-related links can be found at www.OSHO.com/AllAboutOsho

You can search the open access OSHO library for your favorite topic at www.OSHO.com/Library

A complete presentation of all the OSHO meditations and related music can be found at www.OSHO.com/Meditation

To plan a visit to OSHO International Meditation Resort you can visit www.OSHO.com/MeditationResort

Latest updates about events, festivals, media releases and quotes are updated daily on www.facebook.com/OSHO.International

All latest happenings, including information about the OSHO Multiversity courses, are updated daily on www.facebook.com/OSHO.International.Meditation.Resort

You can wake up to a daily OSHO quote at www.twitter.com/OSHOtimes

Your instant access to OSHO video channel can be found on www.youtube.com/OSHOInternational

To make OSHO available in your local language you can register and transcribe or translate OSHO Talks at www.OSHOtalks.info

Please take a moment to **register and browse** these sites as they provide much more information about OSHO. You may also discover many fun and exciting ways to **get involved** in making OSHO available around the world.

Happy reading.